Innovation for the Masses

Innovation for the Masses

HOW TO SHARE THE BENEFITS OF THE
HIGH-TECH ECONOMY

Neil Lee

UNIVERSITY OF CALIFORNIA PRESS

University of California Press
Oakland, California

© 2024 by Neil Lee

Cataloging-in-Publication Data is on file at the Library of Congress.

ISBN 978-0-520-39488-9 (cloth : alk. paper)
ISBN 978-0-520-39489-6 (ebook)

Manufactured in the United States of America

33 32 31 30 29 28 27 26 25 24
10 9 8 7 6 5 4 3 2 1

Contents

Acknowledgments

This book came out of the COVID-19 pandemic. I'd intended to work on a very different topic, but the pandemic initially made travel or research impossible. With hindsight, its publication is one of the few silver linings of a difficult period. The research for it started more than a decade before the pandemic, during my PhD. It has had a long gestation, and I have accumulated many debts.

First of all, I'd like to thank everyone I interviewed while working on the book. This included over a hundred policymakers, representatives of organizations and firms, academics, and other experts. I'm immensely grateful for their honesty, openness, and insights.

My colleagues at the London School of Economics contributed hugely. David Soskice encouraged me to write a book. Many of the themes developed in it come from our discussions and collaborations. My PhD supervisor, Andrés Rodríguez-Pose, has been a wonderful collaborator and friend. Simona Iammarino has also been influential in shaping my thinking. Michael Storper, Vasillis Monastiriotis, Riccardo Crescenzi, Erica Pani, Nancy Holman, and others in the LSE Geography and Environment Department have also been fantastic to work with.

The Cities group at the LSE's International Inequalities Institute provided great discussion and critical insights. In particular, Frieder Mitsch, Andrew McNeil, and Max Herbertson read and commented on chapters, helped with data, and provided critical advice. Mark Fransham, Pawel Bukowski, Jingyuan Zeng, Joel Suss, Margarida Bandeira Morais, Bea Jambrina Canseco, Hilary Vipond, Liza Ryan, Tom Kemeny, Davide Luca, Sebastian Breau, Rania Ramli, Kirsten Sehnbruch, and Yorga Permana, among others, have been wonderful friends and colleagues. Kyung Lin Park, Javier Terrero-Dávila, and Owain Tsang-Wetherald were great research assistants. Paul Yu taught me loads about Taiwan, often at very short notice. Christy Yang, Serena Sih-Yu Chen, and Cedrik Hoffman provided invaluable help on Taiwan, and Martina Pardy, Franz Huber, and Jakob Eder on Austria. Johan Miörner, Katy Morris, Thomas Kurer, Delia Zollinger, Carter Block, and Sarah Jack helped me with Swiss and Swedish (originally Danish) work. I also received fantastic feedback and help from Theis Hansen and Josephine Rekers. Heroically, Han Wang answered an emergency call to translate Chinese-language data when I realized my initial hypothesis about Taiwan was wrong.

The project was funded in part by the REDINN project at the Inland Norway University of Applied Sciences. I'm particularly grateful to Atle Hauge, Trond Nilsen, and Markus Grillitsch for very useful discussions and ski tips. I worked on a related project with a great team from Metrodynamics and the Connected Places Catapult, primarily Eleanor Springer, Anoush Darabi, Alex Gardiner, Mike Emmerich, Emma Frost, and Claire Eagle.

At Oxford, Vlad Mykhnenko and Ben Ansell were generous sponsors. I also thank the Canadian group of Shiri Breznitz, Shauna Brail, and Dan Breznitz, whose work I built on. I received invaluable tips over pints or coffee from Tom Scott Smith, Mike Savage, and Mark Henderson. All mistakes are, of course, mine.

I'm very grateful to Michelle Lipinski, Erika Büky, and Emily Park at University of California Press for being so open and communicative, and to LeKeisha Hughes for answering so many questions about things which were probably in the author's guide.

I also have a personal life. The Utrecht group of Camilla Vogler, Wolfgang Fister, Francesca Grott, and Gabi Wolkerstorfer provided inspiration, teasing, and freezing cold swimming. My kids—Linc, Super-La, and Lochie—have been wonderful, and I'm pleased I got a Tintin reference in for them. My dad and Sue and Rosario and John provided much appreciated childcare.

But there is only one person I could dedicate this book to. My wife, Emma, was patient with my frequent absences and organized two house moves while I was rattling on about Swiss vocational education. You're a wonderful woman, and I'm a very lucky man. Thank you.

Preface

I wrote this book while on sabbatical in my hometown of Oxford, England.

The so-called City of Dreaming Spires is famous for science. As a child, I was taken on school trips to the Atomic Energy Research Establishment, a short drive away, where my friends and I would giggle about three-eyed mutant fish while watching scientific experiments. As we walked through town, my father would patiently explain the achievements of two seventeenth-century scientists, Robert Boyle and Robert Hook, who are commemorated with a plaque on the High Street. The dinosaur in the forum of the University Museum is overlooked by statues of Victorian scientists but overshadowed by the ominous presence of the shrunken heads in the Pitt Rivers Museum next door.

Oxford's reputation for science has led to a reputation for innovation. There are plenty of startups and spinouts, and many multinational corporations have links with the university. It was an Oxford task force that created the Astra-Zeneca vaccine for coronavirus.

The United Kingdom government has placed Oxford at the heart of its innovation strategy. With Cambridge and London, it forms the UK's Golden Triangle—a center of world-leading science and innovation.

Oxford's story appears to be one of incredible success. Yet I'm not so sure. Moving back, I found that few of my friends remained in my lovely but unfashionable suburban neighborhood. Only those with the most lucrative jobs, best luck in the housing market, or largest inheritances had managed to stay in the streets we grew up in. Others, including academics at the university, found themselves squeezed out by high prices. Things were worse for those who didn't go to university: it is too expensive to live in Oxford on a normal wage. Its ratio of house prices to earnings is the highest in Britain. There are plenty of jobs, but many of these are in casual service work and don't pay a genuine living wage. Oxford is a wonderful city, but its economy delivers for too few.

These problems are not exclusive to Oxford. The most innovative cities in the world—including San Francisco, Singapore, Seoul, and Beijing—struggle in similar ways with polarized labor markets, expensive housing, and political economies that lock in these problems. There is a localized dark side to innovation, but we think too little about it.

There are plenty of books exploring how to spur innovation, inspired by places such as Oxford. In this book, I want to ask a different question. Learning from places that promote innovation but also deliver prosperity and well-being for residents who work outside the high-tech economy, how can we share the benefits of innovation?

Introduction

The economics of innovation, growth, and welfare is complicated. Academics like to make it even more so by adding layers of complexity and nuance. Some portray innovation as a linear process, others as a chaotic one. Some recommend policy that is transformative, mission-oriented, or finely tuned for specific local ecosystems. Others think the state should avoid these fads and simply fund basic research. There is little agreement on how best to spur innovation. But most do agree on one thing: innovation matters for people's living standards.

There are, fundamentally, three types of rich country. The first group is rich because of extractive industries. Norway, Kuwait, Saudi Arabia, and other countries have high incomes because they sell the hydrocarbons found in their lands and waters. It is easy to waste such assets, of course, and many countries have done so. But most countries don't have the assets to squander in the first place. Having oil or natural gas reserves is a matter of luck, not judgment. Extractives are a viable route to prosperity only for a lucky few nations.

A second set of countries—such as Luxembourg, Ireland, and Singapore—has grown rich through what can be euphemistically called *openness*. These countries tend to be small financial hubs. They have skilled populations, locations next to large markets, and, often, very low taxes for international firms. A charitable interpretation of this strategy is that they are dynamic, open economies that attract global capital. A less charitable one is that they are tax havens. There is probably some truth to both characterizations. Competing on very low corporate taxes is, however, an option for only a few countries. Tax competition is a zero-sum game, a strategy that moves wealth around rather than making more of it. If all countries did it, there would be a race to the bottom, with states competing by reducing welfare standards and public services.

A third route to prosperity is innovation, or the development and application of new products and processes. Because natural resources are finite and tax havens are small, most rich countries have innovation at the heart of their economic model. If you plot their gross domestic product (GDP) per capita, a measure of national income, against research and development (R&D) intensity, a measure of the share of national income devoted to innovation, you find a strong relationship (see figure 1).[1]

I'm not arguing that R&D is the only measure of innovation, nor that it is the best. Neither am I arguing that increasing R&D spending, or spending on any type of innovation, inevitably leads to economic growth.[2] It is easy to waste money subsidizing pointless R&D. And I'm not saying that all countries fit perfectly into one of these three categories: some, such as Singapore, combine both innovation and free-trade models. But there is a huge body of academic work supporting the basic claim that innovation matters for economic development. Unless a country has oil or suspiciously low taxes, innovation is the best route to prosperity.

Most of the success stories of economic development—from the old world of the United Kingdom and France to later developers such as Taiwan and South Korea—have involved the identification,

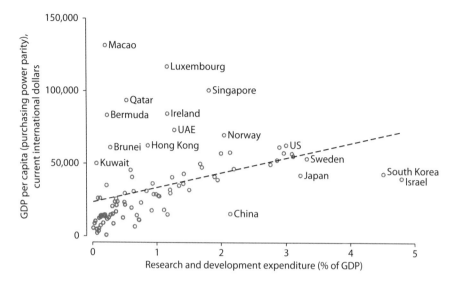

Figure 1. Innovation and economic performance, 2019 or nearest year. *Source:* World Bank development indicators, 2019 or nearest year.

production, and commercialization of new technologies. Policymakers know this. They use tax credits to subsidize R&D, fund expensive labs for blue-sky research that expands the frontiers of knowledge with no obvious application, and set out "missions" around which policy is supposed to focus. Innovation has become a central goal of most national governments.

But there is a problem with this strategy. High-tech innovation has revolutionized the world, but it has concentrated income and wealth in the hands of a few, polarized labor markets and led to divides between a small number of superstar cities and other regions. Inequality in advanced economies has been rising since the 1980s: the ratio of the income of the top 10 percent to that of the bottom 10 percent of earners across member nations of the Organisation for Economic Co-operation and Development (OECD) increased from 7:1 in 1980 to 9:1 in 2013.[3] In the United States, between 1980 and

2017, the share of national income going to the lowest-income 50 percent fell from 20 percent to 12.5 percent.[4] The 1 percent (of highest earners) have been the biggest winners, and their incomes have been increasing since the 1980s across the English-speaking world. Except in a few holdout nations, such as France, most of the advanced world has seen long-term growth in income inequality.

If the richest are gaining an increasing share of output, someone else must be losing theirs. Most of the evidence says that it is the middle classes (or, at least, middle-income earners) whose relative position has declined. The OECD investigated what happened to middle-income households, defined as those earning between 75 percent and 200 percent of median national income. Across the OECD, between the mid-1980s and mid-2010s, the share of households defined as "middle class" declined from 64 percent to 61 percent.[5]

These macro-level problems hide a host of intersecting inequalities. Ethnic and racial inequalities have been prominent in public debate, for good reason. Racial inequalities in the United States are longstanding and stark. In the United Kingdom, the situation is different but little better, with people of Bangladeshi or Pakistani ethnicity having the lowest median household incomes of all ethnic groups. These inequalities are intersectional with other lines of distinction and discrimination. Most notably, gender wage gaps are pervasive across the "advanced" world and have changed depressingly little. Women earn less than men, even when performing the same jobs.[6] Even where you live matters. Evidence shows that growing up in a deprived neighborhood or town can have a long-term impact on your living standards, even if you move elsewhere.[7]

These inequalities—and many others that are less visible and less well reported—have significant social, economic, and political consequences. If people feel their life chances are predetermined by parental income, class, gender, ethnicity, or where they live, it is hardly surprising that they may vote for populist parties that claim to offer simple solutions for these entrenched social problems. They are less likely to trust national governments, vote, or participate in civic life. And they are more likely to become rent seekers, increasing their own income at the expense of others, rather than collaborating and building the social structures necessary for a functioning economy. As a result, inequality can threaten economic success.

Yet many of the world's most important hubs of innovation, from Shenzhen to Seoul, are characterized by high levels of inequality. San Jose, California, the home of Silicon Valley, is one of the most unequal metropolitan areas in the United States. There is a clear link between employment in high-tech sectors and localized inequality.[8] Oxford and Cambridge are two of the most unequal places in the United Kingdom, despite their success in innovation. The new products and processes created in these cities are producing real economic gains, but those gains are not shared among all residents.

The fact that innovation is vital for economic success but often linked to gross inequality is a challenge for policy and society. But growing inequality is a general trend, not a universal law. There are significant national and regional differences in both the magnitude of increases in inequality and their patterns. For example, while the income share of the top 1 percent of earners has increased in the English-speaking countries since the 1980s, it has remained flat in much of continental Europe. Growth since 1980 hasn't benefited those with below-median incomes in the United States, but in Western Europe the poorest 50 percent have seen their incomes rise by 40 percent (in contrast to a 3 percent increase in the United States). The United States is richer than Europe, but the bottom 50 percent of the population earns around 15 percent less than the equivalent group in Western and Northern Europe.[9]

Such divergent trends are difficult to reconcile with the conventional explanations for inequality, which center on the differential impact of technology on workers depending on their particular skills, and the pervasive impact of trade with less advanced economies. The universal pressures caused by technology and globalization do not play out the same way in all countries. National institutions and policy choices matter in moderating the effects of these changes. Plenty of prosperous economies have managed to grow without succumbing to the high levels of inequality of the English-speaking world.

LOOKING BEYOND SILICON VALLEY

When policymakers aim to boost innovation, they search for models from the most innovative places—and from one, Silicon Valley, in particular. Countries from Saudi Arabia to Vietnam have attempted to emulate its success by building business parks in deserts, setting up state-backed venture capital funds to support disruptive innovators, and investing in high-risk innovation agencies. A cliché of Silicon Valley has inspired countries all over the world to develop their own Silicon-Somethings, from Kenya's Silicon Savannah to the United Kingdom's Silicon Canal (Wikipedia lists eighty-one examples). Innovations from the San Francisco Bay Area have shaped the world, from Google's search engine to social media platforms such as Twitter. The Silicon Valley model of innovation policy is itself one of these, and it has gone viral.

Yet for all its success, the Silicon Valley model of innovation is highly problematic. The Bay Area is home to many important tech startups, but there are homeless encampments on its streets. The United States may be the home of more tech unicorns (privately held startup companies valued at over US$1 billion) than any other country, but its life expectancy has been falling. GDP has grown, but the middle classes have declined. The most successful startup founders have made billions, but real wages for the least well-off Americans have not increased since 1979.[10] Some scholars have argued that Silicon Valley has concentrated investment in superstar cities, locking in regional inequalities.[11]

Other examples are similarly troubling. South Korea has become one of the world's leading producers of advanced technologies such as smartphones, but it struggles with stagnant wages and gross inequality (if you doubt this, watch some of its most famous media exports: *Parasite, Squid Game,* and even "Gangnam Style"). The capital city, Seoul, dominates the economy so much that the government is pushing for more balanced national growth. The UK model—less innovative, but still important for policymakers internationally—has strengths in higher education, but spinouts from Oxford and Cambridge concentrate the benefits in already affluent parts of the country, while high house prices squeeze the real wages of those who live there.

The Silicon Valley model of radical innovation, startups, and elite, exclusive universities does not lead to broadly shared prosperity. This problem has been noted in the classic texts about Silicon Valley. In one of these, UC Berkeley's Annalee Saxenian highlights the problems of less-well-paid workers in factories who were being priced out of affluent areas.[12] Bennett Harrison has argued that the widespread view of Silicon Valley as a center of global tech often ignores problems of inequality and disadvantage.[13] Yet researchers and policymakers have too often assumed that this inequality is inevitable. Focusing on Silicon Valley alone has led us to conclude that a truly innovative economy comes at the price of high inequality.

Innovation policy is fixated on the basic question of how to increase innovation. The answers matter, of course, and should provide a foundation for policy. Yet there is no point being "one of the most innovative countries on earth," "a leader in the fourth industrial revolution," "winning the global race for innovation"—or whatever hyperbole is currently in fashion—unless innovation translates into broadly shared prosperity. The US model, despite its great strengths, is problematic: the true purpose of technological leadership is not to win Nobel prizes or develop the most disruptive technology but to increase living standards. Policy for innovation should aim to create good jobs and ensure prosperity is widely shared. Innovation itself is vital but only half the answer.

While there are many studies on innovation and inequality, most of these are attempts to look at where one leads to the other, whether by considering the impact of technological change on labor markets or by studying the divided labor markets of high-tech hubs. In this book, instead of looking at cases where innovation drives inequality, I focus on places where it is a more positive force: where innovation leads to widely shared prosperity.

My approach challenges the conclusion of US studies showing that innovation inevitably results in high levels of inequality. My core argument is that, too often, innovation policymakers ask the wrong question and then look for answers in the wrong places. In addressing the question of how to increase innovation, they focus on models from places such as Silicon Valley, drawing up shopping lists of policies that are then haphazardly transplanted to other parts of the world. It is hardly surprising that these policies fail so often to increase the welfare of people in the national and local economies in which they are applied.

GOOD INEQUALITY, BAD INEQUALITY

There are good reasons to see inequality as a bad thing. Basic ethics suggests that inequality is undesirable, and a simple utilitarian principle is that the least well-off gain more value from a marginal increase in income than someone whose needs have already been met. But things are more complex when considering the link between innovation and inequality, as it might be the case that innovation leads to inequality but still benefits society. A new technology—for example, a lifesaving vaccine—might make someone rich, but others gain from the vaccine's existence as well. Moreover, in the long term many people might be able to build on this initial innovation, leading to more widely distributed benefits. In this case, innovation begets inequality, but it is not clear that inequality is necessarily a problem. The Industrial Revolution led to a major increase in inequality, as some parts of

Britain rapidly grew rich, but other places followed in time. Where it provides the incentive for behavior that increases living standards for others, inequality can be justifiable. With tongue in cheek, I'm going to call this sort of reward for risk taking "good inequality."

The problem is that "good inequality" too often leads to "bad inequality." We know that income inequality is associated with inequality of opportunity, as those who have higher incomes pull up the ladder and foreclose opportunities for those who have less, and social structures become more rigid. For example, faced with competition for jobs, employers may start to demand expensive graduate degrees that are out of reach of intelligent students from low-income households. We can see similar processes at work in the economy if innovative firms can use their success to restrict the gains of others. In some tech industries, for instance, firms gain a first-mover advantage and then build strategic "moats" that stop others from gaining market share and competing with them. Worse, these firms may maintain their market share through anticompetitive practices or the strategic use of lawsuits. The unequal rewards of innovation can, in such cases, reduce innovation in the long term.

A second challenge to this view is that the gains from innovation rarely derive from one firm or worker alone. Innovation tends to be the result of effort by a range of actors in both the public and the private sectors who provide the infrastructure and knowledge on which innovative firms build. While some inequality might be the result of just rewards for the risk and talent required to commercialize these activities, the gains need to be shared.

It is helpful to think clearly about when inequality is and isn't acceptable and what should be the goal of public policy. There is a clear rationale for ensuring that the benefits of innovation are shared within the firm, industry, or city in which it occurs. There is also a strong justification for offering incentives to those who introduce innovations, provided these incentives do not become distortions.

In this book, I consider the innovation-inequality link in several different ways. First, I consider aggregate measures of inequality, such as the Gini coefficient, which characterizes a nation's income distribution on a scale between 0 (perfectly equal) and 1 (perfectly unequal). This measure is useful but partial, as it doesn't tell us much about what is happening within the distribution. Another measure is related: the share of income going to the bottom 40 percent of the population. It is probably better to be less well off but surrounded by the rich than in uniform poverty (although it is better yet to be rich and equal). There's a question about the extent to which we would tolerate the development of elites if it came with higher living standards for the rest of the population, a question that can only be answered on a case-by-case basis. I try to draw out the distinction between good inequality—temporary rewards for genius, risk taking, or hard work—from the bad inequality that can result. I also focus on wages and job creation, with a particular focus on income for the "middle classes" (although these are quite problematic to define). The extent to which inequality is tolerable if everyone's incomes are increasing is a more challenging question.

INNOVATION AND EQUITY: FOUR CLUBS

Which countries manage to combine innovation with broadly shared prosperity? It is hard to answer this question. Innovation is hard to define statistically. Common measures, such as R&D spending or number of patents, give only a partial reflection of innovation. They give no indication of the significance of innovation, and they fail to represent many innovative parts of the economy.

Shared prosperity (or, its inverse, inequality) is equally hard to define. A higher Gini coefficient indicates greater inequality. Yet underlying this simple measure are a host of complexities. Should income be measured before or after tax? Should it be considered as individual or household income, and how should children be taken into account? How should we treat inequality between

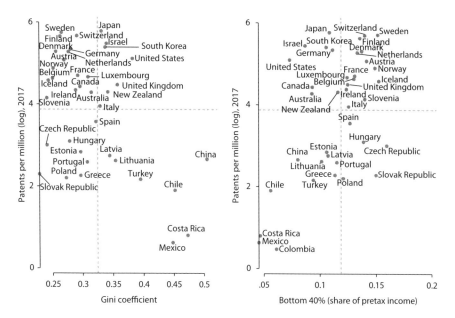

Figure 2. Patenting versus two measures of inequality in the OECD and China, 2017. *Sources:* Patents from OECD (2023). *Main science and technology indicators.*OECD. www.oecd.org/sti/msti.htm; Gini coefficients and bottom 40 percent shares from Alvaredo, F., Atkinson, A. B., Piketty, T., and Saez, E. (2022). *World inequality database.* WID.world. httpsa://wid.world/data.

different genders or ethnic groups? A single aggregate measure can hide significant variation within the income distribution.

I consider these complications in more detail in chapters 2 and 3. The clearest test of the innovation–equality trade-off is given in figure 2, which presents two simple scatter plots of several countries, with different measures of inequality on the horizontal axis, and patenting per capita on the vertical axes. The plots effectively divide the nations into four clubs. In the left-hand plot, at the top left are countries with high innovation and low inequality—countries where the proceeds of an innovation-led economic model are, broadly, shared. In the right-hand plot, where innovation is plotted against the bottom 40 percent share of pretax income, the club of equal and innovative countries appears at the top right.

The first conclusion from these plots is obvious: there is no clear relationship between innovation and equality. Innovation does not come at the cost of inequality; nor does high inequality necessarily spur innovation. The East Asian economies are highly innovative, at least according to the measures shown, but also highly unequal. The United States is in the same category. Canada and the United Kingdom are closer to the average.

But there is a club of countries that combine innovation with equality. These include Finland, Sweden, Denmark, Switzerland, Austria, and Germany. Even Belgium, traditionally overlooked, has relatively low inequality and relatively high innovation by this measure.

But in this book I focus on those in another club: nations that are highly innovative, but where the benefits are shared more equitably. How do these countries achieve this outcome? This is a difficult question to answer, in part because innovation policy tends not to be directly focused on improving living standards, but also because policies that lead to innovation and those that ensure it is broadly shared are often developed and implemented in parallel, with little coordination.

MY ARGUMENTS

In this book I make three arguments, each of which I support with theory, empirical literature, data analysis, and case studies of countries that achieve this balance in very different ways.

First, the dominance of Silicon Valley and, increasingly, China, obscures models that are better at linking innovation with shared prosperity. Europe is too often either dismissed because of the poor performance of southern Europe in the early 2010s or because the focus is on Germany or clichés about the Nordic nations. Yet other European countries have been highly successful at innovation. Switzerland is regularly ranked the most innovative country on earth, and its inequality is below the OECD average. Austria has seen the fastest growth in R&D of any OECD economy bar South Korea and has a strong record of creating skilled, middle-class jobs. And Sweden has long been an economic poster child, combining entrepreneurship and high median wages with a strong welfare state. These countries present important lessons for policymakers in other countries, yet they have too often been ignored in favor of other models.

Second, the state plays a vital role in distributing the benefits of innovation-led growth. Despite rhetoric about a global playing field, national and local context still matters hugely for the development of innovation systems and how those systems affect living standards. The states listed above have succeeded by maintaining and developing their own local models. Innovation policy should be considered not in isolation but with reference to the wider policy frameworks ensuring that workers benefit—including education and training policy, housing, and welfare policy. The state plays a role both in spurring innovation and in ensuring that the benefits are shared. It manages education and training, providing a cushion that allows entrepreneurs to fail, establishing a policy framework that can help ensure the innovation economy is inclusive, and so on. The role of the state goes far beyond funding basic R&D. It also goes beyond providing a strong welfare state. In many of the countries I studied, state actors had, intentionally or not, aligned policy in a way that that gave workers the ability to gain from, adapt to, and shape the nature of innovation. They had also helped provide institutions that facilitated diffusion of frontier knowledge through the economy.

Third, policies for innovation and broadly shared prosperity are mutually reinforcing. Policies that enable broader participation in the innovation economy provide an important comparative advantage. High-quality public services in Switzerland and Sweden attract skilled international science, technology, engineering, and mathematics (STEM) employees who contribute to the economy. The Austrian skill system creates highly productive mid-skill workers, and Austrian firms restructure production processes to create jobs for these workers. Taiwan balances skill development with innovation-led growth strategies. Each of these is an example of the coevolution of state and economy.

Building on these arguments, I argue that three sets of institutions are at work in these countries. The first are institutions that generate innovation. Much of the academic and policy literature has focused on the development of these institutions—with good reason, as they are crucial to the success of advanced economies. A second set of institutions—those that allow diffusion, adaptation, and increased access to innovation—is more important in ensuring that the benefits are broadly shared. These include applied research organizations, networks of small firms, and skill structures focused on diffusion of new technologies. Such institutions focus on incremental innovation and adaptation rather than radical new technologies. A final set of institutions focuses on redistribution and basic public service delivery. Given the tendency of innovation in many leading-edge sectors to concentrate wealth, these institutions remain important.

The immediate challenge to these arguments is likely to be an objection to the idea that policies which are successful (or otherwise) in one place can be packaged up and reused in a very different context. This idea, sometimes called *fast policy,* is a real concern for anyone doing comparative work.[14] Policymakers, desperate for success in a difficult world, may rely on superficial learning from other countries, with "prefabricated" solutions that are decontextualized—in that they are not necessarily appropriate in other geographies—and depoliticized—in that their proponents downplay the need for hard choices or trade-offs. Yet such problems of fast policy are exactly what this book is trying to address. The emulation of Silicon Valley I outline above is fast policy. Instead we need a deeper understanding of the systems in which certain policy measures succeed or fail.

A second challenge is that these outcomes are simply about the welfare state. One variation of this argument is that the only solution to inequality is redistribution and a larger state. Yet while redistribution matters hugely, it can only ever provide a partial explanation for the income distribution. General government spending is just under half of GDP in Sweden and Austria, but in Switzerland it is only 33 percent, less than in the United States (39 percent).[15] (Figures for Taiwan are unavailable.) While redistribution is important, increasing taxation is not the only way to deal with inequality. According to estimates by Thomas Blanchet, Lucas Chancel and Amory Gethin, the lion's share of the difference in posttax inequality levels between the United States and Europe can be explained by the pretax distribution.[16] To put it another way, the income distribution is already largely determined by institutional frameworks, the skill distribution of the population, and other factors. Redistribution is vital, but its importance is also a symptom of something going wrong elsewhere. If the right institutions are put in place, redistribution becomes less necessary. Innovation allows growth, which allows redistribution and so reduces inequality. This is partly true: Sweden and Austria have high levels of redistribution. But it is not the case in Switzerland, which has the third *lowest* difference between pre- and posttax inequality in the OECD.

This book is about realism. It is not about clichés of Nordic perfection nor breathless hype about digital technology. Austria's persistent gender gaps are shameful, Swedish populism is embarrassing, and the neutrality of the Swiss model has a dark side. These are countries, not football teams, and I'm not going to pretend that they are perfect. But if we were looking for a perfect country, a perfect model, or a perfect policy idea, we would be looking for a long time. Instead, we need to learn from the real world.

The first part of the book provides a framework for analysis. I define innovation, look at how it improves living standards, and consider the conditions necessary for this relationship to hold. While rents from innovation contribute significantly to modern economic performance, we should be thinking more about sharing the benefits. Many studies consider the risks of innovation—for example, that it will displace workers—but it is far better to ensure that workers are in a position to benefit from it. Next I develop this analytical framework, building on data on the link between innovation, inequality, and living standards. I show that countries that combine innovation with equity are not the exception. There are basically four groups of countries in this category: the Nordics (Denmark, Finland, and Sweden), two low countries (the Netherlands and Belgium), the Alps (Switzerland, Austria, and—stretching the definition a little—Germany), and two island nations of East Asia (Taiwan and, by some measures, Japan—although Taiwan is not a clear-cut example for inclusion in this category).

Each of the subsequent chapters develops a theme, drawing on an in-depth example. First, I consider Switzerland, a country that combines strengths in radical innovation in digital technology—it is home to Google's largest research hub outside the United States—with incremental innovation in manufacturing industries. The Swiss model is one of historical development in long-cycle industries such as pharmaceuticals, where competitive advantages can be sustained over a long time. The origin story of high-tech growth in Silicon Valley typically dates to the 1950s; in Switzerland, many pharmaceutical firms date to a hundred years before that. This history has led to some Swiss cities being highly innovative, although this fact rarely forms part of the popular narrative. Whereas the US middle class has been in decline, in Switzerland there has been robust growth in high-wage jobs for the middle classes. My argument is that the Swiss model is unusually good at both radical innovation and diffusion of new technologies because of the skills system, regional balance, and applied research.

Next, I consider Austria—a very different model of innovation. By many of the conventional Silicon Valley metrics, this country should barely be competing. Austria has little venture capital, low broadband penetration, and one of the lowest shares of university graduates in the labor force in the OECD. Yet the Austrian model works: the country has the fourth highest median wage in Europe. The Austrian story has been one of innovation in traditionally low-tech industries such as steel and timber, supported by a strong social partnership model. As a result, industrial decline has been less stark than in other countries.

My third case is very different. Taiwan is unique among the Asian Tigers in having achieved rapid economic growth alongside equity. It has balanced growth in skills with a greater focus on small and medium-sized enterprises (SMEs) rather than large firms, and educational development has been accompanied by growth in the welfare state. Taiwan is no Nordic nirvana: inequality has been rising fast, real wage growth for younger workers has been slow, and there are pronounced inequalities. But the island tells us something important about the need to balance economic development and skill strategies to ensure that workers can gain from new, high-tech development.

Finally, I consider what is probably Europe's most successful economy in digital tech. Sweden is the archetypal example of the Nordic model that apparently combines low inequality with economic competitiveness. The strong welfare state is supposed to be a barrier to competitiveness, but in Sweden it is not: per capita, the country has more rapidly scaling unicorn firms and tech billionaires than the United States. I argue that the strong state contributes significantly to Swedish competitiveness in innovation-intensive industries. Yet even in Sweden the growth of digital tech is increasing inequality and straining housing markets in Stockholm, the leading tech hub.

I start with history. Current economic and institutional conditions in each of these countries can be understood only with reference to its development over time. My work is based on data analysis, interviews with policymakers, executives, and academics, a review of the literature, and data on living standards that comes—where possible—from standardized sources.

As I argue in chapter 3, many of the benefits (and costs) of innovation are felt in the local economies in which it takes place. Because of this, in each chapter I conclude by focusing on a region or area of particular interest.

My focus is, deliberately, on the extent to which the benefits of innovation are shared. In presenting an overview, I make some inevitable simplifications. One of these is relatively easy to justify. Trying to draw simple, tractable messages from a messy reality necessarily requires omitting detail that some will feel is important. Sadly, there is no alternative. A second consequence is more concerning: I can give only a broad overview of individual living standards in each place I study. Yet inequality is complex, intersectional, and hard to measure. I have tried to acknowledge ethnic, racial, and gender inequality but cannot do justice to these issues in a book that is primarily about linking innovation to living standards in the aggregate. They are worthy of fuller research. Moreover, I focus on income inequality rather than wealth inequality, which is often closely related to the role of the state in the provision of public goods. For example, where home ownership is less common, wealth inequality is often more pronounced, as individuals do not need to save and so have lower wealth.

While innovation is central to our understanding of different economic models, other features—such as trade and institutions— are also important. I don't think it is possible to separate these out, and so I have chosen not to. But I acknowledge that not all the economic outcomes in the places I study are a result of innovation.

Innovation matters. But policymakers must consider how innovation can improve living standards. No model is perfect, but some countries provide clues about what the benefits of innovation are and how these benefits can be shared.

1 The Economics of Innovation

In popular media, innovation is about a lone genius creating radical new inventions. We are first exposed to this cliché in childhood: my children read about Tintin's friend Professor Calculus solo-inventing a shark-shaped submarine, and they watch Doc in *Back to the Future* invent a time-traveling car. Adult media is no more grown-up. In *Iron Man,* the billionaire Tony Stark builds a bionic bodysuit; and Dr. Frankenstein became the world's most ambitious (and ultimately least successful) transplant surgeon.

These are good stories but terrible portrayals of innovation. While we rightly lionize the achievements of individuals such as Benjamin Franklin, Sarah Gilbert, and Tim Berners-Lee, they rarely act alone, and they should not be considered innovators simply because they have invented something. The so-called lone-genius theory, holding that innovation comes from individual inventors, misrepresents modern science. It confuses innovation with invention and with the entrepreneur, and it ignores the networked, global nature of modern science and technology. People talk about innovation a lot. But often they are talking about very different things. Innovation is a messy, contextual, and cumulative process dependent on relationships. To understand how innovation influences living standards, we need to understand what innovation is (and isn't). This chapter starts by defining innovation and giving some stylized facts—simplified representations of a complex reality—before looking at which countries are more innovative than others.

DEFINING INNOVATION

A search for "innovation" on Amazon yields over sixty thousand books, and airport bookshops are stuffed with manuals on how to nurture it. But there is little consensus on the meaning of the word: one study found that academics use more than sixty different definitions.[1] A familiar shouting match at an academic conference of economists would start with someone talking about commercialized R&D in a rich country and being "corrected" by another researcher who focuses on grassroots innovation in a poor one. There are so many definitions and conceptualizations that using the word *innovation* isn't always helpful.

There is consensus, at least, that innovation is distinct from the inventions produced by the fictional scientists my kids read about. This distinction, between the initial spark of an idea (invention) and its successful application or commercialization (innovation), was first made by Joseph Schumpeter, the Austrian political economist whose work shapes modern thinking about the economics of innovation.[2] Schumpeter argued that the personal aptitudes required for invention—inspiration and intellectual ability—are quite different from those of the "businessman" [*sic*], whose skills are "volitional" and who can successfully apply these new inventions—or, rather, innovate.[3] For Schumpeter, it wasn't enough simply to have a good idea; you also needed to exploit it.[4]

Innovation is also distinct from technology—which itself is another fuzzy concept. One of the leading scholars of technology, Brian Arthur, offers three core definitions.[5] The first is probably the most commonly understood: technology can be "a means to fulfil a human purpose"—whether that purpose is clear, simple, and defined (like that of a frying pan) or open, complex, and changing (like that of an iPad, whose functions update over time). The most famous example of this pragmatic type of technology is the wheel, but the definition would also cover an advanced artificial intelligence program.

Arthur's second definition of technology is as an "assemblage of practices and components," such as biotechnology, chemistry, or computing. This is not a single "thing" or a means to a specific end but rather a way of referring to whole bodies of knowledge and equipment in a specific field. This what we mean when we talk about Information or Communications Technology (ICT) or digital technology.

Finally, Arthur considers technology as the "collection of devices and engineering practices available to a culture"—in other words, technology as everything we are able to do. These three definitions—from specific to more general to grand—are all used to refer to technology in different dimensions and contexts. But for many people, technology is simply a new way of doing things. It has become shorthand for new, particularly digital, tools. Innovation is the process through which the technologies we use evolve.

The most important and coherent definition of innovation comes from the Organisation for Economic Co-operation and Development (OECD), a think tank and membership organization for rich(ish) countries, in its *Oslo Manual*—a text intended to standardize definitions of key terms. The Oslo definition of innovation for each commercial firm or part of one is "a new or improved product or process (or combination thereof) that differs significantly from the unit's previous products or processes and that has been made available to potential users (product) or brought into use by the unit (process)."[6]

The OECD definition is useful because it provides a consistent definition, albeit one unlikely to sell many books in airports. However, it leaves many questions open: How exactly is *new* defined? How significant an improvement is necessary to count as innovation? What about innovation in public services or the creative arts? Even the clearest definition of innovation is blurred round the edges.

INNOVATION AS "A MASSIVE SOCIAL PROCESS"

Given the inconsistencies in defining and measuring innovation, it is hardly surprising that the economics of innovation has some gray areas where it is hard to draw clear conclusions. But a few key generalizations can reflect the balance of academic evidence about innovation and how it works.

First, innovation is combinatorial. New technologies work only in combination with older ones, and the integration of two distinct technologies can be seen as an innovation in itself, a process Schumpeter described as "the bounty of new combinations."[7] Examples of combinatorial innovation include mobile phones and payment terminals. Both technologies first appeared in the 1970s as clunky machines. As these technologies improved and became widespread, they allowed new forms of mobile payment technology to develop. Merging the two has allowed phones to be used for electronic payment via mechanisms such as Apple Pay (a process that may have improved further by the time you read this book). The development of the technology hasn't centered on one company or inventor but has been a cumulative process of development of new and better technologies and supporting infrastructure (such as regulatory changes). Technologies don't come into being fully formed: they evolve through incremental innovations in regular and occasionally larger leaps. Indeed, evolutionary conceptions of innovation have become increasingly popular.

The second stylized fact is that innovation is systemic. Mobile payment technologies were built on earlier technologies, but they also required widespread social adoption and changes to regulatory and banking systems. The companies that constructed phones and terminals needed financing, and in order for mobile payments to enter the market, they had to be adopted by other companies. The production of phones and terminals required a complex mix of skills (taught by universities, vocational schools, and so on), finance (from entrepreneurs, retained profits, banks, and maybe venture capitalists), and a means of commercialization or distribution. In a famous text on innovation, the Norwegian economists Jan Fagerberg and colleagues observe: "Arguably, mastery of physical processes is of dubious value if one doesn't know how to embed these in a well-organized production and distribution system."[8]

Third, innovation is a nonlinear process: there is no automatic link between innovation inputs and outputs. This seems obvious if most new innovations are combinatorial and systemic. Yet the idea of an automatic linear relationship, whereby R&D spending automatically generates innovation and then growth, still dominates policymaking (in part, to be fair, because graphs like the one I used in the introduction misrepresent things). But it is now more generally understood that much of innovation takes places outside the firm (the "open-innovation" paradigm) and that innovators need to capture outside knowledge (often through commercializing applied research).

These three stylized facts reflect innovation's complexity and messiness. Innovation isn't about a single inventor, firm, or product; it is combinatorial, systemic, and path dependent. It isn't about individual inventors working in isolation; it is about teams building on each other's work, often in incremental ways and at different scales. It isn't about a single final product; it is about the continual development and refinement of new products. And it is as often about incremental improvements in existing technologies as it is about radical new technologies. On reading Schumpeter's book, one 1934 reviewer described his theory of one as a "massive social process," and this remains an accurate characterization.[9]

INNOVATION BEYOND INVENTION

A fourth stylized fact reflects clichés of scientific progress: innovation is broader than the production of shiny new technologies. The lab-coat, science-focused conceptualization obscures a plethora of alternative measures of innovation—social innovations, managerial innovations, and so on. Neither is innovation simply about the first stage of a process. It happens at all stages of the supply chain—from the first production of a good to the rebranding and reinvention of historic products or services. There are many routes to innovation-led growth.[10] Innovation isn't simply about R&D; it also involves design, engineering, and training.[11] Economies can grow not only by producing radical new innovations at the technological frontier but also by adapting lower-tech innovations to improve local production processes.

Yet innovations are not always commercialized in a standard sense. The innovations that have made the greatest difference to people's lives include changes to public-service delivery, such as the introduction of new teaching methods, new medical treatments, and improved management processes. They can involve changes to processes, such as new methods of ICT that guide public services, or to products, such as a new benefit or a new type of university.

Too much of the literature focuses on a single radical innovation, such as the smartphone, and portrays it as arriving fully formed and with an immediately obvious use. But innovation doesn't work like this. Instead, the economic historians Ralph Meisenzahl and Joel Mokyr argue that we should think about innovation as involving three different groups of people: major inventors; tweakers, who make "cumulative microinventions," improving and adapting existing technologies; and implementers, who find themselves "building, installing, operating, and maintaining new and complex equipment."[12]

Dan Breznitz, a University of Toronto professor who is one of the most original thinkers on this topic, attacks the myth that "innovation equals high-tech industries, new businesses, and/or new gadgets" and argues instead that we should see it as a systematic process:

> Innovation is the complete process of taking new ideas and devising new or improved products and services. It comes in all stages from the first vision, design, development, production, sale, and usage, to the after-sale aspects of products and services. The true impact of innovation was not in the invention of the internal combustion engine, nor even the invention of the first automobile. The true impact of innovation is represented by the continuous stream of implementation of large and small inventions to make the car a better and cheaper product, to improve the way it is produced, and to continuously find ingenious ways to sell, market and service cars. If innovation was invention there would be no continued progress and growth in welfare. For example, without innovation, there would be no smartphones, since a phone would still be a very large wooden box with a rotating dial, and it would take about a minute to even attempt a call.[13]

Breznitz hints at the myths of innovation. The great-man theory of innovation has become a great straw man, but one that we still think about too often. The great-product theory of innovation is the view whereby innovation stops at the first iPhone, rather than its continual development, marketing, reinvention, and embedding in complementary innovations such as the App Store or iTunes. And the great-company theory of innovation stops with the contributions from leading-edge companies such as Apple, Facebook, and Google, and so ignores the contributions from a wider ecosystem.

Both the Meisenzahl-Mokyr and Breznitzian views of innovation point up the misconception that "novel product" innovation is all that matters. Instead, as Breznitz sets out clearly, there are different stages of production, and the need for innovation at each stage differs. Of these, the most famous, and the stage that dominates policy, is the novel-product stage—the Silicon Valley model of disruptive, new, and shiny innovations that may or (more often) may not have their moment of commercial success. This stage is risky but brings high rewards, which tend to accrue to a small number of innovators and venture capitalists.

The second stage of innovation involves design, prototyping and engineering. Breznitz uses the example of the Taiwanese semiconductor industry. While many of the routine tasks in Taiwanese semiconductor production are now performed in China, the design of semiconductor chips is still a major source of employment in Taiwan. This stage of innovation offers jobs at a range of skill levels—not only for engineers with PhDs but also for those with vocational skills in prototyping and testing.

The next stage involves the reinvention and improvement of existing products as the technologies they are based on evolve. Major companies continually upgrade and improve their products. To use a clichéd example, the iPhone in your pocket is not the same iPhone that was launched in 2007. Another example involves what is, whether we like it or not, one of the most innovative and successful firms of the modern era, Amazon. Much of its innovation has been in subtle organization design rather than the introduction of radically new products: slightly better algorithms recommending products to consumers, improved logistics delivering products more quickly, better fonts that allow people to read ebooks more rapidly (and so purchase more ebooks). The result has been major increases in productivity: labor productivity in US mail-order retail (more precisely: electronic shopping and mail-order houses, according to the standard industrial classification) has quadrupled since 1987, while overall productivity, outside of farming, increased by only 60 percent.[14] The gains from this process have been real for shareholders and consumers, but unequal, as workers have lost out and communities have lost their local shops.

The final stage is production and the logistics that follow. As Breznitz argues, this stage is as important to the functioning of modern capitalism as the others, even if it is often overlooked. It is particularly important for the commercialization of inventions.

This accords with Breznitz's central point: economic development through innovation does not need to be about disruptive innovation in high-tech sectors. It can happen through smaller, incremental innovations in less technologically advanced parts of the economy. Moreover, innovation away from the technological frontier can have benefits that are more broadly shared.

INNOVATION AND DIFFUSION

The fifth stylized fact is that innovation is as much about the diffusion and adaptation of new technologies as it is about the production of entirely new ones. As noted by Lars Coenen, Teis Hansen, and Josephine Rekers, three Nordic economic geographers, there is little point in producing raw technological solutions to problems unless these solutions are distributed more widely into society.[15] Innovation comprises not just the idea but also its application. Innovation isn't simply about titanic shifts in technology; it is also about smaller and incremental changes to an existing technology or product lines. Indeed, the adaptation of new technologies for new circumstances is one of the most important routes to economic development. All the countries that have achieved rapid, innovation-led growth—including Japan, Singapore, South Korea, Taiwan, and even China—had conscious strategies for learning the best technologies from elsewhere while developing the capabilities needed to exploit the benefits themselves.

Thinking about innovation in a Breznitzian sense leads to another distinction. Innovation can mean major, disruptive changes at the technological frontier: for example, the introduction of silicon for making semiconductor chips. But it can also be about more marginal innovations, such as the minor software updates that improve the performance of computers over time (and the diffusion of these innovations across the economy). Yet many policymakers focus on disruptive innovation when marginal improvements would be more beneficial. The United Kingdom is a good example here. One of the canonical principles of UK science funding is that it should be allocated according to the Haldane principle (named after Richard Burdon Haldane, the politician and philosopher who established it in the early twentieth century), by an impartial jury of scientists on the basis of quality alone. We should fund the "best science." While there is some debate about Haldane's true intention, this approach has driven science funding policy in the United Kingdom.[16]

There is good reason for science and innovation policy to be independent of government and placed in the hands of experts, but an exclusive focus on the leading edge neglects the later stages of innovation, which are often where the value is. The United Kingdom, again, is an exemplar of this problem. The national artificial intelligence strategy aims to make Britain "a global AI superpower" and proclaims that the United Kingdom is a "world leader" in this area.[17] The R&D roadmap proclaims the "excellence of our scientific institutions" and recommends linking up with "other world leading research and innovation nations."[18] Where politicians lead, academics follow, and we are no less guilty, selectively publicizing rankings in spurious university league tables, overstating the significance of our work, and forgetting that publicly funded innovation should serve a purpose beyond our own benefit.

Focusing only on the very best science and technology skews incentives and means that many worthwhile projects are not funded. It would be better to think about the diffusion of new technology through innovation. Moreover, diffusion often leads to learning, adaptation, and additional innovation.[19]

The question of *how* diffusion occurs is less clear. Academic research has concentrated on the initial spark of innovation, which is easier to measure than its diffusion. Moreover, the diffusion of innovation differs by business sector, the nature of the innovation, and the place where it happens. Josephine Rekers compares innovations in two very different sectors, theater and pharmaceuticals. She convincingly shows that innovation is a social process, with validation and acceptance of new innovations driven by intermediate institutions.[20] Part of this process involves the mechanics of commercialization:

sales organizations are important in ensuring that even basic medicines are taken up, and innovation diffusion is local, as individuals follow and learn from their peers. Rekers's work updates the common assumption that institutional structures are central to innovation processes: it shows that institutions also play a vital role in the diffusion of innovation.

THE GEOGRAPHY OF INNOVATION

My sixth and seventh stylized facts seem paradoxical: innovation systems are both highly localized and highly internationalized. The spatial clustering of innovation is obvious. In addition to Silicon Valley, examples include the tech companies along Route 128 near Boston, London's financial sector, and the concentration of aeronautics industries around Toulouse. These hubs often have very different bases and have evolved in different ways. In China, the three major regional centers of innovation—Beijing, Shanghai, and Shenzhen and the Pearl River Delta—all specialize in different types of innovation.[21] Research from Europe shows that regions that share very similar industrial bases, such as the medical technology sectors in Scania in Sweden and Vienna in Austria, may differ significantly.[22]

The idea that local innovation systems are important dates back at least to the work of Alfred Marshall, the British economist of the late nineteenth and early twentieth centuries. His work contrasted the innovation impact of a single large firm with that of a geographically proximate set of smaller ones. He argued that while internal scale economies—the benefits of being a big firm—offered advantages, industrial districts consisting of small, interrelated firms could compete with larger individual firms. Proximity allows firms to share pools of specialized labor and provides incentives for workers to develop their skills; it enables entrepreneurs and workers to maintain regular contact with specialist suppliers and customers; and it facilitates knowledge sharing between geographically proximate actors, leading to Marshall's famous phrasing that the skills of trade were "in the air" in certain innovative industrial districts.[23] These three forces, or agglomeration economies, provide incentives for the clustering of economic activity in general. They are particularly powerful for the type of knowledge-based economic activity that drives innovation. Key innovation actors often pay a premium to locate near each other, suggesting that there are powerful forces driving the clustering of innovation.

It is now common to argue that we cannot understand the most innovative places in the world economy at the level of the nation-state but instead need to consider them as local or regional systems. The argument was made most strongly in the early 1990s, as employment in advanced economies was in the late stages of the shift from a Fordist economy, based on extractive industries and the mass production of manufactured goods, to a post-Fordist or knowledge economy, based on high-skilled work in fast-changing sectors that relies on exchanges of tacit knowledge.[24] Some major metropolitan regions provide ideal conditions for these exchanges, partly because they have the institutions required for successful urban economies but also because they provide fertile ground for the exchange of knowledge and information.

Yet localized innovation clusters also have strong international links. Silicon Valley's success has been underpinned by the migration of skilled workers from around the world.[25] To make successful products, most countries rely on outside sources of technology, adapting and changing these technologies in ways that make them useful. South Korea and Singapore began their economic development not by creating new technologies (that comes later) but by absorbing technologies from elsewhere.

INNOVATION IS NOT NEUTRAL

Innovation is not neutral: the direction of technological change is not predetermined but shaped by human action. Decisions about where innovation happens, what new technologies are developed, and how much is devoted to them are highly consequential policy choices. One result is gross disparities in the money devoted to the important versus the trivial: more money is spent seeking cures for baldness than for malaria, according to Bill Gates.[26]

Given the vast sums spent on innovation and the immense technological advances made, it's fair to ask why we don't use it more directly to address socioeconomic disadvantage. This question was provocatively asked by Richard Nelson in his 1977 book *The Moon and the Ghetto*. He posed the question of why, if humans could achieve the technological advances needed to land a man on the moon, they couldn't solve the earthly problems of poor living conditions in the ghetto. The answer, according to Nelson, was partly political, in that people making decisions were focused on a particular type of problem. But he also argued that because there were "no clear paths to a solution" to these socioeconomic problems, nobody attempted to solve them.

Nelson later suggested that the concept of the innovation system was helpful in understanding why innovation does not solve urgent social challenges.[27] The complex web of interactions that lead to the solution of a particular technological problem cannot easily be refocused on new challenges: they are evolutionary processes rather than pathways carved out anew to address specific problems. Contrast two problems: the development of a COVID vaccine and the development of new technologies to combat climate change. The former problem is tightly bound and quickly solved. The latter is unfocused and requires actors to adopt innovations in ways that are hard for them to achieve. It requires multiple, complicated solutions (quite apart from addressing the entrenched interests of oil producers). A focused, limited challenge is easier to address than a complicated, diffuse one.

Some innovations can even be harmful. Even seemingly virtual innovations, such as Bitcoin, consume enormous computing power and emit carbon dioxide for little, if any, welfare benefit. Many of the canonical technologies of the modern world—from the airplane to the aerosol spray can—have later been shown to have damaging environmental effects. Innovations can have important benefits to the individual, but they can also have a major social cost.

THE ECONOMICS OF INNOVATION: PRODUCTIVITY, GROWTH, AND DISTRIBUTION

While definitions of innovation differ, all serious economists agree that innovation is vital for economic growth. Innovation can help make things in better ways, or it can help make better things.

Let's start with the first of these. In a simple model, production is determined by two things—the quantity of inputs (number of workers, hours worked, raw materials) and the productivity of those inputs (how much each worker can produce per hour). Innovation affects productivity and so is a crucial part of the economy. Yet there is disagreement about the exact nature of its effects. There are two basic sets of explanations. Neoclassical theories view innovation as being ordered and steady-state; evolutionary theories focus more on change, complexity, and growth patterns that are "turbulent" and determined by historic circumstances.[28]

The evolutionary perspectives on innovation and growth originated with Schumpeter. Drawing on Karl Marx—who suggested that capitalism tended toward destruction, with old factories, shops, and companies being replaced by new ones—Schumpeter highlighted the positive results of this process: "The fundamental impulse that sets and keeps the capitalist engine in motion comes from the new consumers' goods, the new methods of production or transportation, the new markets, the new forms of industrial organization that capitalist enterprise creates."[29]

In this "organic process," new products, processes, and sources of supply reduce the margins and profits of existing firms in a process of creative destruction that is different from, and more effective than, the textbook model of competition between identical firms. They lead to gradual, path-dependent changes: "The essential point to grasp is that in dealing with capitalism we are dealing with an evolutionary process."[30]

Schumpeter put innovation at the forefront of processes of economic renewal and growth. Innovation was about entrepreneurs—dynamic, powerful individuals who recognized and sought to exploit opportunities. But in his later work, he also considered the impact of large firms in bringing new products to market. In his view, creative destruction was destructive only to the losing parties. His theory spells out powerfully how innovation leads to better products at lower costs.

The idea that technological change can spur growth also underpins "classical" models of growth and development. In the simplest of these models, production (and so living standards) in an economy is determined by two things: the inputs (work and capital, such as machinery) and the productivity of these inputs (how much each worker produces per hour worked—a figure that is assumed to diminish as output increases, reflecting reducing marginal returns). In this type of model, termed a neoclassical or a Solow model (after one leading developer), growth results from increases in the number of inputs or in technology, which are exogenous (outside the model).

INNOVATION POLICY

Given the potential of innovation to raise living standards, it is hardly surprising that policymakers spend huge sums on innovation policy. Innovation spending can be national, regional, or local; it can support firms, universities, or applied research labs; and it can take the form of direct payments or subsidies to firms. Because of this complexity, definitive figures are hard to come up with. But figures on R&D subsidies give an indication of the scale of spending: OECD countries spend an average of 0.18 percent of GDP on R&D subsidies. In France, no great innovator, this figure is around 0.4 percent;

in the United Kingdom, it is around 0.32 percent; but in more innovative countries, such as Switzerland, the figure is below 0.14 percent. Firms in the most innovative countries do not need public
subsidies to encourage them to invest in R&D.[31]

Innovation policy isn't just about R&D: it is connected with science policy and technology policy.[32] There are important questions
about the extent to which scientists should be autonomous and the
extent to which funding should be directed to blue-sky or to more
applied science. Technology policy focuses on encouraging production and absorption of the most important new technologies. But it
overlaps fuzzily with other forms of industrial policy, as it involves
prioritizing technologies or sectors. Innovation policy is yet broader,
concerned with establishing the framework conditions for innovation or about developing a specific type of innovation system. But
because of the diffuse nature of innovation systems, innovation policy can become a sprawling area with conflicting targets: a labor-
market policy focused on innovation would likely have a different
outcome from a policy focused on inclusion.[33] Innovation policy
tends to be focused on economic growth, but there are also high-
profile examples of its focusing on noneconomic goals.

If we view innovation as a system, almost any form of policy can
influence innovation. For example, David Soskice of the London
School of Economics and Political Science identifies four related
"generative institutional structures" that underpin the American success in radical innovation. They are, first, a flexible, decentralized,
and highly competitive research and higher-education system; second, a flexible, decentralized system of finance, particularly risk
finance; third, a combination of a large market—enabled by a unified
legal system—and a weak antitrust legislation (and labor unions);
fourth, a large, highly skilled, and flexible labor market. This list suggests that innovation is complex and involves a broad range of business activities, many of which are shaped by the state. So the state
plays an important role in influencing both the quantity and the type
of innovation in ways that go beyond innovation policy.

The work of comparative political economists such as Soskice helps us see the connections between innovation policy and wider social and economic structures. Similarly, the political scientist Peter Hall uses the notion of growth regimes to reflect the "distinctive institutional shape" of capitalism in different countries. In his words, "tracing changes in the character of capitalism" is "central to understanding changes in the wellsprings of economic growth and the dramatic shifts in the distribution of material benefits that affected so many people's lives." Growth regimes are, for Hall, "constituted by the principal institutional practices that firms and governments use for securing and distributing economic output." Hall focuses on the broader workings of the economy over specific periods, but his approach helps us think about what is happening at any given point in time.[34]

Institutional approaches to innovation and growth point at the importance of interactions between actors and actions in determining outcomes. A similar approach comes from work that considers the effect of the "policy mix" on innovation: how innovation policy interacts with other processes and policies in the same place, the same economic sector, and so on.[35] Innovation policy is messy, but these approaches attempt to simplify it and make it more tractable.

MEASURING INNOVATION

If defining innovation is hard, measuring it is even harder. We need to measure innovation to think through its economic impact, determine benchmarks for the success or failure of policy, and understand the world. Zak Taylor distinguishes four measures of innovation: (1) inputs, such as the STEM workforce and the measure of R&D that I used in the previous chapter; (2) outputs, such as patents, trademarks, and scientific papers; (3) survey measures—for example, surveys asking particular groups about current technology levels, or businesses about whether they are innovating, and (4) innovation indexes, which combine the three previous indicators into a single metric. Taylor argues that output measures of innovation are, in general, more reliable measures than inputs, which may be misspent and may vary by sector. Moreover, inputs are often influenced by policy activity.[36] These are all good points—but the same problems apply to outputs.

The most commonly used indicator of innovation is patents, for reasons that are both pragmatic and theoretical. Each new patent is an output, something normally seen as a good thing. It is evaluated independently, and because applying for a patent involves a cost, the process discourages trivial patents. Patents can be consistently measured over a long period, are easily available, and can be linked to other patents to map chains of invention over time. It is possible to infer the significance of a patent by the number of subsequent patents that cite it over later years. However, patents are not necessarily a good indicator of innovation. In the first place, they measure invention, not innovation, and tell us little about successful commercialization. They are biased by sector: some sectors are more likely to produce patents than others. By this metric, pharmaceuticals, an industry strongly reliant on patent protection, will always look more innovative than financial technology.

In addition, a major problem with using patenting as a metric is that people game the system. It bears out Goodhart's law, a concept named after the economist who highlighted the problems of the use of metrics in monetary policy. If the metric becomes the target, actors skew their actions to meet that target rather than to fulfill the more general aim of a policy. For example, patenting in China in the 2010s was driven partly by the country's technological progress but also partly by the fact that patenting was a criterion for evaluating managers. To improve their performance ratings, managers began patenting increasingly trivial inventions. In contrast, UK firms grew tired of the cost of patenting and so began to patent only the most important innovations. By the number of patents, China looks better than it should and the United Kingdom worse.

A second common measure of innovation is the number of researchers. This is a strong measure of innovation inputs and avoids some of the problems of gaming the system. But it is no measure of quality: a large number of poor-quality researchers is less effective than a smaller number of good ones.

A final measure is R&D spending, commonly designated as a percentage of GDP. This input measure has its own biases. Because R&D spending is often subsidized through tax credits, firms have an incentive to overstate the amount of R&D they are doing. Few inspectors can tell the difference between routine testing (which is not part of R&D) and experimental testing (which is). Yet there is a robust literature on R&D spending suggesting that, despite these flaws, it is associated with growth at the firm, regional, and national level.

All three of these indicators—patents, research workforce size, and R&D spending—tend to produce similar rankings of countries (see table 1). Switzerland, Japan, Sweden, Israel, and Luxembourg do well on patenting, but Germany and South Korea are also strong. Similarly, the countries that have the largest research workforce are South Korea; Sweden, Denmark, and Finland (Norway is close); and Singapore and Taiwan. Rankings by R&D spending are somewhat different: Israel ranks highest, but other East Asian and European countries perform well.

But these indicators are not measures of radical innovation. Some patents, for example, are relatively trivial, and some R&D leads to only minor improvements. Radical innovations are hard to show statistically. Two potential indicators are Nobel prizes per capita and the number of unicorn firms (see table 2). Nobel prizes are not really a measure of innovation at all, but rather a biased indicator of breakthrough science. The United States has had 1.14 Nobel prize winners (affiliated with US institutions) per million population, far more than any country except Norway—and, in absolute terms, more than the next three countries combined.

Another indicator is more closely related to commercialization, in a sense. Unicorn firms are privately held startups valued at more

Table 1 Key science and technology innovation indicators, top 20 countries worldwide, 2020 or latest

Patents per 1,000 population[a]		Researchers per 1,000 population[b]		R&D expenditure as % of GDP[c]	
RANK	COUNTRY	RANK	COUNTRY	RANK	COUNTRY
1	Switzerland 0.15	1	Korea 8.63	1	Israel 5.4
2	Japan 0.14	2	Sweden 7.74	2	Korea 4.8
3	Sweden 0.08	3	Denmark 7.64	3	Sweden 3.5
4	Israel 0.07	4	Finland 7.54	4	Belgium 3.5
5	Luxembourg 0.06	5	Singapore 7.44	5	United States 3.5
6	Germany 0.06	6	Taiwan 6.94	6	Japan 3.3
7	Korea 0.06	7	Norway 6.75	7	Austria 3.2
8	Denmark 0.05	8	Austria 5.81	8	Switzerland 3.2
9	Finland 0.05	9	Netherlands 5.81	9	Germany 3.1
10	Netherlands 0.05	10	Belgium 5.77	10	Denmark 3.0
11	Austria 0.05	11	Switzerland 5.52	11	Finland 2.9
12	United States 0.04	12	Japan 5.49	12	Iceland 2.5
13	Belgium 0.04	13	New Zealand 5.48	13	China 2.4
14	Taiwan 0.03	14	Germany 5.43	14	France 2.4
15	France 0.03	15	Portugal 5.16	15	Netherlands 2.3
16	Norway 0.03	16	Luxembourg 4.88	16	Norway 2.3
17	United Kingdom 0.02	17	Slovenia 4.88	17	Slovenia 2.2
18	Singapore 0.02	18	United States 4.81	18	Czech Republic 2.0
19	Ireland 0.02	19	France 4.74	19	Singapore 1.9
20	Canada 0.02	20	Ireland 4.73	20	Australia 1.8

[a] Triadic patents (registered in the United States, the European Union, and Japan) per 1,000 population, three-year average, 2018–20.
[b] Full-time equivalent researchers per 1,000 population.
[c] Gross domestic expenditure on R&D (GERD) as a percentage of GDP.

SOURCE: OECD (2020). *Main Science and Technology Indicators, Volume 2020 Issue 2*. OECD Publishing. R&D data for Switzerland, Singapore, and Australia is from 2019. Researcher data for Canada and New Zealand is from 2019.

Table 2 Indicators of "radical" innovation (per million population)

Nobel Prize by institutional affiliations			*Unicorn firms*		
RANK			RANK		
1	United States	1.14	1	Singapore	3.45
2	Norway	1.12	2	Israel	2.80
3	Israel	0.76	3	United States	2.12
4	Switzerland	0.69	4	Hong Kong	1.35
5	UK	0.68	5	Switzerland	1.03
6	Sweden	0.39	6	United Kingdom	0.84
7	Finland	0.36	7	Sweden	0.67
8	Denmark	0.34	8	Canada	0.65
9	Netherlands	0.29	9	Ireland	0.60
10	France	0.25	10	Netherlands	0.46
11	Japan	0.25	11	Germany	0.43
12	Canada	0.21	12	South Korea	0.43
13	Germany	0.19	13	France	0.40
14	Australia	0.12	14	Australia	0.39
15	Belgium	0.09	15	China	0.17
16	Italy	0.03	16	Brazil	0.09
17	Russia	0.03	17	Japan	0.09
18	China	0.01	18	Mexico	0.07
19	India	0.00	19	India	0.06
20	Austria	—	20	Indonesia	0.03

SOURCES: Nobel affiliations adapted from Soskice, D. (2021). The United States as radical innovation driver: The politics of declining dominance? In J. S. Hacker, A. Hertel-Fernandez, P. Pierson, & K. Thelen (Eds). *The American political economy: Politics, markets, and power* (p. 323). Cambridge University Press, adapted from Urquiola, M. (2020). *Markets, minds, and money: Why America leads the world in university research*. Harvard University Press, table 1.1. Unicorn firms data sourced from Crunchbase (2022). The Crunchbase unicorn board. https://news.crunchbase.com/unicorn-company-list.

than US$1 billion. Assessing the number of unicorns in a region or country shows where rapidly scaling new tech firms are developing. But many unicorn firms are only clever replications of new technologies developed elsewhere, adapted to serve local markets. Moreover, because unicorns are defined on the basis of market valuations, they may signal asset bubbles rather than real commercial activity. But a number of small economies—including Singapore, Israel, and Hong Kong—perform well on this measure, along with the United States, Switzerland, and the United Kingdom ,which has a strong focus on scaling financial technology firms.

Others have broadened the measures of innovation to capture "soft innovation" in services. For example, Carolina Castaldi and Sandro Mendonça consider trademarks as an innovation indicator.[37] These are another form of intellectual property, albeit one that does not require technological novelty. It can give a clearer indication of commercialization than patenting measures do and account for innovations that are not captured by standard indicators such as R&D spending.

MEASURING COMPLEXITY

International organizations play a futile parlor game producing league tables of countries ranked by a combination of factors such as R&D and patenting. These rankings make good headlines but bad policy. The question of which country is the most innovative is impossible to answer, like asking which country is best at sport. (The United States dominates the Olympics but is poor at soccer and mercifully uncompetitive at cricket.)

It is more useful to view different innovation systems as having different specializations. This insight underpins Breznitz's assertion that Germany beats the United States at innovation. The United States is clearly the leader at producing the dynamic, frontier-tech firms that have shaped so much modern capitalism. It is hard to imagine Google, Facebook, Apple, or other highly innovative companies developing anywhere else. But other countries succeed in other forms of innovation, such as the incremental *Feinmechanik* that has sustained German carmakers.

Constructing a single metric for innovation performance places an artificial structure on a complex concept and can yield some unfortunate results. There is no perfect measure of innovation; few are even particularly good. But this doesn't mean that we cannot come to any conclusions. A group of countries—the United States, the Nordic countries, East Asia, and some countries of central Europe—tend to be more innovative than others by a range of measures. Yet these countries differ hugely in the extent to which they manage to translate this innovation into improved living standards. If innovation is complex, then it feeds into living standards in many different ways , which are contingent on the type of innovation and the context in which it takes place. Innovation is hugely important in raising living standards, but the benefits are not always equally shared.

2 Innovation and Living Standards

My great-grandfather, Harry Lee, was born in 1880 in Stockport, an industrial town near Manchester. There's a running joke about the tough lives of people in the urban north of England, and Harry's was no exception. He had both rheumatic fever and typhoid as a child and was proud to take a cold bath each morning. At fifteen, he started work at Furnivals of Reddish, a company that designed and manufactured printing presses. These printing presses were not a new technology, but they were improving rapidly as companies like Furnivals made continual minor improvements.

A condition of his employment was that he study geometry and mathematics at the Stockport College of Technology, his local technical college. This was one of the institutions founded by Victorian-era municipal governments to improve technical education. Harry Lee's work led to several patents. He shared the practical knowledge he gained at work by teaching at the college where he had studied. His work was skilled, and he was well rewarded: he lived in a big house with a tennis court in the garden, something unattainable to his ancestors.

Harry Lee's life tells us three important things about innovation and how it translates to living standards. First, to lead to higher living standards, innovation doesn't have to be at the cutting edge: the application and reapplication of existing technologies is enough. Second, innovation requires skills. Third, local circumstances are important in making sure the benefits of innovation are felt. The innovative firms in Stockport made it easier for my Stockport-based great-grandfather to succeed.

Stockport's economy isn't as innovative as it once was. But there are places that do manage to combine the institutional frameworks for innovation with those that distribute the benefits. Innovation can lead to higher living standards, but some places manage the relationship better than others.

INNOVATION AND WAGES

As my great-grandfather's story shows, innovation can create jobs, raise living standards, and improve lives. While much of the literature on innovation focuses on its downsides, such as the cost of disruption, the commercialization and use of new technologies can create huge benefits. To see these, let's start with a situation where all firms are the same, producing the same products with the same technologies. In this model, without innovation, there should be no wage differentials between firms. Firms sell the same goods and make no rents (a term used here to describe the difference between the price charged for goods and the cost of production). If a firm tried to charge more than the going rate, they would sell nothing at all, so no firm could pay higher wages than another. Wages would be equalized between firms.

Such a basic model is clearly at odds with empirical reality. Observationally, workers with similar qualifications and personal characteristics may earn quite different salaries in different firms. The reasons for these disparities are complex and sometimes unpleasant: they have to do with market structure, selection, discrimination, and so on. But one major reason is that innovation allows firms to charge an economic rent.

Innovation creates rents in two ways. An innovation may allow a firm to increase prices: for example, a firm's innovative design of a product makes buyers willing to pay more. In this case, the basic relationship is

innovation → higher prices → higher wages

Innovation may also reduce the cost of production (thereby increasing productivity per worker). Innovation allows workers to produce more and, as a result, their wages rise. The relationship is also simple:

innovation → higher productivity → higher wages

As with all good models, there is some truth to these statements. Innovations that enable firms to produce more with less may translate to higher wages. These two fundamental mechanisms—making better things or making things better—provide the core rationales for innovation, for the firm at least.

Such a basic model is useful, but partial. The economy is a complex adaptive system with multiple feedback loops. Innovation too is complex, involving not only new products but also new processes. It can be labor augmenting, increasing the productivity of labor, or labor replacing. Wages don't automatically respond, and workers can capture the rents (or quasi-rents, as they diminish over time) to varying degrees. Labor markets are shaped by formal and informal institutions, muddying the relationship. They are messy places that do not completely reward success (or failure). If you doubt this, look at your colleagues: some are probably less competent than others, but it is unlikely that their wages reflect the differences.

Despite these imperfections, workers still gain from being in innovative firms—and increasingly so. The rents that are the benefits of innovation can be discerned in wage data. Workers in innovative companies are more productive and tend to earn higher wages than other workers.[1] Firms use higher earnings as a way of retaining workers who are good at innovation, thereby preventing them from sharing knowledge with rival firms. One estimate is that US workers gain thirty cents for every dollar of surplus created by a new patent.[2]

Surprisingly, these benefits extend to less-well-educated workers in a firm—even those unlikely to be directly involved in the innovation. To see why this might be the case, Philippe Aghion, an economist at the Collège de France, presents a simple model in which highly skilled R&D workers need support from other, less-well-educated workers in their firms. It is hard to screen the non-R&D workers for the skills they need in advance of hiring, so if they are successful once in place, R&D-intensive firms bid up the wages of existing staff to prevent them from leaving. A good receptionist in an innovation-intensive firm earns more than one in a less innovative company.[3]

But while the benefits of working in an innovative firm are widespread, they are not equally shared. The gains accrue mainly to senior staff and the inventors themselves. The highest rewards tend to go to those in the upper quartile of earnings.[4] And the entrepreneur tends to be the biggest winner. One Finnish study showed that the lion's share of benefits from a new patent went to the founder of the company.[5]

Next, let's think about how the benefits of innovation extend beyond the specific firm that introduces them. One of the classic arguments in economics is that the benefits of the creation of new knowledge extend beyond the individual firm. Ideas are nonrivalrous, meaning that they can be used by many others, so that investments in production can have wide benefits. One estimate is that the social return on R&D is four times the private return. Of course, there are losers as well as winners from R&D: new products may divert demand from existing products.[6] But there is still a strong justification for public investments in R&D.

Innovations are often protected—through patents, for example. But these protections expire. The benefits of innovation, such as they are, start to leach out into the wider economy. The result is a process of innovation-driven technological change that has far-reaching implications across labor markets, for national and local economies, and for policy.

The existence of these rents provides a justification for some inequality. The world is better because of innovation such as new pharmaceuticals, microchips, and other forms of improved technology. But these rents should dissipate over time, as other firms and workers catch up through imitation or through developing their own new products and processes. One reason intellectual property rights exist is to ensure there is an incentive to capture these rents; one reason they often expire is to allow others to catch up.

Yet often rents don't derive from the actions of the firm alone. In the first place, as Mariana Mazzucato has argued strongly, the public sector often plays a key role in the promoting innovation, through funding applied research and by providing education, infrastructure, and so on.[7] Rents may also derive from unjust protection of new technologies, through lawsuits and other anticompetitive practices. Moreover, because many of the gains of innovation arise from its diffusion into new uses, there can still be a net welfare gain, even if the state does not recoup its investment.

ROBOTS VERSUS REALITY

Although innovation can produce real benefits for workers, it is more commonly seen as a malign influence on the labor market. A vast number of articles and books portray a dystopian future for work as new technologies divide labor markets. The fear of automation is not new. But each wave of technological change comes with the fear that, next time, it will be *your* job that is replaced by robots.

The worst of the horror stories come from those looking at the impact on occupations. Carl Frey and Michael Osborne produced the stark finding that 47 percent of US employment is in occupations at high risk of automation.[8] On this basis, the paper has become one of the most cited—and perhaps misunderstood—in the social sciences. Low-paid occupations are, as might be expected, at greater risk. But the paper is concerned with change, rather than redundancy, so it makes no predictions about unemployment. Misreadings of occupation-based measures such as this assume that workers in an occupation threatened by obsolescence don't switch to more productive tasks (for example, moving from working as a typist to one organizing meetings). Indeed, the number of jobs at risk is lower if we account for this process of within-occupation adaptation. A related OECD study focuses on the tasks performed rather than occupations—a switch in assumptions that reduces the number of jobs lost to automation to only 9 percent.[9]

In challenging the view that innovation leads to unemployment, a starting point is to ask whether innovation and new technology have led to widespread unemployment in the great technological shocks of the past. Fortunately, we have great time-series data on employment and unemployment. The Bank of England (the United Kingdom's central bank) dates to the 1700s and has been keeping records for most of that time. If new technologies were really taking jobs, we would expect to see this trend reflected in their data, particularly during the industrial revolutions of mechanization, power, and electronics.[10]

Yet three key measures of UK labor market performance during periods of rapid technological change show little sign of technological unemployment. The unemployment rate is defined as the share of those unemployed among those who are either in work or actively looking for work. It reflects major economic shocks, such as the Great Depression and the United Kingdom's difficulties in the 1980s. But despite rapid technological change, there is no sign of a long-term increase in unemployment. Because people leave the labor market and stop looking for work when the labor market is weaker, the unemployment rate can be volatile. So another measure of employment is the employment-to-population ratio. This is falling slowly over time, but much of this fall is good news, resulting from

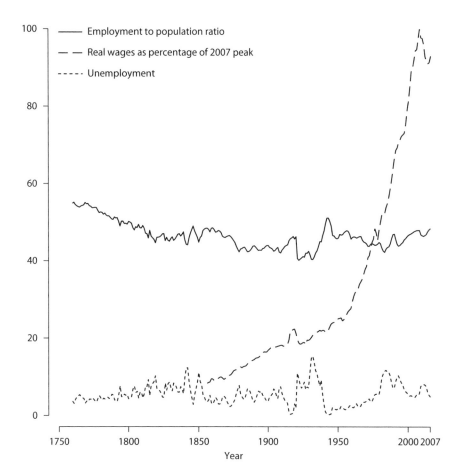

Figure 3. Long-term patterns of employment, unemployment, and wages. *Source:* Bank of England (2023). *A millennium of macroeconomic data.* www.bankofengland.co.uk/statistics/research-datasets.

people choosing to stay in education or retire. There is no clear trend of declining employment.

The third measure, real wages, is unambiguously positive, at least until the last few years (see figure 3). To fit this on the same axes as the other measures, I've plotted it as a percentage of the peak, 2007.

There was an extraordinary increase in real wages from the 1950s right up until the 2008 financial crisis. If technology has led to widespread unemployment and reduced average wages, it has happened only recently.

But technology has, of course, still had an influence on the labor market. Although it has not led to widespread unemployment, it has triggered widespread change in the nature of occupations people do and the types of tasks performed within those occupations.

The dominant explanation for these changes is that technology leads to a polarization of the labor market. In the basic model, consider all jobs on a scale from most skilled to least skilled, where the most-skilled jobs tend to earn the highest wages. (*Skills* is a horrible term here—care worker is a very skilled job, just a poorly paid one—but it is the clearest shorthand for these processes.) The initial prediction of the impact of information and communications technology (ICT) on the labor market is that skilled workers will be made more productive by ICT, and less-skilled workers will be replaced. The result is a process of skill-biased technological change (SBTC), where ICT increases employment at the top of the skill distribution and decreases it at the bottom. Less-skilled workers are more likely to become unemployed; skilled workers earn more.

But this view does not seem to fit the data, at least that coming out of the United States. Instead, the 1990s and 2000s saw growth in so-called low-skilled employment, often in personal services. The reason is the nature of the tasks that ICT can, or rather cannot, perform. While computers are good at routine tasks such as adding up numbers, they are poor at tasks that are nonroutine, manual, cognitive, or social. They have complemented the tasks performed by skilled professionals and reduced the jobs in the middle of the income distribution. The opportunity cost of time for the growing band of professionals who benefit from ICT has led to an increased demand for personal services—such as cleaning and waiting tables—from a growing middle class. (Incidentally, these new jobs must be done geographically near the high-paid workers who have benefited from ICT.) This idea, the "routinization hypothesis," has since been supported by analysis of data from the United States and the United Kingdom in the 1990s. The result is a process of employment polarization, rather than upgrading.

Initial studies supported claims regarding the polarization of the labor market. The canonical studies include Goos and Manning's "Lousy and Lovely Jobs" and Autor, Levy, and Murnane's work on the routinization of skills.[11] These studies shaped the narrative about ICT and work, but they were based on two relatively similar economies and a specific period (the United Kingdom from 1979 to 1999 and the United States between 1978 and 1998) notable for the decline of manufacturing. The evidence for employment polarization outside this period has been weaker.

Much of the economy, in particular the parts that are likely to grow in the future, involves nonroutine activities predicted to be relatively unaffected by automation. It is likely that workers in one part of the economy will move into other roles, particularly as productivity increases wages at the top of the labor market. For example, the US labor market has seen a growth in well-paid professional workers. But this shifts the nature of demand in the economies where they live. Money-rich but time-poor professionals outsource household tasks such as cleaning, caring for children, walking dogs, and preparing food, creating local demand for other workers. As the high-skill economy in advanced economies has grown, there has often been a shift into low-wage services.[12]

But, again, it isn't clear that the theory generalizes beyond this specific period and these specific countries. Studies of countries with different institutional structures show quite different outcomes. For example, one study of Austria ranked occupations by skill level and used data from public employment offices to investigate polarization between 2007 and 2017.[13] The study found little evidence for polarization. A study of Switzerland over a longer period came to a similar conclusion.[14]

Even when we do find evidence of polarization in these countries, the dominant force is upgrading. The OECD has produced good data on job changes by country between 1995 and 2015. They divide jobs into three types: low-skilled jobs in service work, shops and market sales, and elementary occupations; mid-skilled jobs such as clerks, craft and related trades, and plant and machine operators; and high-skill jobs such as senior officials and managers, professionals, technicians, and associate professionals.[15] Across the OECD, the data shows evidence of polarization: there is growth in high- and low-skilled occupations and a decline in the middle. But there is far more growth at the top than the bottom, and the process is closer to professionalization than polarization. The two countries that have experienced the largest increase in high-skilled jobs are Austria and Switzerland, for reasons I discuss later.

Innovation and new technologies have changed the tasks we perform at work. The job of a university professor, for instance, has changed significantly over the past fifty years. Journal articles used to be typed and submitted in paper envelopes through the post; today they are written on computers and submitted online. Secretaries who used to take dictated letters have been replaced by professors sending their own messages. Pigeonholes are now full of standardized, colorful messages from publishers rather than informative, personalized messages from students. And universities are not exceptions: technology hasn't killed office work, but it has significantly reshaped it.

The next wave of technological change is likely to come from advances in artificial intelligence (AI) that make it more useful, reliable, and widespread. There is no question that this will lead to important changes to many people's working lives. If past history is a guide, it still seems unlikely that humans will become redundant, but there will be major changes. Those who can use AI to make themselves more productive will gain, those who perform tasks that can be done by AI will see shifts, and many will lose out.

But the impact of AI will depend on the policy frameworks put in place to shape its impact. A host of other factors beyond technology—skills policy, labor market regulation, and so on—shape the extent to which technological change influences the labor market.[16] Indeed, it is clear that AI will lead to much-needed growth in productivity in advanced economies. While new technology is often seen as a malign force, much of its impact comes from diffusion at a local level.

TECHNOLOGY DOESN'T KILL JOBS, IT MOVES THEM

The narratives on innovation and jobs often miss an important fact: while the total number of jobs may seem to be similar, their location may change. An important study by Hilary Vipond of the London School of Economics and Political Science shows this vividly. She considers a massive technological shock in a single industry—boot making. In 1850, there were over a million people making boots in England. Two of the most important occupations in the sector had been cordwainers, who made the boots, and binders, who sewed together the uppers. In 1852, a new technology—the Singer sewing machine—mechanized much of this process. (Isaac Singer didn't actually invent the sewing machine but improved others' versions and bought up patents.) The next thirty years was a period of massive disruption for these occupations: according to Vipond, "Nearly every county in England lost 90 per cent of its binders."[17]

But this shift didn't mean that jobs disappeared: there was an occupational shift. New workers were required to use sewing machines. This was seen as a woman's job, and so men lost out. But there was also a geographical shift: the new occupations were concentrated in Leicestershire and Northamptonshire in central England. Overall, technology hadn't killed employment, but it had changed where workers were employed.

The unambiguous winners in this change were in the distant town of Elizabeth, New Jersey, where Singer sewing machines were first made. Its population doubled between 1850 and 1860 and almost doubled again in the decade after that. The result was disruption rather than revolution. Certain groups lost out, but aggregate welfare still increased. One point of note is that this was a geographically distributed shock, which affected areas differently. While the result of technological changes is painful for those affected, when concentrated in a single, small local economy the effects can be far worse—a negative-demand shock from which it is hard to adjust. Many stories of the harms of technological unemployment, such as dock workers being put out of work by the containerization of shipping, come from the shock being localized.

Innovation and new technology are, too often, framed in negative terms. Innovation can of course destroy jobs, but it can also create and modify jobs. It is generally better to be producing the innovations, particularly in markets where innovations are protected through intellectual property rights, than to be on the receiving end of them.

SKILLS, INNOVATION, AND EQUITY

The problem for many of the boot binders in Vipond's study was that the skills used to design the sewing machine in New Jersey made redundant the skills used to bind boots in England. Skills are the ability to complete a task well. They come in many forms: physical skills (such as sporting ability), cognitive, emotional, and so on. They are not necessarily learned through education but can be gained on the job or through hobbies, and they are developed and adapted throughout the life course. Because skilled workers are, almost by definition, better at updating their skills than those with lower skill levels (or at least more practiced), they can upgrade their skills throughout their lives.

Many people find their skills aging rapidly, particularly in fast-changing, innovation-intensive sectors. The massive rise in computational power has allowed academics to do more advanced work, but it has also led to higher expectations, with papers requiring better data, more complicated models, and more polished graphics. As the technology has changed, so have the skills required to be at the leading edge.

Obsolescence is widespread across rapidly changing sectors of the economy. A study of graduates with applied STEM degrees in engineering and computer science in the United States shows that although they start with a substantial wage premium over non-STEM graduates, this declines significantly over time, as skills become obsolete and newer ones become important.[18] Skills need to be both learned and renewed. This generally happens in three ways: through learning on the job, through formal training and education, and through learning from people nearby. Skill acquisition is thus geographically based, as we learn from those around us. Not only do skills represent an opportunity for innovation, but the lack of skills can represent a constraint. Lacking workers with the necessary skills, it is impossible to translate invention into innovation.

Innovation policymakers often think of only two sources of skills: skilled migrants and world-leading universities. These are good ideas, but not necessarily the best recipe for equitable prosperity. As my great-grandfather's story shows, innovation in profitable niches, along with continual upgrading of applied technical skills, can be a better way of aligning innovation with shared prosperity. There is a strong correlation between investments in vocational education and innovation.[19] Indeed, a factor common to all the countries in the club of innovative, equitable economies is a strong focus on technical and vocational education. Nobody doubts the importance of skills for innovation, but skill development also provides a vital route for sharing the benefits of innovation equitably.

THE BENEFITS OF INNOVATION ARE LOCAL

As the residents of Elizabeth, New Jersey, found, it is much easier to benefit from innovation when it is happening nearby. The best way to see this is to go somewhere where innovation is scarce. The Welsh valleys are a beautiful part of the world, but their residents have struggled to adapt from a coal-mining past. As a share of output, R&D spending in Wales is similar to that of Greece, GDP per capita is similar to that of Malta, and gross disposable household income (GDHI), a measure of living standards, is low—around 77 percent of the UK average. In contrast, affluent Cheshire has the R&D spending of Denmark, is almost as rich as Sweden, and has a GDHI 7 percent higher than the UK average. While we need to be careful about assuming causation from this sort of correlation, it is clear that innovation affects living standards in regions as much as it does at the national level.

If a firm innovates, the impact ripples through the local economy. A local economy is a bundle of interrelated activities: firms compete for land and labor, people compete for houses, and the production choices in various parts of the economy are determined, at least to some degree, by the activities of the firms around them. A firm that successfully innovates has a knock-on impact on those around it.

Now consider two different firms. The first is a high-tech startup— say a firm that makes satellite technology. Imagine that this firm develops an innovation, such as a product that allows satellites to swarm in space without risking collision. This technology is innovative, in that nobody has done it before; its complexity would make it hard for others to replicate, even if intellectual property laws allowed them to; and there is an established market for such technologies that underpins much modern ICT. And, crucially for this story, such a technology is produced in one place but consumed (or used) elsewhere. A radical innovation in one place concentrates returns in that place. The impact on the market of other local satellite firms, if there are any, is minimal. This sector is defined as *tradable*, because production can happen in one place and then be traded elsewhere.

Now consider a radical innovation in a very different sector: hairdressing. Hairdressing is the archetypal nontradable sector, because a haircut cannot be produced in one place and consumed elsewhere: you have to physically sit in the chair to have your hair done. Few people travel long distances to reach a better barber. So if a barber creates a radical new haircut, the barber may benefit by attracting more customers. But most of these are simply customers who would otherwise go to another local barber. Because the innovation simply displaces other nearby barbers, it is unlikely to serve as a motor of the local economy.

Of course, the distinction between tradables and nontradables is fuzzy, particularly in sectors such as specialist retail and tourism, and the internet may be making things fuzzier still, as individuals are able to order retail products and food online and consume them at home. But this way of thinking about the economy has two significant implications. The first is that tradables are valuable for local economies. Too many politicians aim to encourage new firms in the nontradable parts of the economy. These may create new jobs, and there may be scope for productivity gains. But such firms are unlikely to be the motor of the local economy. Instead, it is innovation that really matters.

But when considering the wider benefits of innovation, a second implication is particularly important. The jobs in nontradable sectors of the economy often depend on the existence of jobs in the tradable sectors. If the satellite company secures a large order, it might expand production locally, increasing the number of jobs in the local tradable sector. But it is also likely to rely on local cleaners, restaurants, and shops. Workers in these nontradable sectors, in turn, spend some of their money locally. Growth in the tech sector has a multiplier effect, with each successive round of spending creating an incremental benefit to the local economy.

The question, then, is who benefits from these multiplier effects. The answer here is complicated because the multiplier doesn't just increase wages; it also increases costs. Urban economists who work on these issues tend to be focused on a model of the housing market, family, and state from the United States—indeed, evidence on this point is disappointingly focused on the Anglosphere. While similar market processes operate in other countries, the complications of social housing, family formation, and other state intervention tend to be abstracted out.

The classic study comes from Enrico Moretti, a UC Berkeley economist whose estimates of the potential multipliers from high-technology industries in the United States, mainly ICT manufacturing firms, were around 4–5, meaning that every new job in tech leads to four or five new jobs in other parts of the local economy.[20] Others have focused on the effect on wages. Tom Kemeny and Taner Osman find the effects are modest, with 10 percent more tech employment leading to 0.1 percent higher real wages in nontradable sectors.[21] In my own work with Stephen Clarke of the Resolution Foundation, we found modest multipliers from high-tech and digital tech industries in Britain, with ten new jobs in the innovation-intensive industry creating around seven in nontradable sectors.[22] The jobs are a net gain, as they go to people who would not normally be working, but they are not well paid, and they reduce average wages for low-skilled workers.

Although these studies have helped us understand the impact of innovation-rich sectors on local economies, they suffer from two problems that are rife in this field. The first is that they draw general narratives from very specific examples. Crazy house prices clearly reduce real wages significantly in San Francisco and London, but this is not a universal rule. And where studies have investigated the impact of tech on real incomes and adjusted for housing costs—as Clarke and I as well as Kemeny and Osman do—we find that while housing markets do reduce the wage gains of a growing tech economy, the reduction is small. But job creation even in the nontradable parts of the economy is partially dependent on what happens in tradables, suggesting that innovation in advanced, tradable sectors can benefit local economies.

DIFFUSION AND LOCAL LEARNING

Growth doesn't have to come from the technological frontier. Productivity growth can come both from innovation, which pushes the technological frontier outward, and also from catching up with the frontier. The importance of the latter process, the diffusion of new technologies, is often understated. It is particularly important at a distance from the frontier, as diffusion allows catching up.[23] For example, the widespread adoption of ICT in the United States led to a productivity surge between 1995 and 2000, driven by productivity growth in wholesale, retail, and financial services and associated with a reduction in US unemployment.[24] It wasn't the production of ICT beforehand that led to this widespread growth, but its subsequent diffusion.

Diffusion is, along with invention and commercialization, one of the three crucial aspects of innovation. The adoption of new technologies in new contexts is the only way to ensure that an innovation has an impact in the wider world.[25] Both the adoption of new technology (whether it is used) and its penetration (how widely it is adopted when used in context) determine how much it increases productivity. Yet too often innovation policy focuses on the initial invention rather than the later phases of use. The result is economically harmful. The Bank of England, for example, pins the blame for weak productivity in many UK firms on the lack of diffusion of new technologies.[26] Small firms in particular can have local market niches that protect them from competitive pressure, and ineffective management that does little to improve productivity. So they have few incentives and little capability to introduce new technologies that might be risky and expensive, offering a long-term reward that is out of their frame of reference.

Just as innovation is geographically based, so is its diffusion. The Swedish geographer Torsten Hagerstrand was the first to set out the idea that diffusion of innovation was geographically bounded. There are three fundamental steps in the adoption of any new technology: becoming aware that it exists, deciding to adopt it, and having the ability to do so. In Hagerstrand's model, innovation starts with a core of local early adopters who know that it exists, and it moves into nearby areas before entering widespread use.[27] Adoption often happens in certain countries or cities, often termed *lead markets,* from which actors can learn from the knowledge that spills over between economic actors.[28]

Diffusion is biased by both skill and geography. At first, use of a new technology tends to be restricted to the skilled workers who have produced it. As it becomes normalized, its use becomes codified, and knowledge of its uses and potential becomes widespread, it starts to spread geographically. Examining growth in US local economies from 1860 to 2010, three economic geographers, Tom Kemeny, Sergio Petralia, and Michael Storper, show that this process of technology creation and diffusion helps explain major patterns of convergence and divergence in US economies.[29] When a major disruptive technology such as electricity comes into being, its benefits are initially limited to the cities and regions where it is created, widening regional disparities. But as it becomes diffused throughout the economy, firms in other locations begin to catch up, with the result that spatial inequality starts to decline. The benefits of major new innovations are initially concentrated in one place. Only later, as the long waves of technological change diffuse those technologies across a wider area, are the benefits more widely shared.

Diffusion also helps less-skilled workers. Complex new technologies are often applied by higher-skilled workers, complementing skills in nonroutine cognitive work. But as they diffuse across the economy, they are more likely to be used by workers in less-skilled occupations. The high-skilled jobs associated with a new technology are more likely to remain geographically concentrated; in contrast, lower-skilled jobs that incorporate these technologies are less reliant on rapid access to the tacit knowledge and experimentation needed to develop the technology.[30]

APPLIED SKILLS AND DIFFUSION

The economic benefit from innovation depends on its widespread diffusion and implementation. Yet the emphasis on invention leads us to focus on high-level skills, missing the crucial role of other skills in the translation of invention into widely commercialized innovation.[31] In a classic 1972 paper on technology, Nathan Rosenberg argued that too much attention was paid to the creation of new technologies and too little to its diffusion. Yet he acknowledged that "the rate at which new techniques are adopted and incorporated into the productive process is, without doubt, one of the central questions of economic growth. New techniques exert their economic impact as a function of the rate at which they displace older techniques and the extent to which the new techniques are superior to the old ones." Innovation was, for Rosenberg, a gradual process of improvement rather than one of radical change. "Continuities are more important than discontinuities."[32]

Mid-skilled workers who can adapt technologies to new circumstances are particularly important to the diffusion of innovations. The benefits of new technologies and concepts aren't immediately obvious to those using them: they need to be applied, tested, and incorporated into workflows. In consequence, those technologies "that stand the test of selection become the new standards in both technological trajectories and formal education."[33] Yet many systems fail to provide the skills needed for diffusion to occur. In the United States, this deficiency has a negative impact on patenting. One study showed that decline in routine work performed by mid-skilled, blue-collar workers reduces innovation: a 1 percent fall in routine occupations leads to a fall in patenting of 1.8 percent.[34] Another example comes from the United Kingdom, where there is too much focus on star scientists and too little on the incremental improvements that can be made by technicians. This focus impedes growth. In a study of the use of new technologies in British life sciences, the political economist Paul Lewis observes: "Where the skills of the technician workforce are deficient—because of shortages of technicians, or because their skills are too specific, or because they lack theoretical knowledge—firms will suffer from poor absorptive capacity, lacking the capability to deploy new technologies to good effect."[35]

Local economies can be trapped in a self-reinforcing cycle, where lack of skills forces firms to adopt particular strategies that then discourage the development of skills. In the most famous analysis of this relationship, David Finegold and David Soskice argued in 1988 that education systems are both a product of and a contributing factor to economic performance. In a damning critique of the UK model, they suggested that the country had fallen into a low-skill equilibrium, or a "self-reinforcing network of societal and state institutions which interact to stifle the demand for improvements in skills," where "the majority of enterprises [are] staffed by poorly trained managers and workers produce low-quality goods and service."[36] Simply investing in skills is useless without considering the institutions and complementary investments in which they are used—both within and outside the firm. In contrast, the most successful local or regional economies develop dynamic ecosystems that allow continual, innovation-driven upgrading of production processes. Finegold describes these as a "geographical cluster of organisations (both firms and research institutions) employing staff with advanced, specialised skills in a particular industry and/or technology."[37]

As ever, the classic example here is Silicon Valley.[38] The initial growth of the cluster of ICT-related activities had many sources, including defense contracts and spinouts from Hewlett-Packard. But these were seeds planted in fertile ground. Elite universities such as Stanford and UC Berkeley provided skilled workers for these new sectors. Firms were attracted by this supply of skilled workers; skilled workers were attracted to the firms; entrepreneurs came from both the private sector and from the universities. In order to monitor their investments, financiers providing venture capital invested according to the ninety-minute rule, which meant they focused investments in firms within easy geographic reach. There was also a good mix of infrastructure, institutions, and culture to support the development of this ecosystem: international airports, technology parks and incubators, a high quality of life, and a risk-taking attitude. Firms in the cluster became interconnected and formed a strong network culture that allowed the area to adapt. This ensured that skilled workers could adapt and upgrade their skills through their careers though informal learning processes, networks of knowledge sharing, and job hopping between firms. The conventional explanation is that these learning processes aid the forms of radical innovation in fast-changing industries in which famous Silicon Valley companies operate. And the model becomes self-sustaining—for example, by attracting skilled workers from all over the world to work in the area and continue the process of innovation.[39]

The incentives for firms to invest in R&D and for workers to invest in appropriate skills are codependent, or strategic complementarities over the long run.[40] If workers know that their employers are focused on R&D and innovation, they have incentives to develop these skills. If their investments of time and effort in developing these skills are likely to be wasted, they won't do it.

BALANCING INNOVATION AND EQUITY

If the gains from innovation are felt particularly where there are innovative firms, where adaptation and diffusion are enabled, and where workers have appropriate skills, then the question is where these things happen. Which countries combine innovation with equity? Given that there is no single measure of innovation or of equity, in this book I try to develop a picture based on multiple indicators. This form of careful triangulation from different data sources is intended to give a picture that reliably illustrates some general trends, but needs careful consideration. I divide advanced countries into four "clubs": those that are neither innovative nor equitable;

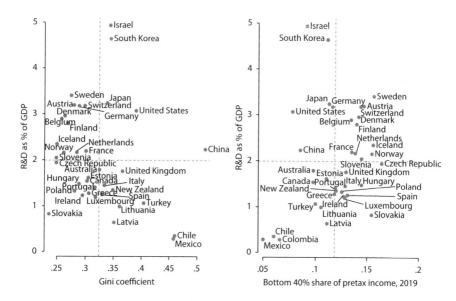

Figure 4. R&D spending and inequality in the OECD and China. *Sources: OECD statistical database.* R&D data from OECD (2023). *Main science and technology indicators.* OECD. www.oecd.org/sti/msti.htm; Gini coefficients and bottom 40 percent shares from Alvaredo, F., Atkinson, A. B., Piketty, T., and Saez, E. (2022). *World inequality database.* WID.world. https://wid.world/data.

those that are low on innovation but equitable; those that are highly innovative but inequitable; and innovative countries with equitable economies. There is much to learn from this last category of country, but we focus too much on those where innovation comes at the expense of equity.

To distinguish the four clubs, I plot a basic measure of innovation—R&D spending as a percentage of GDP—against the Gini coefficient, a measure of inequality. Neither is a perfect measure: R&D spending is an input rather than an output of innovation (although it does include spending on nonpatented innovation and the adaptation of innovations produced elsewhere). The Gini coefficient is a summary statistic for inequality that ranges between 1 (perfect inequality) and 0 (perfect equality), with a higher figure indicating greater inequality. A single summary statistic ignores much variation, something we will consider later. To illustrate the four clubs, I've included a vertical and horizontal line to show the OECD mean for each of these indicators.

All these countries tend to have strong middle classes, according to the OECD definition: the share of individuals in households with incomes between 75 percent and 200 percent of the median. The United States has an extremely high proportion of people in the poor category: double that of Austria or Switzerland, and almost three times that of Denmark.

Major differences are apparent in the size of this middle-income category. In the United States, 51 percent of people are middle-income, compared to 58 percent in Britain and 61 percent across the OECD as a whole. Switzerland has 65 percent in this group and 8 percent in the upper-income category; Austria 67 percent and 7 percent, respectively; and in egalitarian Denmark the proportions are 69 percent and 4 percent. In these three countries 72, 74, and 73 percent of the population, respectively, are in the middle- and upper-income categories combined, compared to just under 70 percent for the United Kingdom and 65 percent for the United States. The relative strength of the middle classes of these countries (even in high-income Switzerland) sets them apart.[41]

Taxation partly accounts for these results, of course. But many of the variables I examine here are pretax. Moreover, evidence suggests that taxation does not explain differences in average incomes between countries as much as some commentators portray, a finding that is perhaps unsurprising when we consider how unprogressive taxation is in many countries. In the most comprehensive attempt to compare inequality in Europe and the United States, Thomas Blanchet and colleagues at the World Inequality Database show that pretax income explains more than 90 percent of the difference between US and European inequality after taxation is taken into account.[42] Other institutions—wider access to education, higher

Table 3   Income classes in selected countries, 2013 (defined by percentage of median income)

	Poor (0–50%)	*Lower income (50–75%)*	*Middle income (75–200%)*	*Upper income (more than 200%)*	*Total middle and upper income*
Switzerland	8.6	19.0	64.5	7.9	72.4
Austria	9.0	17.4	66.5	7.1	73.6
Sweden	10.2	19.6	65.2	5.0	70.2
United Kingdom	9.4	21.0	58.3	11.3	69.6
United States	17.9	16.8	51.2	14.0	65.2
OECD	11.4	18.1	61.5	9.0	70.5

SOURCE: OECD (2019). *Under pressure: The squeezed middle class.* OECD Publishing. https://doi.org/10.1787/689afed1-en.

minimum wages, wage setting institutions, access to healthcare—all explain the wage distribution *before* taxation and redistribution. Instead, these researchers argue, other factors influence income distribution before taxation exerts an effect. Universal education in the Nordic nations, the Netherlands, and Germany allows a form of what has—unfashionably—been called predistribution. This means that taxation explains only part of the effect. There is no single, simple explanation for variations in inequality.

INNOVATION, DIFFUSION, AND REDISTRIBUTION

Innovation clearly affects living standards, particularly through modifications to existing technologies and their adaptation to new circumstances that result in marginal and occasional improvements in living standards. Thinking about innovation in this way means that we should be less concerned about the negative impact of technology on the labor market than about ensuring that workers have the skills and competence required to use and gain from new technology. Much of the research on innovation has focused on star scientists and radical innovation. But if the purpose of innovation is to improve living standards, we would be better off focusing on lessons from places that combine innovation and equity—places that have sustained their middle classes and managed to combine economic performance with equity. The remainder of this book does just that.

3 Switzerland

THE DIFFUSION OF INNOVATION

At first sight, Switzerland is hardly a paradise of equality. It is better known for luxury: private banking, ski holidays, and diamond watches. In 2019 the Gini coefficient of household income inequality was 0.316, far below that of the United States (0.375) but well above that of Sweden (0.276).[1]

Yet Switzerland is one of the best countries in the world in which to be a worker. While the share of national income going to the labor force has declined in many countries, Switzerland has bucked this trend. The share of pretax income going to the bottom 40 percent of income earners is higher than in Finland or Denmark.[2] And it achieves this situation without big-state redistribution: government spending is significantly lower in Switzerland even than in the United States, and the state does relatively little to redistribute income.[3]

Like much else about the country, innovation in Switzerland is unusual. One of the world's most innovative countries, it is one of the few to combine German-style niche production in historic industries with US-style disruptive innovation in radical new technologies. It has strong domestic firms but also attracts multinationals,[4] and there are relatively good jobs, even for those without university education. The result is that Swiss income distribution is relatively more equitable *before* taxes than that of other countries. The Swiss model is one of predistribution, not redistribution.

This chapter examines key elements of the Swiss model that allow the diffusion and adaption of innovation and enable Swiss workers to benefit. A combination of technical skills, niche production, and geographically balanced growth allows Swiss workers to derive significant gains from innovation and the use of new technology even if they are not at the cutting edge. Labor regulation and high costs provide powerful incentives for firms to create good jobs. Switzerland is often feted as a highly innovative country, but it also has an institutional structure that helps distribute the benefits.

THE *SONDERFALL* SCHWEIZ

For a small country with few natural resources, Switzerland is remarkably rich. GDP per capita PPP (GDP based on purchasing power parity) is the fourth highest in the OECD: in 2020 it was just over US $83,000, behind that of Luxembourg, Norway and Ireland.[5] Disposable household income is high, despite high prices. This is the special case (*Sonderfall*) of Switzerland.

Underpinning this success is one of the world's most innovative economies. Innovation is hard to measure. But Switzerland regularly ranks first in the Global Innovation Index, produced by the World Intellectual Property Organization. In one scholarly set of rankings, Switzerland comes first in six of eight measures of innovation, and second in the other two.[6] The country has historic strengths in innovation-intensive niches and more recent strengths in radical innovation and tech. Old, slow-cycle innovation clusters such as Basel's pharmaceutical industry have combined with newer strengths in radical tech in Zurich. The Swiss industrial base is distinguished by its focus on quality production, and this quality is sustained by innovation.

Swiss economic success comes from a diverse set of industries. Major multinational firms include domestic firms such as Nestlé, Novartis, and Roche. But the headquarters of foreign multinationals such as Boots and Glencore are also based there, attracted by the tax advantages offered by some cantons—the semiautonomous states that date to the thirteenth century. The Swiss bankers famous in popular media are important to the economy but not disproportionately so: finance and insurance accounts for around 9 percent of total value added, compared to 8 percent in the United States, the United Kingdom, and Australia.[7]

The great historian of Switzerland, Jonathan Steinberg, links the country's political economy to its geography: it is both at the center of Europe and, because of its mountainous terrain, separate from it. Most of medieval Europe developed feudal societies in which an established nobility owned the land, and a peasantry farmed it in exchange for produce. But this model didn't work in the Swiss mountains. The geography required a form of communalism for people to survive, involving the common maintenance of passes and roads and the regulation of military service.[8] With distinct topographic boundaries between communities, it was clear how to allocate and share civic responsibilities. The mountains made it hard to import food from elsewhere, giving the peasantry unusual leverage: landowners had no option but to buy local. It was also harder to take isolated communities by force: some valleys were allowed self-rule in a tacit exchange for "peaceful compliance," and others were just seen as impossible to control. This meant that "the sheer variety of Swiss and legal authorities prevented uniform control by elites in any of the cantons which in its turn permitted an explosion of 'proto-industrial' activity in the least likely places." Swiss society developed in smaller units, a cellular structure that remain characteristic of national life.[9]

The herder culture of Swiss society—an "archaic, independent, quasi-aristocratic form of life"—still shapes the Swiss political economy. It has had two major effects. First, it molded the political system: a highly decentralized structure based on slow-moving, direct democracy that allowed only gradual change. For Steinberg, "What differentiates Swiss history from the European pattern is the outcome. Swiss communities built from the bottom up, growing out of free peasant or urban associations, are in a curious sense bottom-heavy, rather like those dolls which spring up no matter how often the child pushes them over. The weight is at the base. The communities have a deep equilibrium to which, as the point of rest, the social and political order tends to return."[10] Many of the twenty-six cantons developed from sovereign states. They maintain core powers over tax, health, and education and vary significantly in their size and resources. The principle of subsidiarity means that decisions are made at the most local level possible, and direct democracy means that referenda can change local policy.[11] Policymaking is usually slow, local, and consensual. This reluctance to change can be beneficial but has also had some horrific results: after a failed referendum in 1959, it took until 1971 for women to gain the right to vote in federal elections, fifty-three years after they did so in Germany.[12]

The second consequence of Switzerland's idiosyncratic history and geography is a polycentric economic geography. Historically, cantons were able to defend their economic interests and tailor policy to their specific circumstances. But after the Industrial Revolution, the Swiss economy developed in a distinctive way. The major source of power was coal, which was, to some degree, transportable. Larger countries with lower transport costs often focused on mass production for internal markets, while centralized political systems focused infrastructure investments in a small number of cities. In contrast, Switzerland was already decentralized. Integration into wider European markets helped shape the country's economic geography: from an early stage there were multiple entry and exit points to the country, meaning that commerce did not focus on a single city.[13] The mountainous terrain helped encourage a decentralized economy: "The growth of industry had mainly taken the form of small-scale,

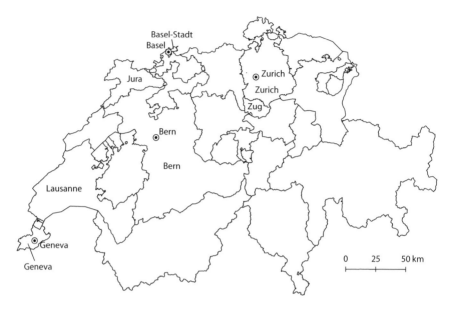

Map 1. Polycentric Switzerland.

high-quality production (watches and precision machinery in the Jura and the textile industry of central and eastern Switzerland). There were no natural resources but there was water power. The free, relatively well-educated population and highly developed mercantile communities were an additional strength of the Swiss economy. As a result industry fanned out in small units of production along the rushing streams." The result of this process was a country with dispersed industrial bases, a strong tradition of local autonomy, and none of the inequality of a feudal system.[14]

The economy started to outpace that of neighboring countries as early as the 1700s, when Switzerland underwent a form of industrialization that led to relative, if unevenly shared, wealth. Growing wealth was reflected in the patterns of economic development of the late 1800s and early 1900s, which, as in other countries, was accompanied by urbanization. Christian Stohr, an economic historian at the London School of Economics and Political Science, identifies three reasons why Switzerland has no single core: a strong federalist structure with no strong central government to draw resources into a capital city, strong transport networks that meant there was no major periphery, and a deeply integrated market and state apparatus.[15]

Today Switzerland is still multipolar and decentralized, but it is no longer isolated. High-quality transport infrastructure has made it one of the most accessible nations in Europe.[16] At the same time, Switzerland's unique economic geography has resulted in pockets of specialized production that enable workers throughout the country to gain from Swiss innovation.

Indeed, the small-town location of some Swiss niche production provides advantages. Lower population density requires that firms invest in the skills of their existing workforce rather than rely on the wider labor market and local suppliers, and that they become more purposive and targeted when interacting and collaborating with other firms. Moreover, this geography reduces division between social (or educational) classes in the local economy.[17] The vast majority of Swiss live in the same canton where they work.[18]

INNOVATION IN SWITZERLAND: INVENTION, APPLICATION, AND DIFFUSION

Switzerland became prosperous early and has stayed so: it was the world's second richest country between 1880 and 1950.[19] Three key features of the Swiss economy have shaped its economic structure. The first is the lack of raw materials. Unlike countries such as Germany and the United Kingdom, Switzerland lacked the coal needed for mass production.

This lack of resources was exacerbated by a second feature of the Swiss economy: its small size and central geographic location. Because of its size, Switzerland had to trade with its larger neighbors. Several cities served as entrepôts for trade with different countries:

Basel with western Germany and northern France; Geneva with eastern and southern France; Zurich with Germany, and so on. This polycentric structure forced the Swiss economy to focus on niche production. Trade could happen only through quality production, not mass production. The Swiss economy was built, as Steinberg observes, with the aim of "dominating markets rather than lands."[20]

Third, Swiss firms have a tradition of sharing new technologies. There was no patent protection in the early period of Swiss industrialization. New technologies did not have the same effect of concentrating production in the hands of the original inventors as they did in other countries.[21] As a result, technologies could be stolen, reconfigured, and integrated into production across Switzerland. This was a form of the diffusion of technology. The cellular structure of Switzerland allowed new technologies of production to develop, and lack of regulation meant they diffused through the wider economy.[22]

This history has made Switzerland strong in niche production in sectors such as manufacturing, where export-focused, medium-sized firms succeed in international markets. Such *Mittelstand* firms are seen as characteristic of the German economy, but they are also important in Switzerland. One good example of Swiss innovation is G Bopp and Co., a manufacturer of wire mesh—which sounds like a product that should be mass-produced in a way impossible in a high-cost economy such as Switzerland. Founded in 1881, the company still makes wire mesh and gauze, including the mesh that protected the microphone in early iPhones. The company has focused on precision, offering services such as design and prototyping, experimenting with new materials, and technical advice along with manufacturing. This is *Feinmechanik,* precision engineering in niche production.

SWISS WATCHES: INNOVATION FOR ADAPTATION

Two of Switzerland's historically successful industries are watchmaking and pharmaceuticals and chemicals. Both are relatively research-intensive manufacturing industries, and both have focused on niche production, quality, and innovation to maintain a competitive position.

The Swiss watch is a classic technology, symbolizing luxury production, craftsmanship, and punctuality. It is possible to see the development of the industry in three phases: a slow ascent to dominance, a near-death technological shock, and a clever reinvention as a luxury good. Although clockmaking technology was developed in China, Europe later took the lead, for reasons that remain opaque. Part of the explanation was that Europe had demand: Benedictine monks needed to know when to pray, aristocrats had the money to purchase these prestigious technologies, and Renaissance cities provided an affluent market of busy people whose time was money. The Industrial Revolution supercharged these trends, as industrialists wanted to get a full day's work from their labor forces, and workers eventually wanted to know when they were allowed to stop work.

Yet these were European advantages, not specifically Swiss advantages, and the Swiss became leading producers of timepieces only later. Initially the dominant producers were the English, who introduced the minute hand of the clock—a significant innovation—in the late 1600s. But English clockmaking was focused on small-scale production for the elites and the navy, and the guild system was resistant to change. The Swiss undercut them on price and then quality, leapfrogging them by copying technologies used elsewhere in a manner akin to recent intellectual property issues in Chinese manufacturing (ironically, the Federation of the Swiss Watch Industry's website now has a Trump-like plea to "stop the fakes!"). In the first half of the 1900s the Swiss were major world producers. When other countries stopped production during the Second World War, Swiss neutrality gave them a near-hegemonic position in world markets.

Swiss watch production was localized in the Jura region. The industry was both horizontally and vertically disintegrated, with multiple small manufacturers producing similar items. Production was small-scale, high-quality, and, apparently, flexible.[23] But while the Swiss watch industry was superb at making incremental improvements, it found it difficult to make giant leaps. So when it was hit by a technology shock—the so-called quartz crisis of the 1970s—it was unable to sustain its position.

In the space of a decade, the state of the art in watchmaking went from mechanical to electronic and then to quartz based.[24] This technology shock led to a trade shock, as it allowed new, lower-cost producers in the United States, Japan, and Hong Kong to gain market share. Ironically, quartz watch technologies had been invented by a consortium of Swiss companies in the 1960s. But they were unable to innovate, clinging to old mechanical technologies as new ones came into being. To paraphrase Amy Glasmeier, science replaced art in watch manufacturing.[25] The artists didn't adapt.

It took four years to train a Swiss watchmaker, and technology was changing rapidly. Small firms lacked the scale to make major investments in innovation and the coordination or leadership to make a big jump to a new technology. The Swiss went from a situation of near–global monopoly after World War II to apparent near-extinction in the early 1980s.

Swiss watch companies had to adapt or die, and many closed. But two changes saved the industry. The first was an innovation of sorts—a new form of watch, building on existing technologies, that opened a new market. Two bankrupt Swiss watchmakers merged to form a new company, SMH, later renamed Swatch—a portmanteau of *Swiss* and *watch*—in 1985. The company launched relatively high-quality, mass-market watches in the early 1980s. The innovation was the brand, not the technology. Fashionable, colorful, well-designed Swatch watches reached new markets.[26]

The second change was new forms of marketing. The problematic characteristics of the Swiss watch—its expense, its reliance on old technology, and its old-fashioned production processes—were repackaged as strengths. This shift in strategy is portrayed in painstaking research by Ryan Raffaelli.[27] Mechanical watches were portrayed as luxurious and precise. Older production methods were portrayed as painstaking rather than archaic.

The Swiss now dominate the luxury watch market: in 2016 the Swiss produced only 3 percent of watches sold, but these accounted for 60 percent of total value. Swiss watches are technically brilliant, but this isn't the point—few people can distinguish between the timekeeping of a $20,000 Rolex and a $20 Timex. Instead they serve as status symbols and holders of value (gold Swiss watches are, apparently, popular bribes in China).[28]

To some extent, both types of reinvention of the Swiss watch—the mass-market Swatch and the luxury production of firms such as Rolex and Omega—are based on an old technology. But to see them only in this light is to misinterpret the nature of innovation. Both enterprises involved heavy spending on research and development and production processes (luxury watch manufacturers often used this R&D to symbolically distance their products from the failed ones of the earlier period).[29] They involved complementary investments in marketing and manufacturing processes that improved and showcased quality. Soft innovations in branding created real value and helped the industry recover.

PHARMACEUTICALS: NICHE INNOVATION

A second Swiss industry is more classically innovative. Basel, the center of Swiss pharmaceutical production, spans the Rhine, crossed by tourist boats and swimmers towing brightly colored floats. On one shore the dominant building is the Münster, parts of which are over one thousand years old. But the other side is dominated by a modern white skyscraper, the headquarters of Roche—a family-owned Swiss firm that is the largest pharmaceutical company in the world. Novartis, another massive pharmaceutical company, has headquarters is a little way downriver. Because of their presence, the city of Basel has more patents per capita than Silicon Valley and a strong claim to the title of the most innovative city on earth. Yet it remains a good place to live. This is not a story of disruptive start-ups, but one of industrial evolution since Roche was founded in 1896.

The roots of the Swiss pharmaceutical and chemical industry are based in the dyestuff industry of the mid-1800s. Some important inventions from the University of Basel were allowed to spread because there was no patent protection. The city specialized in the production of ribbons, the dyeing of which used technologies complementary to pharmaceutical production. Its position on the Rhine facilitated trade. Yet even in the late 1800s, it was clear that the Swiss industry could not compete with the economies of scale in the much larger German market. Instead, it had to compete through niche products, quality, and novelty. These could be achieved only through innovation.[30]

Innovation in pharmaceuticals is generally slow. The long time-scale of developing, testing, and marketing new drugs makes it harder for companies to enter the market—particularly given the need for skills and the capital-intensive nature of the sector. Returns are skewed, with a few new products or processes creating most of a firm's income. Firms need to place a lot of bets in order for one to come off. Firms such as Roche and Novartis have used innovation as a way of staying ahead of market trends.

These firms are bound to Swiss cities like Basel not by low taxes (or they would be headquartered in a lower-tax canton like Zug), but by the need for skilled workers to produce these innovations. Some parts of the Swiss economy are, of course, anchored in tax competition between the cantons or between Switzerland and other countries. But the representatives of firms I spoke to were clear on why they were located in Switzerland, despite the costs: in addition to the country' s long history of innovation in pharmaceuticals, it offers concentrations of skilled workers in cities like Zurich, links to leading research universities, and a system of vocational education.

INNOVATION IN TECH

Pharmaceuticals and watches are classic Swiss industrial strengths, but what marks the country as special is the expansion into newer tech industries. A focus on niche manufacturing understates Switzerland's success in the disruptive, tech-focused forms of innovation: it has one of the highest numbers of unicorn firms per capita of any country in Europe. Zurich has a developing tech scene, with all the costs and benefits that implies. Switzerland is home to the second most important R&D hub for Google, the most important outside the United States. (This facility has not been immune to the recent layoffs in the tech industry: workers walked out in March 2023 in protest at job losses.[31]) Google executives were attracted not only by the city's quality of life but also by the skilled workforce trained at ETH (the Swiss Federal Institute of Technology) and the University of Zurich, and proximity to ETH's research labs. While the country is known for its vocational education, the federally funded ETH is the largest recipient of Swiss "innovation" funding. It is regularly ranked as the best university in Europe and—according to my interviews—has attracted other foreign tech multinationals, such as Facebook and Microsoft.

Switzerland is unusual because it combines radical innovators in high-tech sectors with niche production of domestic small and medium-sized enterprises (SMEs). Given this strength in innovation, it would be natural to assume that Swiss innovation policy is focused, dynamic, and cutting edge. But this assumption would be wrong. The Swiss political system focuses on subsidiarity, with decisions made at the local level, and a liberal economy. The government of Switzerland is focused on concordance and negotiation—often designed to protect the losers from the consequences of change.[32] The result is slow policy. Central policymakers are cautious about the fads of innovation policy. The bulk of innovation funding goes to the ETH and the École Polytechnique Fédérale de Lausanne (EPFL). Both institutions are regularly ranked among the best in Europe and often in the top twenty in the world.

In Switzerland, education is tightly integrated with innovation processes: the federal education ministry is called the State Secretariat for Education, Research and Innovation (SERI). Central policymakers in SERI are cautious, open, and well-educated. This is a strategic federal agency, with responsibilities for this policy area largely at the cantonal level. Strategy means choosing what not to do as well as what to do, and the Swiss are skeptical about initiatives such as the "missions" that feature heavily in policymaking in countries like the United Kingdom. The emphasis is instead on education, including vocational education.

SHARED PROSPERITY IN SWITZERLAND

Switzerland is no progressive utopia. The "gnomes of Zurich," as the British prime minister Harold Wilson described Swiss bankers, have long been seen as shady characters colluding with the world's richest people to conceal their wealth. Swiss banks profited in the Second World War; the Swiss were slow to make amends and return money to victims of the Holocaust and slow to come to terms with this legacy. Switzerland remains the center of tax evasion and shady finance. Swiss women gained the right to vote shamefully late, and there are still glaring gender disparities. There is a neoliberal side to the Swiss economy that makes some nervous, and tax competition between different places is a problem.

Yet the Swiss economy delivers for most Swiss people. The Gini coefficient of income inequality is below the OECD average. The share of income that goes to the richest 1 percent is below the OECD average, although it is rising. Relatively few workers are low-paid: in 2021, about 12 percent of workers earned less than two-thirds of median earnings, compared to an OECD average of 13.6 percent. (In contrast, in the United States the figure was 22.7 percent.[33])

One useful measure here is household gross disposable income—income adjusted for expenses such as health and education.[34] In

2019, Swiss gross disposable income was around US $42,000 per capita. On this metric Switzerland comes fourth in the OECD—above Norway and below only the United States, Luxembourg, and (by a fine margin) Germany.

The performance of the Swiss labor market has been underpinned by two unusual, related features. The first is that the Swiss haven't suffered the decoupling of wages from national income that has plagued many developed economies. Across the OECD, the share of national income going to employee compensation started to decline in the mid-1990s, falling from around 56 percent of national income to 46 percent in the late 2010s. But Swiss workers have seen their share of income increase in this period—from near the OECD average in 1995 to around ten percentage points higher now. (See figure 5.)

Second, although Switzerland has seen the same decline in middle-skilled jobs as many other advanced economies, that shift doesn't seem to have increased wage inequality. In Switzerland, the period 2008–15 was accompanied by declining employment in jobs paying less than two-thirds of the median wage, and growth in the middle and the top of the earnings range. The country has experienced job upgrading rather than polarization with growth at the bottom.

This trend may be due to the high cost of living (although PPP calculations partially adjust for this). That is, Swiss wages need to be high because the country is so expensive. High prices force firms to adapt and underpin the Swiss focus on niche production. There is no route to mass production in a high-cost economy such as Switzerland's, and policymakers do not attempt to create one. The structure of the Swiss labor market minimizes low-paying jobs. The strong economy keeps job vacancies low and creates demand for less well-educated workers.

There is no Swiss federal minimum wage, but some cantons have introduced one. Wages are regulated more generally through collective bargaining between employers and trade unions. Wages are high by international standards, and this affects the nature of available jobs.[35] Finally, the population is highly skilled, particularly in

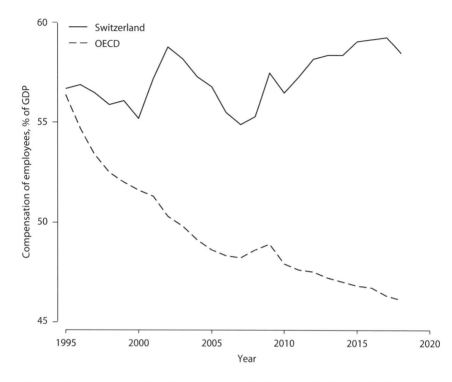

Figure 5. Compensation of employees in Switzerland compared with OECD. *Source:* OECD (2019). *OECD economic surveys: Switzerland 2019.* OECD. https://doi. org/10.1787/7e6fd372-en.

mathematics and science.[36] Around 43 percent of the labor force have tertiary education, compared to 37 percent across the OECD. And a strong vocational education system means that even those who do not go to university have relatively high skills.

Yet even the Swiss labor market faces the two familiar challenges of advanced economies. There are significant differences in employment and earnings between immigrants and natives. The number of migrants in Switzerland has increased significantly since 2000, in particular because of a process of labor market integration with the European Union that began in 2002.[37] Unemployment rates for

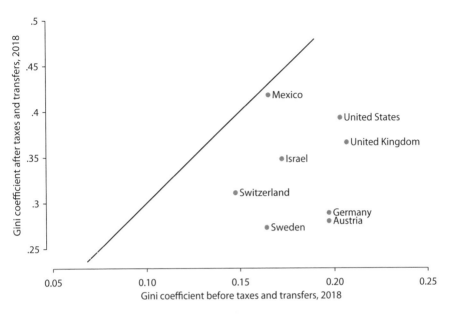

Figure 6. Swiss income inequality before and after taxation. *Source:* OECD (2022). Gross domestic spending on R&D, OECD, http://stats.oecd.org/Index.aspx?DataSetCode=IDD.

non-Swiss residents are higher and wages lower, especially for men.[38]

Alongside this, there are gross gender inequalities. The median income for women in 2021 was 13.8 percent less than that for men, higher than the OECD average but comparable with countries like Germany and the United Kingdom.[39] Research by the Swiss government shows a gap of about 18 percent in average monthly pay between men and women. Of this, around 56 percent can be "explained"—if not excused—by factors such as years of service, work experience, qualifications, and sector. But the remainder of the gap likely results simply from labor market discrimination in some form.[40] It is particularly acute in some sectors, including those that are R&D intensive. Swiss women are underrepresented in STEM fields and in patenting. Only nine out of one hundred Swiss patents are filed by women inventors, only just below the figure of the United States (9.6), but well below that of France (13.8).[41] The share of national income going to workers is extremely high and has remained so even as it has declined in other economies. Yet Switzerland is not redistributive. The Gini coefficient before taxes is even lower than after transfers are taken into account (see figure 6). This comparison illustrates the Swiss form of predistribution. The Swiss model gives workers the skills to benefit from innovation and ensures that there are good jobs in their location. A process of continual evolution has—so far—helped the country weather change.

DIFFUSION THROUGH APPLIED SKILLS

Switzerland tends to do well in league tables of innovation because it is an all-rounder: it has disruptive innovation as well as more incremental improvements and *Feinmechanik*. But these characteristics alone cannot explain its success in innovation. The Swiss model of innovation is unique because it combines leading-edge innovation in disruptive, short-cycle sectors such as tech with incremental innovation in other parts of the economy. In addition, elements of the Swiss economy—in particular, its vocational education system, its mix of research organizations, and its relatively low regional disparities —help encourage the diffusion of innovation among nonleading firms. Combined with distinctive labor market regulations, these features allow Swiss workers to gain.

Vocational education in Switzerland still provides a plausible career path for ambitious young people. Consider an eighteen-year-old with reasonable rather than stellar grades considering what they want to do after leaving school. In the United Kingdom or the United States, middle-class parents would probably be suspicious of vocational education. They would know few people who had taken that route and be uncertain of its benefits. Vocational education relies on employers willing to work with apprentices who learn on the job, and employers are often unenthusiastic. Qualifications are often a confidence trick: employers need to trust that credentials impart (or signal) skills, students need to feel they are worthwhile, and parents need to trust educational institutions as destinations for their children. In countries such as the United Kingdom, vocational education is often seen as a second-class choice, and this problem becomes self-reinforcing. (There are some significant exceptions, of course: apprenticeships at major engineering companies and defense contractors can be very competitive.)

By contrast, in the Swiss system, apprenticeships are common. Around 38 percent of Swiss young people go into vocational education, compared with the OECD average of 32 percent.[42] The success of the Swiss model depends in part on the strong involvement and influence of employers. Apprenticeship places are, by definition, available only when employers offer them, and this ensures a strong link with labor demand. Second, there are no dead ends in the system. Learners do not complete an apprenticeship and then stop learning: the system is designed to allow them to pursue higher education if they want to.[43] A high share of workers participate in adult learning. Forty percent of Swiss aged 25–34 and 24 percent of those aged 55–64 take part in adult learning, compared to 18 percent and 6 percent in the European Union.[44] These figures are high even relative to countries with strong vocational education systems: the figures for Germany are only 19 percent and 3 percent. Vocational education in Switzerland is not a period of learning followed by employment but emphasizes lifelong learning.

Uschi Backes-Gellner, a professor at the University of Zurich, and colleagues identify three main features of the Swiss vocational system that makes it so strong. First, the curricula are advanced, linked to business needs, and flexible: they are redrafted every five years in consultation with businesses, ensuring that they stay fresh and focused on the skills businesses need. Second, apprenticeships can exist only if businesses provide them, the result being a system driven by business needs rather than those of the educational provider. Finally, Swiss vocational education combines occupational and general skill training. Vocational education systems do more than teach learners to do a job: they give them the skills to learn throughout their lives. The system produces better labor outcomes for some than others—incomes are higher for men who go through the system than women—but the labor market prospects for students in vocational relative to general education have deteriorated little over time.[45]

The Swiss system balances high-quality university education with high-quality vocational education. Switzerland spends more on education per student than any other country in the OECD except Luxembourg.[46] It has more elite universities per capita (defined as among the world's top one hundred) than any other country in the world.[47] But it also has a vocational system that companies, learners, and their parents see as a route to both a good job and personal respect. It is adaptive, meaning students can start at a low level and progress. The result is a system that gives workers the skills to ensure the diffusion and adaptation of innovation.

There's a virtuous circle in Swiss skill adoption: the acquisition of skills may provide incentives to develop new skills.

Technical skills → diffusion of new innovations → incentive for skill creation → higher wages

The supply of skills can create its own demand, in a variation of Say's law that production can lead to demand for that product. Swiss firms operate in a niche production mode, and they are enabled do so by the availability of skilled workers.

In addition, when workers gain high skills, these skills let them benefit from innovation. The supporting infrastructure of the labor market rests on a characteristically Swiss combination of minimum wages in some cantons and a mixed economy of institutions. Around half of Swiss employees are covered by collective bargaining, much higher than the proportion in the United States (12 percent) or the

United Kingdom (27 percent) but well below the level of Austria (98 percent) or Sweden (90 percent).[48] Labor markets are regulated through wage bargaining, rather than union-employer conflict, there are very few strikes, and it is relatively easy for firms to hire and fire staff.[49] The result of this situation is relatively high wages for many workers.

CELLULAR GEOGRAPHY

It is hard to measure spatial inequality in income, but the best guesses suggest that Swiss regional inequality is low.[50] This is partly because of the country's urban structure, with major cities serving different external markets. But it is also due to the legacy of powerful decentralized institutions. The result can be perverse. Some of the twenty-six cantons are smaller than the major corporations located in them. (Zug, with a population of around 130,000, is host to the cryptocurrency platform Ethereum, which had, at one point, a US $1.2 trillion value). At one company, a representative told me that their headquarters might be located in low-tax Zug, but if they needed to scale up their R&D activities they would be able to do so only in Zurich.

Swiss policy has tried to encourage nationwide innovation. One example of this effort is the Swiss universities of applied science. Policymakers had long been concerned about bridging the gap between the apprentice system and higher education, enabling students on the vocational track to jump to the academic track. Between 1997 and 2003 the Swiss government established nine universities of applied science, carefully located so as to be accessible to students everywhere in the country. Based on the model of the German *Fachhochschulen*, teaching the applied knowledge of technical and engineering disciplines, these universities had a legal mandate to focus on applied research and to collaborate with firms and other research institutions.[51]

These institutions are not Stanford or Cambridge; they rank nowhere on international league tables. But they train workers whose skills are tailored to local business needs. They also provide local firms with opportunities for collaborative research, reducing the barriers to innovation. Throughout the country they produce highly skilled graduates with both practical and scientific knowledge, thereby fostering the direct transfer of knowledge and technology between research institutions and the firms that can profit from that knowledge and technology. They help new technologies to be adapted and to diffuse through the economy.

Economic studies show a 7 percent increase in the number of patents and a 10 percent increase in the quality of patents filed by firms near these institutions a decade later.[52] Over the long term, local economies become more focused on innovation-led industries that benefit from this proximity. Institutions that focus on the modest diffusion and adaptation of technology can have a powerful local impact, benefiting local workers.

EQUITY THROUGH DIFFUSION IN SWITZERLAND

Switzerland is full of paradoxes. Despite its mountainous terrain, it is highly accessible. It has a reputation (undeserved) as unwelcoming to foreigners, but it has one of Europe's highest shares of foreign-born residents. It is traditional, with an economy based on old-school industries such as watchmaking, yet it is also hypermodern, leading in niche technological fields and home to some of Europe's best universities. The Swiss model of innovation melds niche production on the German model with a US focus on disruptive, radical tech. Switzerland is also unusual in its mixture of historical, family-owned multinationals and SMEs that coexist with startups founded by migrants and funded by venture capital.

But the key strength of the Swiss model is diffusion. Vocational education gives Swiss businesses the skilled workers they need; it gives workers the ability to earn high wages; and it allows diffusion of innovation into other parts of the economy. Its multiple population hubs exist for historic reasons. But policy has reinforced this situation with new institutions that facilitate innovation, built to evolve with local economies over the long term.

Switzerland's political economy is dominated by slow-moving institutions, but it encourages a long-term perspective. I was struck by the honesty of the firms and policymakers I spoke to. There was no wishful thinking about the future. Innovation policymakers were resistant to fads of innovation policy. The vocational education system was designed to give a realistic view of the labor market, and where the jobs are, rather than offering learners false hope. Firms were clear about their comparative advantages, rather than boosterist about the next phase of growth. This approach sometimes felt dour, but it has created a system which—for now—means that many people can benefit from Switzerland's success in innovation.[53]

4 Austria

The southern Austrian town of Leoben should be the archetype of industrial decline. The economy has traditionally been based on two labor-intensive industries, steelmaking and mining, which have been shrinking across much of Western Europe. The nearest big city, Graz, is an hour away by train, just out of range for most commuters. Its population, at only twenty-five thousand, doesn't seem big enough to sustain the innovation-intensive industries of the knowledge economy. It is a pretty town, but not pretty enough to attract many tourists—and few outside Austria have heard of it. On paper, it is a lot like the industrial towns of South Wales, northern France, or northwestern Germany; isolated, dependent on big industry, and in decline.

But Leoben is a prosperous, pleasant place. Houses are clean, municipal buildings show signs of investment, and when I visited, residents were eating ice creams in the sunny, if chilly, main square. This is not San Francisco, with tech startups driving the local economy, but neither is it Detroit. Near the town is a 3.5-kilometer-long steel-fabrication plant run by Voestalpine. The local university, the Montanuniversität Leoben (sometimes called the Mining University of Leoben) specializes in disciplines relevant to the important local industries and is often ranked the best university in Austria.

Leoben is an exemplar of the changing Austrian economy: between 1998 and 2016, Austria saw the largest increase in R&D intensity of any OECD economy bar South Korea. Much of this growth occurred in industries such as steel, rather than the advanced digital technologies so fashionable with policymakers. In Austria the number of mid-skilled jobs declined more than in any other OECD economy. The country also saw the largest increase in high-skilled jobs. Yet the result wasn't spiraling inequality. All these changes happened in a way that benefited workers. Increases in inequality have been smaller than in most other countries, income growth at the bottom of the distribution has been higher, and growth in top incomes has been relatively constrained.

How did Austria achieve such a significant increase in R&D intensity? What were the consequences? And what can other countries learn from its experience? Austria's success has been a race to innovate from irrelevance. A consensus, first among politicians and then among bureaucrats, to increase R&D spending enabled the country to compete in the low-tech industrial sectors, such as steel and paper, in which it specialized. Combined with a social-partnership model with ongoing dialogue between management and labor, this approach has sustained wages for workers, ensuring they benefit even as employment in many of these innovative but low-tech industries has fallen. This strategy is clearest in the industrial regions that, in other countries, declined.

EMPIRE AND INDUSTRY

Whereas Switzerland's history is marked by stability, Austria's is one of change. Austria is a Western European economy that is geographically part of the East. Austria started the twentieth century as the center of an empire and finished it as a small country of only nine million people. It has gone from being a neutral power in the Cold War to becoming part of the European Union, and from being a poor country after World War II to being one of the richest countries in the world. Underpinning Austrian success has been innovation, but not innovation in the disruptive Silicon Valley sense. Austrian innovation has often been in traditional, low-tech industries.

Austria's history is rich, complicated, and conflicted. It began the twentieth century as the core of the Austro-Hungarian Empire. At its peak this included most of central Europe, including parts of present-day Italy, Croatia, Bosnia, Czechia, Slovakia, Romania, and even Ukraine, with Vienna as the capital. The ruling dynasty, the Habsburgs, had run much of Central Europe since the 1400s. The late 1800s and early 1900s were an astonishing period of intellectual productivity in the city: Sigmund Freud, Elise Richter, Theodor Adorno, Joseph Schumpeter, Friedrich Hayek, Karl Popper, Lise Meitner, and Ludwig von Mises were all educated at, or taught at, the University of Vienna.

Defeat in World War I broke up the Austro-Hungarian Empire, ending Habsburg rule and Vienna's central importance. This had major economic consequences: a well-integrated customs union was divided by eleven new national borders, and Vienna lost its hinterlands.[1] The loss of market access and established trading relationships meant hardship. At the same time, authoritarianism was becoming rife. This position worsened after World War II, as Austria was left further isolated by the Iron Curtain to the east.

Postwar Austria suffered poor harvests, food riots, and starvation. The celebrated historian of Europe Tony Judt argued that it was never obvious that the country would be of the capitalist West. Geographically it was closer to the East, bordering Czechoslovakia and Hungary.[2] The Allies saw it as part of Nazi Germany, and so it was divided up in a similar fashion into zones of occupation, with the United States, Britain, France, and the Soviet Union in control of different parts of the country—with Vienna split. The Red Army occupied southern Austria until the mid-1950s, cautious in case Austria became a military asset for the West. But a negotiated neutrality prevailed: Austria became an independent country but had to stay out of NATO.

Through cultural, geographic, and economic proximity, however, Austria was swept up in West Germany's *Wirtschaftswunder*, or economic miracle. The Marshall Plan provided significant income: fully 14 percent of Austrian national income from July 1948 to June 1949 came from the plan, a greater share than in any other European country.[34] But Austrian growth in the 1950s and 1960s was also driven by technological innovation.[5] An Austrian Research Council was established shortly after the war, as exiled scientists returned and saw the parlous state of Austrian universities.[6] New industries developed, and older ones became more productive. Although invented in Switzerland, the Linz-Donawitz process for making steel (named after the Austrian city and a nearby town) was commercialized in Austria and made the Austrian steel industry the most productive in the world. Many heavy industries were nationalized to protect them from Soviet intervention, but they remained productive.

Austria's geography—between Eastern and Western Europe, close to both Europe's richest and its poorest countries—was both a blessing and a curse. After the war, the Iron Curtain reduced Vienna's access to overseas markets, exacerbating the problems caused by the fracturing of the Austro-Hungarian empire. But the result was greater regional balance (although Vienna remained larger than would be expected for a capital city in a country of Austria's size). The states of Upper Austria, Salzburg, and Tyrol benefited economically from proximity to Germany. And there were benefits from neutrality. Becoming home to parts of the United Nations helped Vienna return to its position as one of Europe's most important cities.

AUSTRO-SCANDINAVIA AND THE SOCIAL PARTNERSHIP

Austria's growth was accompanied by social spending and the development of a Western European–style social safety net. There were suggestions, according to Judt, that the country was, "outside of Scandinavia, the closest approximation to the Social Democratic ideal" and even talk of an "Austro-Scandinavian model."[7] But Austria's approach was different. Widespread state spending was allocated according to political affiliation, often according to the *Proporz* system, which allocated decisionmaking positions proportionately to electoral support. The country's politicians pushed for an inclusive social model because they believed that without it the country might implode. Neutrality meant lower defense spending and more money for welfare.[8] An informal pact between unions, workers, and the political parties led to rising living standards.[9]

The result was a country that grew in a negotiated way, with strong state control of the economy and a significant social safety net. Austria became a classic corporatist economy, in which "major aspects of economic regulation rely upon a system of organised cooperation between labor and capital"; but in contrast to Switzerland's, its markets were subject to political control.[10] Particularly after World War II, a form of Keynesianism guided the economy, characterized by central control of monetary and income policy, state intervention in an otherwise liberal economy, and strong trade unions.

The Austrian model has historically been classified as institutionalized neocorporatism, with "strong links between the social partners and the political system and a bargaining system containing sectoral agreements with exceptionally high coverage rates."[11] The idea is to achieve consensus: business and labor participate in government decisionmaking, wages are balanced against price stability, and decisions are made, nominally at least, in the common interest. In this *Sozialpartnerschaft* model, organized labor is represented through trade unions and their umbrella organization, the Österreichischer Gewerkschaftsbund (ÖGB); workplace councils that negotiate with employers on behalf of employees on social, personnel, and economic issues; and the Arbeiterkammer, or Chamber of Labor, which represents Austrian employees and consumers. Membership is compulsory for employees, and the nine regional and one central Arbeiterkammern play a role in negotiating prices and wages. Collective bargaining is central in the Austrian model. Labor contracts are negotiated by the Federal Economic Chamber (WKÖ), which represents employers, and the ÖGB, which represents employees. Wage negotiations generally take place at the industry level.[12] They stipulate wage floors, but, in practice, workers often negotiate wages above the minimum. Organized labor is thus far more important in the economy than trade union membership would imply: 28 percent of workers are union members, just above the figure in the United Kingdom (26 percent), but 95 percent of Austrians are covered by collective bargaining, compared to only 29 percent in the United Kingdom.[13]

The Austrian corporatist system has been watered down since the postwar period, particularly during two periods of right-wing government, in 2000–2006 and 2017–19.[14] The labor movement remains powerful but, as in most countries, has been losing ground.[15] A series of reforms pushed for by the right-wing ÖVP party weakened the social partnership: these included reforms of social security and pensions, reducing spending, and efforts to speed up decision-making. The political influence of the unions declined, and strike activity began to increase as unions tried to assert their position.

Social partnership is based in the idea that coordination and cooperation improve policy by ensuring price stability, allowing systems to respond to crises, and increasing flexibility. But partnership requires a shared belief in the system, particularly when sacrifices from one party are required. As Franz Astleithner and Jörg Flecker observe, "According to today's mainstream economic textbooks it is inconceivable that strong unions and comparatively rigid regulation could help a backward agrarian country to become one of the richest economies in Europe, but that is what happened."[16]

Underpinning Austria's labor market performance is a strong vocational educational system, similar to that of Switzerland. Around 40 percent of young people enter vocational education, spending around a third of their time at vocational colleges while also learning on the job. Unemployment rates among this group are much lower than in other groups.[17] Students are streamed into different types of secondary education, in a manner similar to that of Switzerland and Germany.[18] According to the political scientists Niccolo Durazzi and Leonard Geyer, this means that alongside industrial relations and labor-market institutions, vocational educational systems can "combine economic efficiency, by providing firms with a broad base of specifically skilled workers, and social inclusion, by integrating academic low achievers rather smoothly into the training system and subsequently the labor market."[19] The training offered by vocational colleges differs from that of Switzerland, which is more employer led. The Austrian approach comes with significant costs, as the supply of skills is not as closely linked to employer demand.

This system has adapted over time. The 2008 Vocational Training Act altered the apprenticeship system by allowing young people to study for supracompany apprentice training, a hybrid scheme. In 2016–17, 37 percent of students at upper secondary level were undertaking apprenticeships.[20] Recently fewer firms have been offering apprenticeships, and apprenticeships have become higher skilled. As the skill requirements of jobs have increased, the apprenticeship system has struggled to stay relevant.[21]

Although high taxes on labor theoretically restrict labor demand, Austria's labor-market performance has been strong, with employment above the OECD average.[22] Earnings are high, and labor-market insecurity is very low. Few people live on low incomes, and compared to the OECD average, disadvantaged groups do well. The Austrian economy is small, open, and productive. In 2022, Austrian workers produced US$75 of GDP per hour worked, placing the country sixth in the OECD—just ahead of Sweden.[23]

This isn't to say that Austria's model lacks flaws. While wage inequality is relatively low, gender inequality is grossly high. In tandem with a conservative welfare-state regime reliant on cash benefits, the social-partnership model doesn't work well for women, particularly those on low incomes.[24] Austrian women are much more likely to work part-time than Austrian men, so they benefit less from high wages.[25] Across Europe, women earn—on average—14 percent less than men. Austria ranks third worst among the twenty-seven EU countries on this measure, above only Estonia and Latvia. Austrian women earn 19 percent less per hour than Austrian men.[26] And the efforts of Austrian policymakers to address gender inequality have been weak. Equal-pay reports have so far had little effect in redressing gross gender disparities.[27] Other disadvantaged groups include older workers: in Austria those aged 55 to 64 are less likely to be working than in most other European countries, particularly countries such as Switzerland or Sweden. And immigrants are still likely to be in low-paid work.[28]

The social partnership model has been breaking down. In the past, crises were overcome through "mutually agreed readjustments," with high growth and political stability being "mutually reinforcing."[29] The high tax costs of Austria's social partnership are irrelevant to firms but dissuade some skilled migrant workers. The country's political system is often unstable, extreme right-wingers have come close to gaining power, and politicians often cross the line that separates consensual governance from self-interest and corruption. Sebastian Kurz, elected chancellor in 2016 aged only 31, pulled together an unprecedented coalition of the right-wing People's Party and the left-wing Greens. But the wunderkind of Austrian politics was forced to resign in a corruption scandal in 2021. (He went on to take a job with Peter Thiel, the Silicon Valley venture capitalist and Donald Trump supporter.[30]) This distinctively Austrian mix of political instability, policy stability, and high-level corruption has consequences. The *Financial Times* reported the chief executive of Berndorf, a highly successful Austrian firm, as saying that if he had to start his firms afresh, he would do so in Switzerland, "where labor costs are even higher but the political system is far more predictable."[31]

SHARED PROSPERITY IN AUSTRIA

The Austrian story is one of extreme growth in R&D spending and significant growth in high-skilled employment achieved while maintaining relative equality. Since 1980, income inequality in Austria has been comparatively flat. The share of pretax income for the bottom 50 percent has decreased slightly, while the share for those between the median and the top 10 percent has increased slightly. The income share of the top 10 percent is little higher than it was in 1985, while the share going to the top 1 percent of income earners is lower now than in the 1980s.[32] This pattern of constrained income growth at the top is unusual, and differs from similar economies such as Germany. Moreover, although Vienna is home to around 20 percent of the population, regional inequalities are relatively low.

As in most countries, inequality in Austria has increased over the medium term, but it remains low. Growth has benefited those on below-average incomes. The World Inequality Database provides data on the difference between the income growth per adult of the bottom 40 percent and the average national income growth per adult between 1980 and 2017—a measure of the extent to which growth benefits those on lower incomes. Of thirty-one countries considered, Austria ranks fourth.[33] The bottom 40 percent saw their relative incomes fall—incomes for this group grew around 10 percent less than the average—but they lost less ground than their counterparts in most other advanced economies.

Like Switzerland's, the Austrian model is does not rely solely on redistribution. The tax-to-GDP ratio is relatively high, according to WIFO, the Austrian Institute of Economic Research: "Before redistribution, income in the top decile of the income distribution was 30 times that of households in the bottom decile; after redistribution it was only 5.5 times higher." Most of the redistribution involved benefits in kind, through state provision of education and health care, rather than direct financial redistribution.[34] Nevertheless, the state plays a significant role. Transfers are relatively high in the Austrian tax and benefits system: just under 20 percent of national income consists of transfers to those below the median income, including pensions. This figure is much higher than in the United States (13 percent).[35]

But these redistributive mechanisms don't fully explain Austria's relatively low aggregate inequality. After considering tax and spending, the Gini coefficient of income in Austria moves from 0.24 to 0.23—a comparatively small shift.[36] Instead, the Austrian system is good at predistribution of income, with a complex, corporatist web of activities leading to a system in which at least some of the benefits of innovation are shared. The negotiation culture, labor market institutions, skills and training, and industrial policy of Austria help distribute the benefits. In particular, the evolution of the Austrian economy helps ensure that key sectors are relatively inclusive.

AUSTRIAN INNOVATION

By most rankings, Austria is an upper-mid-table innovator. It ranks seventeenth on WIPO's Global Innovation Index.[37] But some champion Austria's performance. One booster is Bernd Greifeneder, the founder of one of Austria's most successful technology companies, Dynatrace, which provides artificial intelligence services from the north Austrian city of Linz. In an interview for the *Financial Times* he commented, "I see Linz as like Silicon Valley."

Greifeneder is a highly successful technologist. Yet, for the rest of us, it is hard to see anywhere *less* like Silicon Valley than Linz, or Austria more generally. The country lags on the conventional Silicon Valley metrics: venture capital is scarce, broadband penetration is low, the share of university graduates is one of the lowest in the OECD, and Austrian universities have been sliding down the international rankings. Few countries have as rich an intellectual history as Austria, yet it has had fewer Nobel laureates than Argentina.[38]

But maybe Greifeneder is right. All the measures above are inputs into the innovation process, rather than outputs. The reason policymakers are fond of counting venture capital, Nobel prizes, and so on is that they are supposed to lead, eventually, to innovation and then to higher living standards. And on most output measures, the Austrian model works: the median wage is the fourth highest in Europe, and the employment rate is higher than that of the United States. Inequality has been constrained, and some of the world's best-performing recent tech companies have been Austrian. The number of triadic patents—a term for particularly significant patents registered in the United States, Europe, and Japan—per one thousand Austrian researchers in 2017 was the sixth highest among EU member states (plus the United Kingdom), although lower than in 2013.

But it isn't the overall levels of innovation that make Austria interesting: it is the recent change. In 1998 R&D spending in Austria was 1.73 percent of GDP, below the OECD average and closer to that of Canada (1.72 percent) than to the OECD average (2 percent). But in the subsequent two decades, it saw the second fastest increase in R&D intensity in the OECD, behind only South Korea. By 2018, Austria was the second most R&D-intensive economy in Europe. Austria shifted from being a European laggard to level-pegging with Germany.

One of the problems with R&D as an indicator of innovation is that it is biased by sector: some industries, such as pharmaceuticals, are more R&D-intensive than other sectors, such as financial services. It is possible to construct a measure of adjusted R&D intensity that accounts for the sectoral mix of the economy. And by this measure Austria now ranks as the most R&D-intensive economy in Europe. Austria has massively increased R&D spending in industries that are not traditionally R&D intensive.

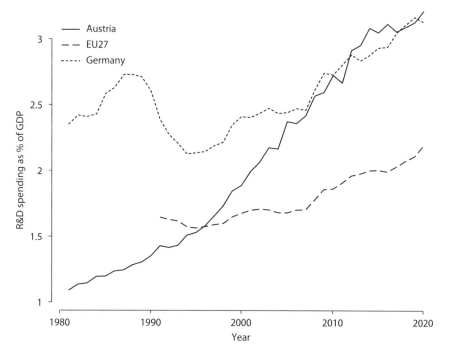

Figure 7. Convergence in R&D spending between Austria and Germany. EU27 refers to the twenty-seven EU member states, after the United Kingdom's exit. *Source:* OECD (2022). *Income distribution database.* OECD. https://data.oecd.org/rd/gross-domestic-spending-on-r-d.htm.

This success stands in stark contrast to most efforts to increase R&D. Because the economic importance of R&D spending is well known, a common policy approach is target setting: focusing the machinery of government on a specific goal. In some circumstances, this can really work—for example, the United Kingdom's success at addressing child poverty in the 2000s was largely due to setting a target. (But it can also have unintended consequences, as Goodhart's law implies. In Britain, child poverty fell, but working-age poverty increased.) Targets are popular with politicians. They sound good, are easy to justify, and often fall into the next political cycle. And they sometimes work.

But setting a target is easy: hitting it is hard. In a classic study, the Portuguese economist Adão Carvalho tested whether countries hit their R&D targets. Collating data on forty-two different countries between 1990 and 2011, he found that they had set a total of 112 R&D targets. Of these, only two were met, in the well-governed and innovation-intensive countries of Denmark and Finland. And Denmark hit only one target of two, Finland one of three.[39]

The European Union is a master at missing R&D targets, to the extent that they are often considered aspirational rather than realistic. In 2002, the EU set a target of 3 percent R&D intensity in 2010—and missed it by a mile. With R&D intensity only at 2 percent, the same target was reaffirmed in 2010 with the Europe 2020 strategy. Yet when 2020 arrived, R&D intensity was only 2.3 percent. What little progress had been made was due to a fall in the denominator: as GDP fell in the pandemic, R&D intensity—defined as the share of total R&D in GDP—increased because absolute R&D spending fell less than GDP did. Although the EU had made apparent progress towards its aspiration, total R&D spending had actually fallen.[40] It has tried again, and its 2030 strategy sets out the worthwhile but now-familiar target for all member states to reach 3 percent R&D intensity.

These failures don't mean targets are worthless or that the European Union shouldn't be setting them. Setting a target might help increase R&D intensity even if it were missed, and the EU has few other powers to force member states to make progress in this difficult area. But it does show that policymakers have no magic buttons to increase R&D intensity. Governments are in a conflicted position, trying, with limited influence, to increase GDP at the same time as they try to influence businesses to increase R&D spending.

Given this context, the growth in Austrian R&D intensity is a rare innovation policy success. Although encouraged by government policy, most of the growth was funded by the Austrian private sector.

According to the OECD, just over 53 percent of the increase from 1998 to 2015 was funded by domestic business enterprises, 34 percent by government (including federal, state, and municipal sources), and 12 percent by sources abroad, including the European Union.[41] Overall, private-sector R&D intensity as a share of GDP more than doubled, from 1.10 percent in 1998 to 2.21 percent in 2015.[42]

The Austrians increased R&D spending through a combination of deliberate action and luck. The Austrian economy was in a difficult position in the early 1980s. Many key firms were still nationalized, and it was clear that this state-industrial complex was not working well. But the industrial base hadn't declined as much as in other countries, and the economy faced two major, favorable economic shocks. Few countries have benefited from the fall of communism as much as Austria, which suddenly found itself close to new markets in Eastern Europe. Moreover, the end of communism meant that Austrian neutrality was no longer necessary, so—along with previously neutral Finland and Sweden—it was able to enter the EU.

Austria needed more spending on R&D. This point was, as one interviewee put it, "so obvious" that there was unanimity among politicians, business, and academics. In 2000, Chancellor Wolfgang Schüssel, looking for ways to ensure the country remained competitive in the single market, made increasing R&D intensity "a personal mission." Higher R&D spending was seen by politicians and civil servants as important to the process of national upgrading. In addition, business interests were aware of the need to upgrade their processes, and the wider policy community was pushing R&D. Social partnership provided an easy route for representing the interests of firms, and new institutions, such as research funding organizations, were developed.[43] One bureaucrat who was there at the time told me that "in the old times leaders had castles built, in our time they build research institutes." For once, political and economic interests were aligned.

The result was, for want of a better term, an R&D partnership. With initial leadership from Schüssel, a consensus developed among politicians, government ministries (including, crucially, the finance ministry), business, and experts. A series of R&D targets were set— and missed, but falling short mattered little as long as the direction of travel was clear, policies were focused, and R&D intensity increased. R&D targets were soon displaced by other priorities, but because the idea of increasing R&D had become an important part of government policy, it became a wider goal of civil servants and society. The bureaucracy sustained the initiative even after the politicians had moved on to other priorities.[44]

No policy can succeed unless the local conditions suit it, and the Austrian context was well suited to these efforts. The economic base was often in industries which, while traditionally low- or medium-tech, had the potential to upgrade. Because Germany was not offering the same level of R&D tax subsidies, a form of R&D tax competition developed, with German firms moving into Austria to take advantage of skilled workers, cultural affinity, favorable taxation, and Austria's "unique know-how" in areas of heavy engineering. Firms had strong technical abilities, even if what they were doing was not specifically R&D activity. Entry into the European Union made Austria an attractive place to do business: it provided rich export markets, standardized legislation, and certainty for non-Austrian firms. Policymakers were planting seeds in fertile soil.

At the core of these efforts were two types of policy: direct financial support, in the form of subsidies and a reformed R&D tax-credit system, and the development of new intermediate research and training institutions. As R&D was increasing in Austria, financial support was becoming more generous. Between 2006 and 2019, business R&D intensity went from 1.66 to 2.2 percent of GDP. This growth was supported by an increase of government support for business R&D that was double the size of the OECD average increase. The bulk of this spending was through tax incentives.[45] The lion's share of funding has gone to large firms. Direct funding also increased between 2000 and 2019, from €311 million to €713 million (2015 prices), and from 0.11 to 0.19 percent of GDP.[46] German firms were able to move R&D facilities across national borders and take advantage of Austrian generosity.

There is little point in the government investing in R&D unless the private sector translates the investment into economic benefits. Subsidizing R&D without a set of complementary investments, particularly in skills, would be a waste of money. Austria's R&D growth has been accompanied by an increase in the number of workers with advanced STEM skills, facilitated by the country's strong tradition of basic training and apprenticeships. A focus on STEM education provided skills for workers in R&D-intensive industries. Yet skills weren't integrated into Austrian innovation policy until the 2010s. Between 1998 and 2019, the total number of employees in R&D increased from thirty-one thousand to eighty-four thousand. Of the new jobs, the lion's share (around thirty-eight thousand) were in the private sector. *Fachhochschulen* (universities of applied science) were established in 1994, with mixed financing from the state and from private companies. They offered accreditation and practice-oriented education but not PhD programs. The twenty-one *Fachhochschulen* aimed to bridge the gap between academia and the job market and to offer a route to a degree for those who lack the grades or motivation for university.

In the same period, Austrian research and innovation institutions were being upgraded. In 2004, four research funding agencies were consolidated to produce the Österreichische Forschungsförderungsgesellschaft (Austrian Research Promotion Agency, or FFG). The Institute of Science and Technology Austria was founded in 2009 on the model of Israel's Weizmann Institute of Science, with interdisciplinary research groups and scientists given a mandate to undertake risky scientific projects autonomously, with little bureaucratic or political oversight.

All these developments were undertaken with a focus as much on employment as on technology. The aim of the FFG is to "promote research, technology, development, and innovation for the benefit of Austria"—with the subsidiary goal to "ensure the long-term availability of high-quality jobs and maintain the prosperity of one of the world's wealthiest countries."[47] The Austria 2030 research strategy justifies R&D spending on the basis that companies that perform R&D create more jobs.

The Austrian model of R&D increase was not a Schumpeterian process of creative destruction, with new firms and industries developing and replacing old ones, but rather of the evolution of existing industries and firms. Bernhard Dachs and Andreas Drach, two Austrian economists, show that most of the growth between 2002 and 2013 was associated with firms that existed at the start of the period: old firms did new things.[48] Increased tax credits provided an incentive for firms to either start doing R&D or increase their R&D. The economy didn't pivot to new, high-technology sectors but upgraded what it had. Policymakers, unwilling to sacrifice earlier accomplishments, worked with existing strengths.

The Austrian steel sector was at the heart of this upgrading. Voestalpine is a Linz-based steelmaker that still maintains just under half its workforce in Austria. Founded in the 1880s, but with a difficult political history as part of a strategic national industry, the company had been one of the leading commercializers of the Linz-Donawitz process of steel production. Like many big Austrian firms it was nationalized after World War II before being privatized in the mid-1990s. Through its history of state ownership it maintained close ties to bureaucrats, who could help guide policy.

High costs in Austria forced the firm into a particular type of production, and the only way it could survive was by moving into more profitable niches. Unable to compete effectively at producing basic steel, it refocused on higher-quality, higher-margin steel such as the thin but strong plates needed for fuel-efficient cars and airplanes.[49] By 2018, Voestalpine had revenues of over US$11 billion. Of this, which only a third came from steelmaking, the rest from related products. The company expanded across Austria, buying other Austrian steelmakers (including the one at Leoben). A new plant just north of Graz was justified as offering proximity to the "company's metallurgy and material science research facilities in Kapfenberg." The company became so important to the Austrian economy that it ended up causing problems. According to one estimate, if it shifted from using coal to electricity to heat its furnaces, it would require half of all Austrian electricity production.[50] It is the largest carbon dioxide emitter in the country, responsible for 10 percent of Austrian CO_2.

A less charitable interpretation of the Austrian increase in R&D is that the generous tax incentives led firms to declare spending as R&D that would not have previously counted as such. The Frascati manual for R&D spending—the OECD document that outlines what counts as R&D—defines it as "creative and systematic work undertaken in order to increase the stock of knowledge—including knowledge of humankind, culture and society—and to devise new applications of available knowledge."[51] This definition includes basic research, applied research, and experimental development. These categories are tightly defined in theory, but in practice they are hard to police. Firms have a powerful incentive to classify routine testing, which is not part of R&D, as experimental development, and thus benefit from the R&D tax credits available. This is likely one explanation for Austrian R&D success, but only a partial one; the same can be said of other, less successful countries.

The Austrian economy has experienced deindustrialization, but the loss of manufacturing jobs has come later than in other countries and been less extreme. In 2019, about 25 percent of Austrians worked in manufacturing. This was a lower percentage than in Germany (27 percent) but significantly higher than in the United States (20 percent) and the United Kingdom (18 percent).[52] The declines since 1991 were sharpest in the United Kingdom (a 12-percentage point fall, from 30 percent), Germany (a fall of 11 percentage points, from 38), Austria (a fall of 9 percentage points, from 34), and the United States (a 6-percentage-point fall, from 26). What's significant about this change is that Austrian manufacturing was stable in the 2010s.

As the Austrian economy has changed, it has been accompanied by significant changes in the labor market. Austria has seen the largest decline in mid-skilled jobs of almost any country between 1995 and 2015, and some increase in low-skilled work. This is a problem driven by those issues of technological change discussed in chapter 3.[53] But while this kind of employment polarization is generally seen as a bad thing, that isn't necessarily the case. By comparison, the Czech Republic has experienced declines in low- and mid-skilled jobs alongside a smaller increase in high-skilled jobs. Even if Austria has polarized, the average Austrian is probably better off with the shift to a high-skilled economy, particularly given that relatively few employees in Austria are low paid.

THE STYRIAN VALLEY

Perhaps the most surprising part of the Austrian story involves one region, Styria. The second largest of the nine federal states (*Bundesländer*), Styria (or Steiermark) encompasses much of central Austria and the region south toward the Slovenian border, including Graz, Austria's second largest city. According to Franz Tödtling and Sabine Sedlacek, two Austrian geographers, the region can be divided into three parts.[54] The core is the city of Graz, a high-income city with four universities, many leading firms in mechanical engineering, and a thriving cultural sector. To the south lies a flatter area, including small hills and vineyards. There are strong culinary traditions in this area and softer innovations in food and wine. North of Graz is Obersteiermark, a mountainous area including some steel towns such as Kapfenberg and Leoben. At the heart of this area lies a spectacular open-cast iron mine, stepped like an Aztec pyramid and symbolic of the natural-resource extraction that led to the area's industrialization. Along with abundant power from coal reserves, mountain rivers, and timber, these resources enabled the area to industrialize. As in many countries, industrial towns sprang up

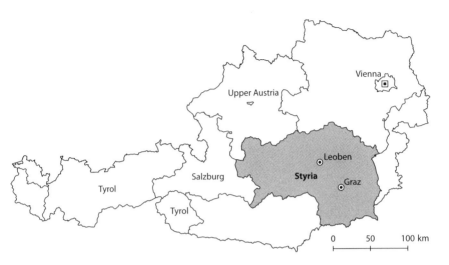

Map 2. Styria in the Austrian context.

because of proximity to raw materials. But in most countries, these towns declined as trade costs fell and proximity to raw materials became less valuable. In Styria, rather than die, industries upgraded and adapted. The story of Styria is one of decline averted.

The old wealth of Styria was based on iron ore and steel production. In 1974, around a quarter of the region's employment was in extractive industries—agriculture, mining, energy, and primary production such as paper mills, sawmills, and smelting.[55] Yet, as elsewhere in Europe, these industries were threatened in the 1970s and 1980s. The oil shocks of the mid-1970s led to a significant decline in demand. The late 1980s saw the collapse of communism and a drop in demand for mechanical products. Although Austria had gained from proximity to Eastern Europe, it was also more exposed to declines in demand for steel and mechanical engineering. Styrian output had been declining as a share of federal GDP since the early 1960s.[56] After a shock of unemployment in the early 1980s, its unemployment rate increased to 18 percent. There were protest marches on the streets of industrial towns, and the region of

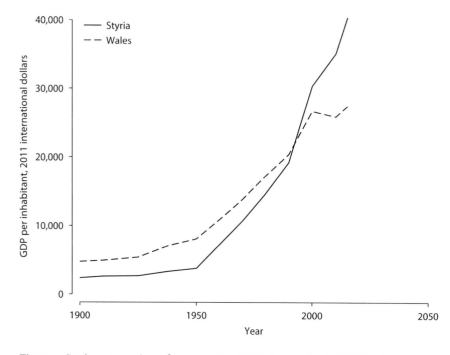

Figure 8. Styrian economic performance since 1900. *Source: Rosés-Wolf database on regional GDP* (version 6, 2020).

Obersteiermark qualified as poor enough to receive regional development funding from the European Union.[57] Styria's economy, based on low-tech, industrial sectors, looked dated and doomed.

We can observe Styria's resurgence by comparing it to the economic situation of Wales. In the mid-1970s Wales and Styria had similar industrial structures, with an emphasis on heavy and extractive industries. GDP per capita in Wales was significantly higher. For the next two decades they were level-pegging, before Styria developed a lead in the 2000s. From an apparently similar starting point, Styria's heavy industry became more innovative while Wales experienced decline.

At the heart of Styria's resurgence were networks between the *Bundesland* government, other institutions, and firms. This partnership approach based economic upgrading on existing local strengths. It wasn't a top-down process (although there were important leading figures) but what one of my interviewees described as "organic, strategic development." A strong set of innovation institutions helped advance this agenda. Styria has five universities: the University of Graz, the Technical University of Graz, Karl Franzens University (in Graz), the Medical University of Graz, and the University of Leoben. Firms collaborated with local applied research organizations, universities, and technology transfer institutions.[58] These networks enabled the diffusion of innovation between firms.[59] The result was that social partnerships, so often seen as inefficient and favoring incumbents, developed into an innovation system through which existing firms could upgrade.[60]

Styria has seen a disproportionate share of Austria's massive increase in R&D, particularly between 1993 and 2007. A state accounting for about 14 percent of Austria's population was, in absolute terms, responsible for about 23 percent of the country's increase in R&D spending. Styrian innovation wasn't innovation in the Silicon Valley sense of digital technology. It was innovation in the low- and medium-tech industries on which Austria thrived.

Styria's strong universities were joined in the late 1990s by *Fachhochschulen*, which were designed to do applied research that is locally relevant. The *Fachhochschule* of Joanneum in Graz, Kapfenberg in the mountains, and Bad Gleichenberg in the south of Styria offered courses based on applied research in areas including health care, low-energy construction, and, later, drone technology. Innovation policy focused on applied research and technology: there are two technical universities and strong competence centers in technology, which received money from the federal and Styrian governments An automotive cluster of interrelated firms developed in connection with the historic steel industry, supported by local cluster policy.[61]

Firms drew on what has been called the "protective role" of a peripheral location. Two Austrian economic geographers, Jakob

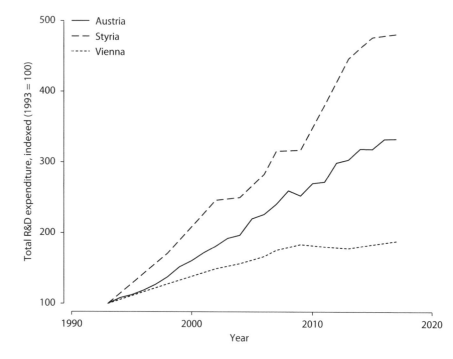

Figure 9. R&D expenditure in Styria relative to Vienna and Austrian total.
Source: OECD statistical database.

Eder and Michaela Trippl, argue that the advantages of such a location include leeway with supportive institutions, high quality of life, price advantages, and access to natural resources.[62] These benefits compensate for the disadvantages of peripheral locations and strategies that seek to take advantage of these disadvantages by, for example, shielding R&D activity from the outside world.

My example of Leoben—the declining mine and steel town which hasn't declined as it should—shows the results. Its problems have often been those of success: as industries have become more productive, they require fewer employees. By the late 2010s, according to the Leoben Stadtmuseum, the steel plant at Leoben needed 1,600 workers to produce as much steel as had previously been made by

11,000. Some university graduates grumbled that students from applied apprenticeship courses earned higher salaries than those with degrees. This story of innovation in low-tech industries has not been "job creating," according to one study, but instead has been "job preserving and job changing as the transforming character of low-tech manufacturing requires new job profiles with upgrading of formal qualifications and skills." [63]

But there has also been an effort to upgrade other traditional industries. South of Graz is Vulkanland, a rural area of extinct volcanoes on the border with Slovenia. The economy is dominated by small, family-run firms and agriculture, with many vineyards. It is a good example of the Austrian model of innovating in low-tech sectors. The agriculture sector has been upgraded, with a greater focus on processing, branding, and local retail. The craft manufacturing sector pays high wages but has found it hard to recruit the skilled workers it needs. Firms such as KGT, which offers ventilation and other building technologies around the world, require skilled workers with technical rather than academic skills. The result has been that the labor market is strong, with significant skill shortages, and job creation has been focused on technical workers. The skill shortages in part reflect the aging of the workforce, as population growth remains flat and in-migration low, but an Austrian-style upgrading has led to economic success in a peripheral region.

You are unlikely to find evidence of Styrian production in your iPhone. But you will certainly find it in lower-tech parts of your local economy. One company produces machines that remove bad grain from production: the grain cascades past a set of light sensors that detect bad grains, which are immediately shot out of the system with puffs of pressurized air. The region produces the world's longest train rails, 120-meter lengths of metal that reduce the cost and problems of fitting multiple rail lines together. The timber industry produces large timber-frame buildings and high-quality paper for magazines. Styria is a good example of the Austrian advances in normally low-innovation industries.

Styria's success has been based on several related factors: innovative local firms, foreign direct investment, diversifying steel companies, and infrastructure to support innovation, and a policy approach focused on upgrading.[64] Firms have upgraded instead of trying to lower costs, supported by collaborations with research institutions and applied universities. They have operated in market niches with inelastic demand that were resistant to Austria's high labor costs Styria has avoided decline by taking the high road—upgrading and creating good jobs.

WHAT DOES AUSTRIA SHOW US?

Austria's stellar R&D performance has been at the heart of a wider economic transformation that has seen good jobs created for many and turned the country into one of Europe's most prosperous. This is not fully shared prosperity—a shameful gender gap persists—but it shows that the benefits of innovation can be felt even beyond the service-based, knowledge economy. It shows that there can be a future for industrial areas, even in high-cost countries, and that industrial decline can be abated. Through innovation, industries that have declined in other countries have, so far at least, thrived in Austria.

Austria's approach is very different from that of other countries. Although many policymakers across the world are fixated on degree-level education, Austrian firms are less concerned. Almost all the Austrian policymakers I spoke to were concerned about low levels of venture capital investment, yet Austrian wages are higher than in countries such as the United Kingdom, where such investment is much more widespread.

But this model of high-innovation in low-tech industries, supported by negotiated politics, might not be sustainable or adaptable to other contexts. Russia's 2022 invasion of Ukraine drove up energy prices, threatening energy-intensive industries such as steel. Policies intended to mitigate climate change will force firms to adopt more energy-efficient production. Austria's economic growth has been uneven: GDP growth exceeded that of the United States only twice in the 2010s. Austria is a high-income country, but real income growth has been flat. There's a perennial concern that its industrial base isn't changing fast enough, and that the economy isn't adapting to new industries. But Austrians have been worried about their concentration in declining industries since at least the 1990s. Bureaucrats are still focused on R&D as a means to upgrade, but they are doing so with different tools. A numerical R&D target has been replaced by a relative one—to improve rankings in international indexes of innovation—and this may reduce the focus of policy on R&D.[65]

5 Taiwan

My previous examples of highly innovative economies are both in slow-growing Europe. But my third case, Taiwan, is different. The East Asian island is the poster child of economic development. In 1980, it was slightly poorer than Jordan; in 2019 it was slightly richer than Austria.[1] It went from being a poor, agricultural country to a rich, highly technologically advanced one. Few Taiwanese firms are household names, but they are crucial parts of global production systems: Foxconn is the world's fourth largest tech company, and Taiwan Semiconductor Manufacturing Company (TSMC) produces half of the world's chips. If you use a smartphone or drive a modern car, the chances are that you use Taiwanese technology.

Taiwan's growth has been well studied by scholars of economic development such as Alice Amsden and Robert Wade. Most of this research focuses on Taiwan's export- and innovation-led growth. Taiwan's growth has similarities to those of the other Asian success stories of Singapore, Hong Kong, and South Korea, but it also has one important difference: while these other countries saw rapid growth in GDP alongside large rises in inequality, Taiwanese growth was relatively equitable. The Gini coefficient of household income inequality actually fell in the 1950s and 1970s, a period when real per-capita income more than doubled.[2] Many commentators highlighted Taiwan's development as a story of "growth with equity."

But the Taiwanese story is more complicated than that. Until 2000, Taiwanese development was characterized by relative equity. A rapid and coordinated increase in the supply of human capital allowed workers to gain in the race between education and technological development. Yet this equitable growth hasn't lasted. The Taiwanese model has, more recently, seen the erosion of younger workers' living standards, with inequality driven by high capital incomes among the richest. The successes, and failures, of Taiwanese development offer important lessons.

INNOVATION-LED DEVELOPMENT IN TAIWAN

At the end of World War II, Taiwan was in a difficult position. When the colonial power, Japan, ceded control in 1945, a new government took charge, led by the Guomindang, a Chinese nationalist political party. When the Chinese civil war resumed, the Guomindang lost power in mainland China to the Communists, but they retained their hold on the island of Taiwan, staging a mass evacuation to the island—the Great Retreat—in 1949. Taiwan became a de facto sovereign state, independent of the People's Republic of China on the mainland.[3] But Taiwan's government was mostly composed of exiled politicians, military officers, and intellectuals who had fled the mainland. It was led by Chiang Kai-Shek, the authoritarian politician who had run the Republic of China from 1928 until losing control to the Communists. His son ran the oppressive secret police.[4] Large parts of the country were still owned by absentee Japanese landlords, and a process of de-Japanization took place. But the country was poor and postcolonial, with complex ties to a much larger neighbor.[5]

Taiwan had some strengths, including road, rail, and port infrastructure, although these largely served the needs of Japan.[6] A skilled population arrived from China. The United States provided significant aid, and, after the Korean War Taiwan also became a foreign-policy priority in the Cold War. While many countries in the 1950s and 1960s tried to develop through import substitution (by stimulating domestic production), early Taiwanese development was focused on export-led growth to meet outside demand. Foreign companies were attracted by cheap labor and welcoming government policy. Once established in Taiwan, they were introduced to local entrepreneurs who could build parts more cheaply and at lower capacity.[7] The result was an industrial base that was more productive than those of many other Asian economies. But many in the government still expected some form of reunification with mainland China. Only when Chang Kai-Shek died in 1975 did it become clear that a return to China was unlikely and that long-term investments were needed.

By the 1970s, Taiwan's infrastructure was stretched and in need of modernization. The Ten Major Projects— investments in rail, shipping, air transport, steel, and energy infrastructure—were undertaken to further national development.[8] Taiwanese development was still characterized by family-owned small and medium-sized enterprises (SMEs). Some researchers have argued that this pattern led to a relatively equitable income distribution compared to the chaebol (family-owned conglomerates) that were developing in South Korea. The relative lack of corporate power meant that the state had more autonomy to act, and so it allowed more interest groups to have a say in growth.[9]

One crucial policy of this period was the reform of land ownership. The motivation was political rather than economic. When governing the mainland, the Guomindang had allied with landowners, with the result that the alienated rural peasantry were easily

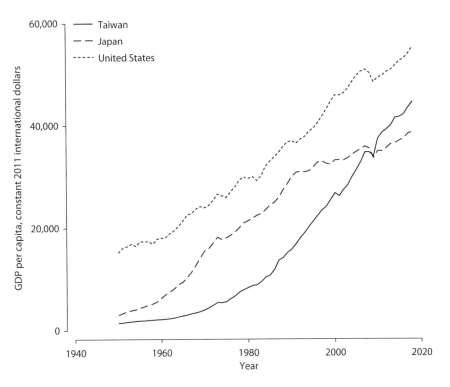

Figure 10. Economic growth in Taiwan compared to Japan and the United States. *Source:* International Monetary Fund (IMF) (2022). *IMF database: GDP per capita.* https://data.imf.org.

recruited by the Communists. The Guomindang had no desire to repeat this mistake in Taiwan, so they began instituting land reforms in 1949, reducing rents and selling land confiscated from Japanese landlords. Through a "land to the tiller" program, landlords were expected to sell any land over a certain quota to the government, receiving bonds and stakes in nationalized government in return.[10] The result was that a commercial elite developed in place of the landowners. It led to a form of stakeholder capitalism, as different interest groups—including farmers, the landless, and capitalists—all had a stake in the country's growth.

The land reforms took place in a period of brutal repression known as the White Terror. Over almost four decades, particularly in the 1950s and 1960s, thousands were executed or displaced. But this period was also, paradoxically, one of economic growth. A terrified leadership knew they needed growth to compete with the mainland, and the restriction of landowners enabled them to divert resources to the sectors they thought would get them closer to this aim.[11]

Taiwan's economic development was rapid. Before World War II, the country had been far poorer than Japan, and incomes were relatively flat. As Japan's economy began to take off in the 1960s and 1970s, Taiwan still lagged. But GDP per capita was on a steady upward trend from the late 1970s, overtaking Japan's in the late 2000s and slowly converging with that of the United States.

Taiwan's rapid growth challenged the conventional wisdom on development in two ways. First, it showed the limitations of the orthodox approach of getting the macroeconomic institutions right and avoiding government intervention. In addition, by achieving growth with equity, Taiwan showed that high inequality was not an inevitable effect of development.

THE TAIWANESE DEVELOPMENTAL STATE

In the 1980s and 1990s, government intervention in economic development was seen as counterproductive, leading to vested interests shaping policy and resources being used to support established firms rather than challengers that might drive growth. Partly due to a view of the economy focused largely on supply-side intervention and partly because of an entirely reasonable suspicion of government mismanagement, international organizations such as the World Bank and the International Monetary Fund had preached that growth was likely to come from openness and government investment. Based on these views, a set of policy recommendations pertaining to fiscal discipline, tax reform, property rights, deregulation, trade liberalization, and barriers to foreign direct investment were pushed by Washington-based institutions onto developing economies as a condition of financial support. The economist John Williamson dubbed these approaches the Washington Consensus. At their heart, they advocated that the focus of economic development should be the allocation of resources. The government's role was to create the conditions that would enable the private sector to succeed.

Yet these norms didn't apply to the most successful set of developing economies, those of East Asia. Countries such as Taiwan did not wholly reject the policies of the consensus—for example, governments built trust in global markets through fiscal discipline, and property rights were secure—but they did not privatize firms or massively deregulate as had been recommended.[12] Sometimes they achieved Washington Consensus–style policy aims by different methods. Rather than reduce export controls to encourage firms to export, as would have been the Washington Consensus recommendation, Taiwan gave firms a target to do so but maintained trade barriers.[13] The role of government in industrial development was seen in a more positive light.

This approach inspired some of the classic works on economic development. In 1990, Robert Wade published *Governing the Market*, in which he argued that Taiwan—along with South Korea—might be first to join the stable "club of innovators" that dominated the world economy. Wade argued that Taiwan's transformation from a poor country to one of the world's development success stories was the result of astute government intervention. Taiwan had actively shaped the economy, constructing an "arrangement of the institutions of capitalism, with government helping to strengthen the competitiveness of selected industries." In Wade's view, the aim of Taiwanese government, along with the governments of South Korea and Japan, was to "build up the international competitiveness of domestic industry—and thereby eventually to raise living standards."[14]

Wade suggested that Taiwan was a "governed market" in which the state, rather than just trying to get the basics right, used a large toolbox of policies to shape the economy. The market was governed through "(1) redistributing agricultural land in the early postwar period; (2) controlling the financial system and making private financial capital subordinate to industrial capital; (3) maintaining stability in some of the main economic parameters that affect the viability of long-term investment, especially the exchange rate, the interest rate, and the general price level; (4) modulating the impact of foreign competition in the domestic economy and prioritizing the use of scarce foreign exchange; (5) promoting exports; (6) promoting technology acquisitions from multinational companies and building a national technology system; and (7) assisting particular industries."[15] This goal was not just developing new industries and new technologies but also promoting diffusion of innovation in existing industries.

More than thirty years on, Wade's list looks strong but incomplete. First, given Taiwanese development since the 1990s, most researchers would ascribe innovation a stronger role in recent development than Wade does. He also neglects the issue of skills development, which was one of the central means by which the success of domestic industry raised living standards in Taiwan.

FROM THE DEVELOPMENTAL STATE TO INNOVATION

Taiwanese development happened in phases, with the country specializing in increasingly high-value products. The early phase was largely based on land reform and increasing agricultural productivity. After 1949, Taiwan's exports were primarily natural resources, food, and textiles.[16] As the country developed, science, technology, and innovation grew in importance. In the 1970s, Taiwan began exporting television and radio equipment, followed by engineering, medicines, and electronic technologies in the 1990s. By the 2000s it was a world leader in several technological fields. The Taiwanese state was active in promoting this evolution. It was sharp at following price signals, selectively working with existing industrial strengths, and upgrading.[17] It failed in sectors such as automobile manufacturing and biotechnology—particularly in the latter, where success is uncertain. But it excelled in more predictable sectors such as information and communications technology (ICT).

The ICT industry began to develop in Taiwan in the 1960s.[18] The country worked to attract foreign multinationals, such as Philips, by virtue of low costs. Export-processing zones were established. But while seeking to keep production costs low, the Taiwanese government needed wages to rise, in part to discourage local workers from protesting for democratization. To raise wages, they needed domestic semiconductor firms to do well. The Taiwanese applied local manufacturing criteria, breaking up the "enclave positions" of multinational corporations.[19] They focused on process innovation and component manufacturing rather than new product creation. Recognizing that they could not compete with richer Korean firms that benefited from economies of scale, they focused on niche production of specialized chips.[20] Innovative local manufacturing, specialization, and local production remain characteristic of the Taiwanese economy.

The developmental state evolved rather than ended.[21] In 2007, Dan Breznitz characterized the Taiwanese model of innovation-led growth: the state identified foreign technology, had research agencies understand, absorb, and develop it, and then helped in the creation of new private-sector companies that could use it.[22] The focus on hardware arose from the specific institutional and political configurations. In hardware, the Industrial Technology Research Institution (ITRI) adopted a strategy of support, whereas in software the state research agency—the Institute for Information Industry—was producing more leading-edge research.

Two Taiwanese economists, Tain-Sue Jan and Yijen Chen, argued in the mid-2000s that ITRI played several distinct roles in Taiwan's economic development. In some technological areas the role was strategic, in that ITRI actually introduced new firms—the activity

for which it is best known. This strategic role was clear in semiconductor production: the company TSMC was spun out of ITRI.
In other areas, ITRI played a facilitating role, by coordinating
R&D alliances among multiple firms or by incubating new firms.
Taiwanese success in the production of laptops, electric scooters,
and so on was all assisted by ITRI. Finally, it played a classic
technical-support role by conducting contract R&D, licensing intellectual property, and providing services such as testing and
certification.

Business groups began to develop in ICT-intensive sectors. Until
the 2000s, domestic Taiwanese firms had not been as successful as
those in South Korea or Singapore. Traditional family-owned small
and medium-sized firms had begun to decline in the early 2000s. As
explained by a Taiwanese economic development official to Henry
Yeung, an economic geographer at the National University of
Singapore, the early strategy of picking winners evolved in the mid-
1990s, as companies developed capacities beyond those of the government. The role of the state shifted to "providing a sound
investment environment" rather than actively guiding the private
sector. National champions no longer needed the state in order to
succeed in global markets. In Taiwan, as in other East Asian nations,
the state helped to ensure that firms caught up with international
leaders. This process of strategic coupling as actors coordinate and
negotiate to achieve their interests has marked the later stages of
East Asian development.[23]

TSMC is a classic example of the rise of the pure-play foundry, a
facility dedicated to producing chips for other companies rather
than designing its own. Running a semiconductor production site is
capital-intensive and expensive, involving wasted capacity and a
lack of economies of scale. Only the biggest chip users and manufacturers, such as Samsung, generate enough demand to justify operating a dedicated fabrication plant. Pure-play foundries allow
producers to scale up production faster and at a lower cost than they
could by maintaining their own facilities.

TSMC was spun off from ITRI in 1987 with the simple aim of producing chips. It was run by Morris Chang, a Taiwanese American scientist and businessman who had been chair of ITRI. For most of its history, it has produced chips from other companies' designs. Recently competitiveness in the manufacture of chips began to outpace design, so TMSC began working with designers to improve chips.[24] For chipmakers, the rapid growth in processing power has meant the need for constant, extremely expensive investments in production facilities and R&D. This trend has led to market consolidation.[25]

TSMC accounts for around half of all contract-produced chips in the world. It gained attention during the pandemic when slowdowns in chip production—caused by President Donald Trump's threats of boycott pushing the Chinese to stockpile, manufacturers canceling orders in anticipation of a COVID-induced recession, and the failure of the monsoon in East Asia, which created a shortage of water needed for chip manufacturing—had a knock-on impact on car manufacturing.[26] Only TSMC and Samsung have the scale and technology for very small (5–10 nanometer circuit) chip production.[27] The huge capital investments required for new production facilities provide a significant barrier to entry for new firms, particularly when there is uncertainty about whether these chips would be used.

TSMC is at the center of a distinctive Taiwanese innovation system, according to a 2004 comparative analysis by Pao-Long Chang and Hsin-Yu Shih. One of its features is that it developed through consensus in the early stages, with five yearly conferences bringing together experts and stakeholders and a Technology Advisory Board producing annual reports to steer policy. R&D was financed primarily by industry and performed by SMEs. Taiwanese patenting by foreign nationals, which was dominated by ICT, increased rapidly from the early 1990s as the country went from playing catch-up to becoming a technological leader, but it was dominated by employees of SMEs and public research institutions.[28] Strong partnerships existed between firms and research institutions, and workers moved relatively easily between them. Firms were also active globally, learning from other countries. As a result, R&D intensity increased massively in the early 2000s. Between 1998 and 2015, R&D intensity increased by almost 1.2 percent of GDP.

Taiwanese growth is often portrayed as a deliberate process, focusing first on the export of low-value products and then on more innovative ones. But this assessment leaves open the question of how this shift came about in Taiwan but not in other countries. Part of the answer is the island's historic relationship with Japan: Taiwan was able to learn from Japanese technological advancement. However, the distinctive Taiwanese political economy also played a role. The insecure relationship with China provided an external threat that motivated elites to focus on science, technology, and innovation rather than their own enrichment.[29] In 1966, China demonstrated a hydrogen bomb at about the same time as the United States cut aid to Taiwan. The result was an urgent need for foreign currency that could only happen through the export of high-value products. The Taiwanese elites, united against China, also needed to ensure that there were no domestic threats. The government was repressive but scared, with a strong incentive to ensure that workers benefited from the country's growth. The result was a period of growth with equity.

GROWTH WITH EQUITY

Just as Taiwan challenged the conventional view that government intervention did not lead to growth, it also suggested that growth could be achieved without skyrocketing inequality. The classic explanation of how growth relates to inequality is the Kuznets curve. Based on a simple model of one poorly paid agricultural sector and one better-paid manufacturing sector, Kuznets predicted that as people moved into the cities to work in manufacturing, the economy would grow, but so would inequality, as wages rose for a small group.[30] After a while, inequality would begin to fall. The result was an inverted-U-shaped curve showing the relationship between growth and inequality, with income distribution first widening and then compressing as more people entered the better-paid sector.

A famous report in 1980—*Growth with Equity: The Taiwan Case*—set out the World Bank's view on how Taiwan had achieved this success.[31] Studies showed that around 1964, growth began reducing inequality.[32] Agricultural income was still relatively unevenly distributed despite land reforms. But industrialization was geographically dispersed and labor-intensive, bringing those on the lowest agricultural incomes into the manufacturing sector before those on higher incomes and thus reducing inequality.

Writing in 1979, Gustav Ranis of Yale argued that land reforms had reduced the average agricultural income in Taiwan, but a favorable pattern of development through an "active balanced rural growth strategy" allowed people to enter new, labor-intensive employment.[33] To some extent this was a matter of happenstance, the result of being colonized by a country that focused on rural development. Jobs were created across the country rather than in the big cities, as would have happened without the colonial infrastructure. Taiwan's small size, along with investments from the 1960s onward in road infrastructure and rural electrification, facilitated economic development throughout the country. Research infrastructure was developed locally and so was appropriate for the local economy. Medium- and small-scale industry contributed to export-led growth, with the result that exports were more employment-intensive than they would have been had large firms been more dominant. Taiwan's industries employed a very high number of researchers, so productivity came through innovation rather than capital intensity.

Reviewing the debate over Taiwan's growth in 1982, Dennis Chinn of Stanford University asked whether this period of high growth and low inequality was more the result of policy or of unique circumstances.[34] This distinction matters because circumstances cannot be replicated, but strategies and policies can. And, as Chinn argued, equitable development was one of the main lessons that Taiwan's growth offered. Chinn saw early land reform as crucial for allowing growth with equity. Land reforms resulted in a relatively equitable distribution of land, and farming associations helped introduce the technology needed to improve it. Equality of assets led to relative equality of incomes and thus to political equality and a tradition of equal benefits. But Chinn further argues that relative equity may have provided the incentive to work hard, take risks, and innovate in Taiwan, because workers knew they would benefit from the fruits of their labor.

Data for Taiwan in this period is poor, and it is hard to assess with confidence what happened. But there are several linked explanations for why Taiwan achieved growth with equity, each rooted in the specific political economy of the island. Under the Guomindang, landowners were given stock as compensation for being forced to sell their land, but much of this stock was quickly sold.[35] Both land and stock prices later appreciated . As a result, the richest lost out, and the country started with relative equity. The Guomindang's fear of communist revolution led it to offer limited representation and the sharing of economic growth in conjunction with authoritarian rule.[36] Semidemocratic farmers' associations were formed, giving the people a taste of democracy and representation.[37]

Alice Amsden has argued that low Taiwanese inequality was due to land reforms. The equitable distribution of land reduced the size and power of the landed elite, preventing accumulation of agricultural wealth; it reduced consumerism, as few people inherited wealth; and it allowed the state free rein to enact reforms.[38]

Taiwan did not see the development of large firms that characterized other East Asian economies. South Korea famously developed by subsidizing large, heavily diversified business groups (the chaebol), but Taiwanese firms were much smaller. Some scholars argue that the Guomindang wanted to encourage growth but did not want private capital to be concentrated in a few hands.[39] Economic stability was prioritized over economies of scale. As a result, there were fewer major owners of capital, and inequality was lower.

The Taiwanese government historically used nonstate action to meet material needs: families and communities were seen as important providers, and economic growth and job creation were seen as the routes to prosperity.[40] But this idea began to break down in the 1990s, as social insurance was expanded to marginalized groups.[41] Three main factors drove this change. The first was the combination of growing democratization and an increasingly highly educated workforce. Modernization theory suggests that a growing middle class increasingly demands a say in policy decisions. Taiwan met these conditions. State welfare spending had initially been focused on state-employed workers, such as civil servants, teachers, and the armed forces. To broaden its political base, the government expanded the welfare state to include low-income households.[42] Second, there were conspicuous needs. Taiwan's model began to creak in the 2000s. As the bursting of the dot-com bubble and the global financial crisis led to increases in unemployment, the government instituted active labor-market policies.[43] Finally, to address the concern of falling birth rates, the state has been expanded as a way of making it more attractive (or at least less costly) to have kids.[44]

EDUCATION AND TECHNOLOGICAL DEVELOPMENT

One factor has been relatively neglected as an explanation for Taiwanese growth: skills. Yet education has played a vital role in growth, the sharing of growth, and processes of modernization that have encouraged shared prosperity. In a famous paper on the role of cognitive skills in economic development, Eric Hanushek and Ludger Woessmann use data for fifty developed and less-developed economies and plot years of schooling in 1960 on one axis (controlling for initial GDP) and GDP growth in the subsequent forty-year period.[45]

The relationship is clear: more schooling leads to more growth, presumably by expanding the skills and capabilities of the population. The development of skills has a long-term payoff for both individuals and the state.

The growth in skilled workers helps explain why Taiwan's economic development was not, initially at least, accompanied by growing inequality. The clearest analysis of this balance comes from the economists Claudia Goldin and Lawrence Katz, who argued that there is a "race" between the supply of education and new technology, with growth in the educated workforce needed to keep inequality down.[46] If the supply of skilled individuals lags but technological change still mainly benefits those with high skill levels, the result is growing inequality. In contrast, if education expands at the same time as skills-biased technological change, the two factors will balance out, and inequality will not increase. While Goldin and Katz were writing about the United States, this basic framework is helpful for understanding what happened in Taiwan. Taiwan's technological development was, initially, balanced out with a massive increase in the supply of skills. So inequality did not increase as it would have done if education hadn't increased.

The rate at which young people in Taiwan are enrolled in tertiary education (an imperfect measure but one that we would expect to be highly correlated with skills) has rapidly increased. In the late 1970s, it was barely 10 percent of the population; by the mid-2000s it was above 60 percent and rising, exceeding the rates of similar countries such as Japan. In 1950, Taiwanese had an average of three years of schooling; by 2010 the average was eleven years.[47] Now the country is near the top of international educational rankings. Taiwanese students do well on the PISA test, a standardized international test of educational achievement. In 2018, 82 percent achieved level 2 in reading (demonstration of ability to glean the main idea from a text), compared to 77 percent across the OECD: 86 percent in math, compared to 76 percent; and 85 percent in science, compared to 78 percent. Not only does Taiwan perform strongly overall, but it does well in the distribution of test scores: there are fewer poorly literate students in Taiwan than in almost any other country.[48]

After 1995, there was a large increase in the number of university graduates. As a result, higher incomes went to those who attended graduate school and, at least until the late 2000s, those with vocational qualifications.[49] As one study concluded, "The demand for technicians in the information industries provided vocational school graduates with opportunities to work in the IT industry . . . , allowing them to use their professional and practical skills."[50]

Taiwan invested heavily in education after 1949.[51] It was a leader in education reform and saw an early increase in university education relative to other developing economies. Educated workers were important for economic growth, but they also drove social change and locked in incentives for further reforms. Taiwan's tertiary education enrollment for those aged 18–21 caught up with Japan's in the early 2000s and soon overtook it, particularly for women.[52]

This increasingly skilled population was the result of a deliberate policy decision. There were 105 higher-education institutions in 1985, 150 in 2000, and 164 in 2007.[53] Skill development was so rapid that in one generation it increased as much as in three generations for other advanced economies.[54] To achieve these results, education reform needed to be dynamic and linked clearly to economic development. Demand and supply of skills were aligned. The result was a strong focus on STEM.[55] The relative egalitarianism of Taiwan meant that education policy, in turn, became egalitarian.[56]

Education played a core role in Taiwan's specialized expertise in semiconductors manufacturing. Morris Chang, the founder of TSMC, argued in a Brookings Institution podcast that Taiwan's strengths in semiconductor manufacturing were "almost entirely people related, talent related."[57] The government not only funds basic research but also continually strives to make new industries competitive, with skills being part of the effort. The country has also gained from the "movement of engineers and researchers back and forth between Taipei and California's Silicon Valley."[58]

In Taiwan, along with the other developed East Asian states, the state played a key role in ensuring the supply of skilled workers. In the early phases of development, the prevalence of SMEs created demand for vocational education linked to these companies' needs.[59] Yet the returns on these skills declined as more people enrolled in universities. Although the premium on vocational skills increased from the 1970s to the mid-2000s, the increase was far lower than for those who attended college or university.[60]

THE END OF GROWTH WITH EQUITY

Taiwan still appears highly equal by some measures.[61] According to some standard income data, inequality has risen over the past twenty years, but by far less than in the other developed Asian economies. For example, data published by the Asian Development Bank allows Taiwan to be compared with China, Japan, and the other newly industrialized economies of Singapore, Hong Kong, and South Korea.[62] Levels of inequality in Taiwan have consistently been far lower than in these other countries. Although inequality has risen over this period, it has declined in Taiwan since peaking in 2012, just after the financial crisis. Taiwan's Gini coefficient is about 0.1 lower than the unweighted average of these other countries, roughly the same as it was in 1980. According to this data, Taiwan has become more unequal, but its position in regional rankings of inequality has remained unchanged.

Sadly, it isn't clear that this data gives a true representation of Taiwanese incomes.[63] Taiwan's delicate relationship with China means that it is not a member of the OECD or party to all its statistical treaties. Three key features of the Taiwanese model make income data particularly hard to trust. The first is one of the features of the economy that was seen as so important in the "growth with equity" phase: the dominance of SMEs in the economy. One result of this dominance of small, entrepreneurial firms is that capital income—

derived from wealth or profits—seems to play a stronger role in the Taiwanese economy than in others. In addition, many Taiwanese have complex links with China. Taiwanese entrepreneurs who set up business in China, a group known as the Taishang, have incomes that are hard to capture in official statistics, so inequality looks lower than it is. Finally, family structures in Taiwan may be obscuring some forms of inequality. In particular, there might be a difference in inequality between household heads (who are predominantly older) and lower-income, younger workers who still live in larger households.

Taking up these problems, Taiwanese economists have used new methods to show that inequality in Taiwan is now in fact higher than in many similar countries. Cyrus Chu, Chien-Yu Chen, Ming-Jen Lin, and Hsuan-Li Su construct distributional national accounts for Taiwan using a method that accounts for the whole income distribution and allows the patterns of growth to be mapped onto income structures. This method allows them to capture the relationship between capital income and household structure and leads to a radical reinterpretation of recent Taiwanese growth. While Taiwanese growth was relatively evenly distributed in the period 1981–2001, the subsequent two decades have seen a pattern of growth that was much less beneficial to those on lower incomes. From 1981 to 2001, between 34 and 39 percent of economic growth went to the top 10 percent. From 2001 to 2017, this share was higher than 50 percent, largely due to capital income.[64] By using individual rather than household income as the unit of observation, they found that inequality increased significantly. They also found that corporate profits accounted for a large share of this inequality.

Data from the World Inequality Database on income shares in different Asian economies similarly challenges the view that Taiwan is an equal country (see table 4). There is gross and rising inequality, largely due to income growth at the very top. In 1980, the top 1 percent of Taiwanese took around 10 percent of national income, comparable with the share in Singapore and slightly above that of South Korea (in contrast to narratives suggesting that the chaebol have

Table 4   Shares of pretax national income in selected Asian economies, 1980
and 2019 (%)

Population segment	Year	Taiwan	Japan	Singapore	South Korea
Top 1%	1980	10	11	11	08
	2019	19	13	14	12
Top 10%	1980	35	36	36	32
	2019	48	44	46	35
Bottom 50%	1980	19	19	21	21
	2019	12	17	17	21

SOURCE: Alvaredo, F., Atkinson, A. B., Piketty, T., and Saez, E. (2022). *World inequality database.* WID.world. https://wid.world/data.

concentrated South Korean income). The Taiwanese top 10 percent also took less than that population segment in Japan or Singapore, though more than South Korea. But the income share for the bottom 50 percent was lower (at 19 percent) than in Singapore or South Korea. To put this in context, the equivalent figures for the bottom 50 percent in the United States and Sweden were 20 percent and 27 percent respectively. These figures were even worse for Taiwan in 2019. Only 12 percent of national income went to the bottom 50 percent, far less than in Japan or Singapore, and close to half the share in South Korea (21 percent). The share going to the top 1 percent was 19 percent—far higher than in any of the other countries.[65] Taiwan is not as equal as it is sometimes portrayed.

The period covered by the national income distribution study maps to two growth phases of the Taiwanese economy. Jenn-Hwan Wang distinguishes between the catch-up phase of Taiwanese development, which mainly drew on innovation from elsewhere, and the innovation phase, during which companies have had to innovate themselves.[66] A simplistic summary here might be to say that the catch-up phase was accompanied by equity but that the innovation phase has seen widening income gaps.

The second phase of Taiwanese growth saw major structural, occupational, and geographical changes in the economy. Intergration into the global economy is often seen as negative for workers, driving up wage inequality between skilled and less-skilled workers.[67] Taiwanese industries had to improve production quality or face price competition from low-cost Chinese firms. This shift was complicated by deep Taiwanese business links with China: between 1990 and 2011, there was about US$120 billion worth of Taiwanese investment in China, according to Jen-Der Lue, a Taiwanese researcher.[68] The growing importance China in the global economy had important ramifications for Taiwan because of geography, cultural links, and the Taishang.

The "growth with equity" phase of Taiwan's economic development saw a major shift from manufacturing to services. In 1980, around 33 percent of the labor force worked in services; by 2004 this was 54 percent.[69] But agricultural work declined from 18 to 6 percent, and production/machine operation fell from 43 to 33 percent.[70] This sectoral shift was followed by within-sector changes, particularly after the new Taiwan dollar (NTD) began to appreciate in the 1980s, forcing Taiwan to shift out of labor-intensive manufacturing. Labor shares in manufacturing were higher in the early 2000s than in other Asian countries, at a level similar to Japan's, but as manufacturing employment declined, this shift had less of an impact on inequality.[71]

A geographical shift in the production of semiconductors has facilitated these changes. As labor-intensive parts of the electronic industry moved to China, Taiwanese industry continued to upgrade. Around 5 percent of the Taiwanese population now lives in China, and Taiwanese firms are major Chinese employers: the Taiwanese multinational Foxconn is the largest private employer in China, with over a million employees there.[72] Overseas production contributes to Taiwanese GDP, but in a highly unequal way, as the benefits accrue largely to capital owners. The jobs that remain in Taiwan are the most highly skilled.

As a result of these sectoral shifts, the share of professional work-ers (defined by the Taiwanese statistical agency as "professionals, technicians, and associate professionals") increased from 12 to 25 percent of the labor force between 1983 and 2004.[73] Growing pro-fessionalization in the workforce was accompanied by growing wage divergence. The most information-intensive parts of the economy have seen the largest increase in wages, the largest of all being in electronic parts and computers.[74] At the start of the 1980s, average earnings in electronics were lower than those in services or textile mills. By the early 1990s, they exceeded those in textiles, and by the middle of the next decade they also outstripped those in services.[75] Unemployment in Taiwan was very low until the late 1990s, when it reached 2 percent for the first time, and it worsened after the burst-ing of the dot-com bubble.[76]

Spatial inequality in Taiwan has also increased. Urban-rural dif-ferences in income were low, at least until the early 2000s, in part because of the distribution of SMEs across the country.[77] The initial growth phase was based on labor-intensive industrial employment, which was often located in rural areas. But the semiconductor-fueled growth of the ICT industry, focused in a few urban areas, has increased regional divergence. Income increased disproportionately in northern Taiwan, in particular Hsinchu, where many semicon-ductor firms are located, and Taipei, the capital, starting in the early 1980s.[78] According to Taiwanese government data, the highest incomes were in Taipei City, where average household incomes were around 1.732 million NTD (around US $57,000), followed by Hsinchu County (1.68 million) and Hsinchu City (1.6 million).[79] Regional and occupational patterns of inequality were linked: returns on education in northern Taiwan were higher than in the rest of the country, but wages were higher for less well-educated workers even in the north.[80] The rise of the ICT industry in northern Taiwan has contributed to the development of a north-south divide.

Inequalities are evident even within the successful cities. The highest wages are paid in Hsinchu City and Hsinchu County, near

the Hsinchu Science Park, which is home to much of the semiconductor industry. Taipei also has high wages and increasing inequality. In 2007, the Gini coefficient of household disposable income
around Taipei was 0.282; by 2016 it had increased to 0.293. By the
same measure, inequality had fallen in the rest of Taiwan over the
same period, from 0.297 to 0.280.[81] Real wages have been further
squeezed by high house prices, which force young people to live with
their parents or outside central Taipei.[82] A familiar story has developed of insiders who benefit from the innovation economy and out-
siders who experience high costs but little gain.

The fulcrum of many debates about inequality in Taiwan has been
the housing market. Housing inequities are ironic given the idea
that land reform was undertaken partly to promote growth with
equity. There are widespread concerns about the use of housing
as investment property, which contributes to higher real estate
prices and squeezed incomes.[83] High housing costs in tech hubs are
a familiar story, but in Taiwan they have been exacerbated by
repatriated finance from overseas, high savings rates, and the
deregulation of housing markets, raising concerns about a political
backlash.[84]

Taiwanese gender inequality is low relative to other countries, but
still high in absolute terms. Industrial expansion in the early phases
of economic growth required a ready supply of workers, and women
were integrated into the labor force fairly early. Higher-education
entrance has long been relatively gender equal.[85] Although Taiwan is
not a member of the United Nations and therefore is not included in
the UNDP Gender Inequality Index, the Taiwanese government has
replicated this data, showing that it has the lowest gender inequality
by this measure of any Asian state.[86] But better-educated Taiwanese
women are particularly and surprisingly well rewarded in the labor
market.[87] As a result, the gender gap is larger for the less affluent
than at the top of the income distribution. Similarly, women account
for about 25 percent of managers in the private sector, much higher
than the rate Japan or Korea (11 percent in each), but much

lower than in Singapore (34 percent) and the United States (43 percent).[88]

GROWTH, INNOVATION, THEN INEQUALITY

Taiwan's growth has been one of the great success stories of the global economy. Like the other advanced Asian economies of Japan, Singapore, South Korea, and Hong Kong, it has grown rapidly on the basis of innovation. Yet, unlike these other countries, it has achieved much of this gain through education. Although the dominant narratives of Taiwan's growth have tended to focus on advanced research institutions and state-led industrial policy, skills have played a crucial role both in generating growth and in ensuring that it benefits the Taiwanese.

Structural shifts in the Taiwanese economy—in particular, trade and the rise of skill-intensive ICT—have reshaped the Taiwanese income distribution. These trends are clearly linked, but empirical work that has tried to evaluate their relative effects suggests that technological progress and shifting industrial structure have probably been the most important factors.[89] Taiwan's later development, shifting from a focus on catching up to achieving development on the basis of innovation, has been problematic.[90] Taiwan is no longer a clear-cut example of growth with equity. Wage inequality has been rising since the 1980s, particularly at the very top, driven particularly by ICT manufacturing and services, as the workers in the most innovative part of the Taiwanese economy have benefited disproportionately from that sector's success.

Taiwanese educational development has been a core part of a balanced strategy of growth that has included development of science parks beyond Taipei and its hinterlands, development of key strategic high-tech sectors such as semiconductors, and the gradual expansion of a social safety net. An increasingly well-educated Taiwanese population has in turn played a role in shaping public policy. This focus on innovation and equity is likely to continue. In her 2016 inaugural address, the Taiwanese president Tsai Ing-wen stated: "The new administration will pursue a new economic model for sustainable development based on the core values of innovation, employment, and equitable distribution. . . . We will prioritize our plans to promote five major innovative industries, with the goal of reshaping Taiwan's global competitiveness. By protecting labor rights, we will also actively raise productivity and allow wages to grow in lockstep with the economy."[91]

But the model has broken down. Taiwan's skills system has not kept pace with its economic development strategy. Because few Taiwanese firms sell directly to consumers, margins are being squeezed as the large companies who are their customers bargain hard. Returns on education increased in during Taiwan's period of rapid growth, probably because education enhances learning ability and mental flexibility, allowing workers to adapt to change.[92] But returns on education have been declining more recently, even though the economy has remained hot. The result has been a paradoxical situation of skills shortages and low real wages for younger Taiwanese.

Perhaps the next phase of Taiwanese development will involve addressing the country's growing inequalities. Tsai Ing-wen, educated at the London School of Economics and Political Science, was elected president for a second time in 2020 in part on the promise that she would help equalize incomes.[93] But Taiwan faces a challenge in maintaining its position in semiconductors while sharing the benefits equitably.

6   Sweden

Sweden has famously low income inequality and a famously large state. According to some commentators, these characteristics should preclude success in the sort of disruptive tech that has become such an important part of the modern economy. Yet it succeeds. Per capita, Sweden has more venture capital investment than anywhere else in Europe bar Estonia. Many of the most successful digital tech firms of the modern era—Spotify, Skype, Klarna, and the companies behind Minecraft and Candy Crush—have Swedish roots. The staid city of Stockholm has been breathlessly described in the *Financial Times* as "a Unicorn factory."[1]

Central Stockholm is full of signs of this activity. One neighborhood, just south of the KTH Royal Institute of Technology and the Stockholm School of Economics, is home to 70 percent of Swedish venture capital investment.[2] The local workforce is highly international, and people speak English with accents from all around the world. When I passed the offices of Klarna, a financial technology firm, two women were loudly discussing coding problems in

American and British accents. Around 20 percent of Stockholm's labor force works in tech. While many tech hubs feel like divided cities, Stockholm just feels prosperous. According to the OECD, the city is more equal than other large Swedish cities, such as Malmö and Gothenburg.

In a two-by-two graph of the share of unicorn firms versus equality, Sweden is firmly in the quadrant that exhibits a good share of both, combining a competitive capitalist economy, an advanced welfare state, and disruptive innovation. Sweden's welfare state has proved no barrier to growth in advanced tech. Moreover, Sweden has a strong set of institutions that ensure the sharing of the benefits of this success in innovation. Yet even Sweden has seen strains arising from the country's success in radical tech.

THE DEVELOPMENT OF THE NORDIC MODEL

Sweden is the archetype of the Nordic model of capitalism—the idea that countries can achieve economic competitiveness while making sure that the benefits are widely shared. For those on the left, the Nordic model represents the idea that welfare states are compatible with a dynamic economy. High levels of welfare spending, according to this view, are a form of social investment, increasing the productive potential of the population through better education, skills, and policies that encourage participation in the labor market. The state plays a role in the economy, funding public research and encouraging the development of firms. This basic idea, of a middle way between US-style capitalism and state-managed socialism, has inspired politicians from Tony Blair to Bernie Sanders.

For those on the right, the perennial challenges, adaptations, and compromises inherent in the model are a sign that it is unsustainable. In this view, high tax rates and government intervention discourage entrepreneurship and limit the functioning of the free market; immigration reduces citizens' willingness to pay for a welfare state that benefits people who are "not like us"; and high taxation erodes incomes, leading to a situation in which workers cannot afford all they want. This position has led to some curious feats of reasoning. Under Donald Trump, the US Council of Economic Advisors published an infamous paper arguing that the price of a pickup truck in Sweden was almost double that in the United States.[3] But while portrayals of a socialist dystopia are wrong, it is equally mistaken to lionize Sweden as a Nordic utopia.

The Swedish model dates from the 1930s,when Social Democrats began a long period in power. They ruled either in coalition or in a minority government from 1936 to 1973 and developed a framework for economic policy based on macroeconomic control and welfare through public-sector provision.[4] The model had three pillars.[5] The first was tripartite consultation among the state, employers, and workers, represented by trade unions. Management and unions coordinated a wage policy designed to ensure equal pay for equal work, rather than according to the sector or the company. This policy was designed to reduce variation in wages across different parts of the economy and so reduced wage inequality. It also penalized uncompetitive sectors and so shifted labor into more productive uses, increasing productivity but widening the gap in profits between more and less successful firms.[6]

The second pillar was a comprehensive welfare state that provided services and shielded the disadvantaged. To mitigate the threat of unemployment, Swedish labor market policy focused on providing the unemployed with new skills and information and on subsidizing the relocation of workers to areas of stronger demand. Income was kept equal through a progressive income tax.

Third, economic and industrial policy aimed to sustain a fiscal environment with high levels of investment and a labor market that supplied the skills required by businesses. This approach kept the private sector competitive and ensured that wages increased only in response to gains in productivity, limiting wage inflation. Active labor-market policies and a focus on high employment created a broad tax base, making the welfare state affordable. Labor-market participation rates remain extremely high, at 82.9 percent of the population aged 20–64 (compared to 72.8 percent in the OECD overall).

This model was highly successful in the postwar period. After World War II, Swedish GDP per capita was about 20 percent lower than that of the United Kingdom. As Sweden's economy modernized, it became one of the richest countries in Europe. Exports quadrupled between 1950 and the early 1970s, driven by a shift away from raw materials toward higher-value and higher-tech production. Its GDP per capita reached parity with Britain in 1957 and is now around 20 percent higher.[7]

Part of Sweden's economic success derived from natural advantages. The country was already industrialized and productive before the war, at least in European terms; it was neutral in World War II and peaceful beforehand; it had significant natural resources; and the population had high levels of mutual trust and was relatively unified, making it easier to build social solidarity. However, productivity per hour worked was half that of the United States.[8] The silver lining of this gap was that it offered plenty of scope for catching up, but Sweden still faced a challenge. While labor costs were cheaper than in the United States, they were still much more expensive than the rest of Europe, so Swedish firms had little scope to compete on price. However, Swedish industry was technologically sophisticated in sectors such as telecoms and focused on knowledge-intensive activities. Investment in mechanization could increase productivity further.

The strong run of the Swedish economy could not last forever, and it didn't. The model began to break down with the oil shocks of the early 1970s. Growth was poor across much of the world, but Sweden did particularly badly: between the 1970s and the 1990s its growth was among the lowest of all advanced economies.[9] People began to turn against the high levels of taxation and to consider reforms. The finance minister in the late 1970s, Kjell-Olof Feldt, argued that high taxes had led to a culture that encouraged people to cheat the system, and this view became widely shared. Once people lost faith in the system, the Swedish model had to adapt.

The late 1980s and early 1990s saw a period of major economic reform. Capital markets were deregulated, restrictions on foreign ownership of firms removed, state monopolies ended, industries privatized, and corporate taxes cut significantly.[10] Income taxes were also reduced: between 1983 and 2013 the marginal top rate of income tax fell by 27 percentage points, to 57 percent.[11] These reforms were accompanied by periodic economic shocks. During the Swedish economic crisis of the 1990s, around 15 percent of all jobs were lost, unemployment rose to 9 percent, and a government budget crisis ensued.[12]

Yet crisis was followed by successful adaptation. Swedish postreform growth often exceeded that of the United States.[13] Sweden joined the European Union in 1995 and became one of the richest member states. In 2019 only Ireland and Denmark had higher real GDP per capita.[14] (Luxembourg would probably rank higher, but it doesn't publish this data.)

These reforms were not simply about reducing taxation. Reforms helped steer private finance toward more productive uses and provided stronger incentives for competition and entrepreneurship.[15] But state spending remained relatively high.

The cost of these reforms was a radical change in inequality. Between 1985 and 2010, inequality increased in Sweden more than in any other OECD country. The incomes of its top 1 percent have increased more than in most of Western Europe; the increase has been exceeded in only a few countries, notably the United Kingdom and the United States.[16] Relative poverty has increased, mainly because of immigration from less affluent parts of the world.[17] But incomes still increased for everyone. Sweden did not experience a US-style collapse of incomes for low- and middle-income earners but rather saw the top pull away from the rest.[18]

The result is that Sweden is no longer the *most* equal country, but it remains in the club of relatively equal countries. Depending on

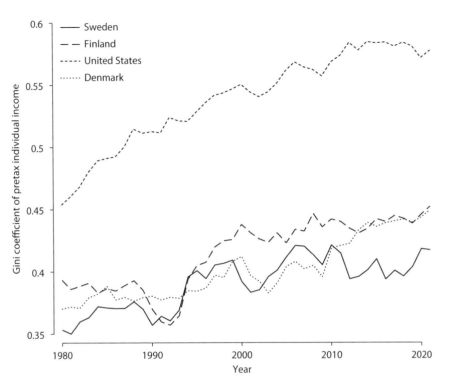

Figure 11. Inequality in the Nordic countries and the United States. *Source:* Alvaredo, F., Atkinson, A. B., Piketty, T., and Saez, E. (2022). *World inequality database.* WID.world. https://wid.world/data.

how it is measured, inequality in Sweden is similar to that of Austria but below that of Norway, Finland, and Denmark.[19] A basic measure of household income inequality includes earnings, self-employment, and capital income after taxes and social security deductions, adjusted for household size.[20] Of the thirty-eight countries in the OECD, Sweden comes tenth by this measure, making it the least equal of the Nordic countries. The employment rate is much higher than the OECD average, at 77.1 percent in 2019. One reason is that Sweden has one of the highest rates of female labor-market partici-pation in the rich world. The male employment rate is 78.8 percent, compared to 76.3 percent across the OECD. The employment rate for women is a little lower, at 75.4 percent, but much higher than the OECD average of 61.4 percent.[21] The result is that inequality in Sweden has risen, as in Denmark and Finland, but it remains far below that of the United States.

The Swedish economy is notable for the development of business dynasties and the super-rich. Per capita, Sweden has more billionaires than the United States (or any other country except Switzerland). Many of the richest Swedes are from established families. The Tetra Pak milk carton was invented by Erik Wallenberg, an engineer, and commercialized by Ruben Rausing, an industrialist. His grandchildren Jorn, Finn, and Kirsten Rausing are all billionaires and among the 150 richest people in the world. The Wallenberg family is descended from André Oscar Wallenberg, a banker who introduced the postal exchange of money to Sweden. Another beneficiary of inherited wealth is Stefan Persson of the H&M clothing chain. But the wealthiest Swedes also include newcomers from scalable, disruptive industries: Ali Ghodsi, the founder of the data analytics firm DataBricks; Martin Lorentzon and Daniel Ek of Spotify; and Lars Wingefors, who set up the Embracer group, a gaming company.

This commercial elite highlights a paradox in the Swedish model, one shared with the other Nordic countries and Switzerland. Income inequality is low, but wealth inequality is not. Three economists from the London School of Economics and Political Science, Frank Cowell, Eleni Karagiannaki, and Abigail McKnight, have shown that wealth inequality in Sweden is higher even than in the United States or the United Kingdom.[22] This is partly a result of structural factors. State provision reduces the need to save. The rate of home ownership is low, and most people don't need large private pensions: these are restricted to the richer groups. Because private wealth is less important to living standards in Sweden than in the United States or the United Kingdom, only the Swedes with the highest incomes make the investments required to build their own pensions. Where

Table 5 Dollar billionaires per 10 million population, 2022

Rank	Country	Billionaires
1	Switzerland	47
2	Sweden	43
3	Norway	24
4	USA	22
5	Australia	18
6	Denmark	16
7	Germany	16
8	Italy	9
9	UK	7
10	France	7

SOURCE: Number of billionaires from Forbes (2023). World billionaire list. *Forbes.* www.forbes.com/billionaires.

people are less able to rely on the state, there is a stronger incentive to save.

The Swedish state is big, but not as big as it was. In 2020, government spending was about 53 percent of GDP, similar to that of Canada or Spain. Relative to the OECD, Sweden spends slightly more on education and public services, less on health, and a lot more on social protection.[23] Nor is redistribution the only cause of relative equality. After considering income taxes and cash transfers, the Gini coefficient of income is lower, but it falls only by around the OECD average.[24] Moreover, the extent to which the state redistributes has declined over time.[25] Yet Sweden is also a good place for entrepreneurship: in 2019, it ranked tenth out of 190 countries in the World Bank's (controversial) ease-of-doing-business ranking.[26]

The key fact about the Swedish welfare state is not its size but its universalism.[27] Public social spending is extremely high, at almost 18 percent of GDP in 2013, compared to 12 percent in the United States.[28] This is not a redistributive state that takes from the rich and gives to the poor, but rather a system in which everyone pays in and everyone gains. This leads to buy-in from the middle classes. There is general interest in maintaining high standards, so strong incentives for doing so need to be provided. This contrasts with the model of less universalistic countries, where public services focus on the poorest, resulting in fewer incentives for more affluent groups to fund welfare.

High levels of taxation in Sweden are something of a chimera. Old people, for instance, earn higher pensions. But they pay taxes on these pensions, as part of a universalist tax policy that doesn't distinguish between sources of income. The recycling of money through the tax system gives Sweden a much lower and more normal level of government spending than basic accounting would suggest.[29]

The Swedish labor market has experienced employment upgrading as the economy shifts towards higher-value, better-paid work.[30] This process has been uneven, however. During the past three decades the share of employment in low-wage jobs in Stockholm has increased even as its labor market has otherwise professionalized.[31] But corporatist institutions of wage setting prevent large Swedish firms from exploiting their market power, as they might in other countries.[32]

The starkest challenge to the Swedish model has been high levels of migration: the number of asylum applications in 2015 was equivalent to 1.6 percent of Sweden's population.[33] Sweden's relative ethnic homogeneity was seen as one reason why people were traditionally willing to support high welfare-state spending, as residents were willing to support the disadvantaged if they were "like us." Some researchers have argued that strong welfare states are possible only in situations of relative homogeneity. Troubling empirical evidence supports this view and suggests that Swedish people are less likely to support the welfare state when they live near others of different ethnicities.[34] When refugees were placed in Swedish municipalities in the late 1980s and early 1990s, support for the welfare state among local Swedish residents decreased.[35]

There are also concerns about long-term declines in the quality of Swedish education. While Sweden still performs relatively well in international tests of performance in reading, mathematics, and science, its scores have declined relative to the OECD average. Scores dropped throughout the 2000s until 2012, when education spending increased significantly. The trend has since been improving, but the gains are uneven. Students from immigrant backgrounds do much worse than those from Swedish backgrounds and have been increasing in numbers—from 12 percent of students in 2009 to 20 percent in 2018.[36] This trend threatens to lock in the problems of disadvantage of immigrant groups, leading to further problems of integration and weakening support for the welfare state.

Because the Swedish model has adapted over time, the old clichés are no longer quite accurate. Income inequality is increasing. Wealth inequality is high, in part because of the size of the state. The state is less redistributive and more universalist than that of other countries. Yet, for all this, it still has some significant strengths: inequality is still low, wages are high, and living standards are excellent. Underpinning this welfare model is an economic model that is far from cuddly Nordic capitalism but instead a form of hard-nosed capitalism in innovative sectors.

FROM BORING CARS TO EXCITING TECH

Even at its peak, the Nordic model was no statist economy. High levels of public spending need to be paid for, and the Swedes ran an advanced capitalist economy to underwrite them The Swedish economy was well regulated, open to trade and investment, and ruthless. Sweden is one of the most innovative and technologically advanced countries in the world. It performs well in all the spurious rankings of innovation: it ranks second in the global innovation index, a composite measure. In 2020, Sweden's R&D spending as a share of GDP was behind only that of Israel, Korea, and Taiwan.[37] Sweden was the home of Alfred Nobel—best known for the prizes he endowed, but also the inventor of dynamite.

Sweden has world-leading companies in several sectors. These include the traditional, boring backbones of Swedish industry. Volvo evolved from a ball-bearing factory in Gothenburg in the 1920s to a major car manufacturer, trading on a Swedish reputation for solidity and safety. The car division was sold to Ford in 1999, but Volvo Group remains one of the world's largest manufacturers of trucks, buses, and engines. IKEA is the world's largest furniture retailer, offering affordable flat-pack furniture and meatballs in sixty-three countries (but now headquartered in the Netherlands for tax reasons). H&M is the world's second largest clothing brand, offering fast fashion in seventy-four countries. Swedish firms tend to be positioned at the high end of global value chains.[38]

One Swedish strength has been telecoms, a sector whose development has been aided by rapid technology adoption and government policy. Alexander Graham Bell patented the telephone in 1876. By 1885, there were around four thousand telephones in London, Paris, and Berlin—but Stockholm, despite its much smaller size, had five thousand.[39] This rapid diffusion aided the development of major firms: Ericsson began in the 1870s, making telegraph machines and then telephones and switchboards, expanding first to the other Nordic countries and then globally. Years later it became the company behind Bluetooth technology. After the crisis of the early 1990s, Sweden became a leader in the ICT sector.[40] Tax breaks were used to encourage personal computer use, leading to a strong programming sector.[41]

Public procurement played a role in technological development. The state provided funding for risky new technologies, allowing firms to invest. Ericsson, for example, collaborated with the Swedish telephone provider to help develop new technologies—a relationship sometimes termed a development pair. Building on locally sourced technologies developed through this model, Ericsson was then able to export overseas and create its own market. The resulting innovations included a type of digital switch for phones, which Ericsson was reluctant to produce because of high R&D costs and risk. The state telecoms company wanted the switch, however, and noted that they could procure it elsewhere, forcing Ericsson to make the investment. This was not monopoly capitalism but rather a form of state cooperation underpinning a competitive market. The approach resulted in a very Scandinavian model: private companies were supported to make long-term investments, but the relationship was marked by a hard capitalist streak.[42]

R&D spending has declined since 2003 but remains high. This trend has been driven by falling business spending, which has meant that the small increases in public spending have been less impactful.

The OECD has identified four key features of the Swedish model of innovation.[43] First, firms tend to be quick to go international. Klarna, for instance, expanded rapidly in the Nordic countries and used this expansion as a base for further internationalization. The relatively small size of the Swedish market makes it harder for firms to scale up, but they have compensated with a focus on rapid internationalization. Second, the Swedish state often operates as a lead market, cooperating with business on the development of key technologies and using procurement strategically to ensure their commercialization. Third, the tripartite model allows interaction between business, government, and social partners: productivity gains are shared. The Swedish welfare state provides a backdrop for this interaction. Fourth, the country has high levels of R&D spending and a highly educated and skilled population. Large multinationals make significant R&D investments, and Sweden has strong universities and research institutions.

THE ENTREPRENEURIAL (WELFARE) STATE

Many observers, particularly those on the right, see Sweden's welfare state as a problem for the economy. In 2006, the *Economist* magazine sneered at the possibility that "the Nordic countries have found some magic way of combining high taxes and lavish welfare systems with fast growth and low unemployment." [44] Sweden combines three features that can be seen as contradictory in the age of globalization. It is an open economy with free flows of capital and open firms, a high-tax economy, and a society that values the welfare state. For some, this is an impossible trinity: if you are open to international competition, your taxes must be low.

This view is expressed most clearly by Magnus Henrekson, a Swedish economist who wrote a famous paper on the topic in 2005. He argued that the welfare state posed four major problems for entrepreneurship. First, taxation of entrepreneurial income encouraged institutional rather than personal ownership of firms, and so reduced incentives for people to launch startups. In his view, this meant that a "highly competent venture capital industry where high-powered incentives can be used to reward investment managers *cannot develop* in Sweden." [45] Next, he suggested that the public provision of education, housing, and social care, alongside unemployment insurance, removed incentives for individuals to save. As a result, new firms could find only limited supplies of equity finance. Third, he argued that state provision squeezed out opportunities for private-sector entrepreneurship: who would set up a company that had to compete with the state? Finally, he argued that the welfare state reduces the push factors for entrepreneurship. Unemployment benefits provide a floor on earnings—a so-called "reservation wage"— that removes the incentive for workers to set up businesses.

One problem with arguments like these is that they confuse general entrepreneurship with more specific forms of high-tech entrepreneurship. Consider two potential entrepreneurs: one setting up a bakery, the other with an idea in the tech industry. The former business will tend to be replicable and local. It is worthwhile but not particularly transformational: the bread and cakes may be better than those available before, but these improvements are unlikely to scale up. State provision may crowd out some enterprises of this kind (for example, particular types of doctors' surgeries). Many arguments about the role of the state in disincentivizing entrepreneurship are likely to be most applicable where the rewards of entrepreneurship are low. In the case of high-impact, Schumpeterian entrepreneurship, the disincentives are likely to be relatively small. So the welfare state is likely to influence the type of entrepreneurship as much as the quantity. And it is the quality of entrepreneurship that matters. But it is clear that some parts of the Swedish tax code—such as treatment of stock options—historically reduced entrepreneurship. Henrekson had a point.

But Sweden is now arguably a more entrepreneurial country than the United States, where the growing influence of major firms has been documented by economists such as Thomas Philippon, and the number of young firms has been falling. In contrast, Sweden has seen a growing number of new firms. Promarket reforms in the 1990s redesigned and reduced corporate taxes, while product market reforms made it easier to start firms.[46] The economy was liberalized, with employment protections being relaxed and staffing agencies opened up. Corporate taxes are lower than in the United States, and Sweden now has a higher share of entrepreneurial firms. Perceptions of Sweden have been changing: six years after the *Economist* sneered about the "magic" of the Nordic model and predicted its imminent collapse, it had changed its view. A 2012 cover feature heralded the Nordics as "the next supermodel."

DISRUPTING THE WELFARE STATE

A core area of Swedish success has been high tech. The star firms of Sweden's industrial success—Ericsson, Volvo, and even IKEA—had historical roots. This history, along with the corporatist structure of the economy, high tax rates, and a strong welfare state, led many observers to assume the Swedish economy would struggle to adapt. But Sweden has become one of the leading economies in disruptive digital tech.

The classic Swedish tech success story is Spotify, a music streaming service that makes heavy use of data science. In many ways its emergence was a classic Silicon Valley–type story. The company was founded in Stockholm in 2006 by two entrepreneurs with coding backgrounds, Daniel Ek and Martin Lorentzon, both of whom were flush with early success. Lorentzon had worked for AltaVista in Silicon Valley; Ek was a coder who had started in business aged just thirteen. Both could have retired on the profits of selling earlier firms, but instead they chose to create a new company. Spotify has become the most-used streaming service, with over four hundred million users in 183 countries.[47]

The parallels with Silicon Valley parallels go beyond the positive results. Like Uber or WeWork, Spotify is barely ever profitable. High valuations have been supported by expectations of future growth rather than by profits and dividends. The company achieved its first profit in 2022, after thirteen years in operation. It has been controversial, for example by keeping a COVID-denier podcaster on air for longer than many commentators thought appropriate. In 2016, Ek and Lorentzon complained about the problems of Swedish policy: tight planning restrictions, a lack of top programmers coming out of the Swedish education system, and restrictions on stock options that impeded entrepreneurship.[48]

A second example is Klarna, founded in 2005 by three students at the Stockholm School of Economics. The company specializes in processing payments for online shopping, offering payment-after-delivery and installment plans that reduce the friction involved in online purchases. Clever algorithms and analysis of user data allow the company to offer credit that is effectively interest free, provided consumers pay up on time. The winners are consumers, who can make purchases more easily, and companies, which see expanded sales. The losers are credit card companies, whose services are no longer necessary. Yet there are also concerns that Klarna makes it too easy for consumers to access credit, meaning they can become indebted rapidly.

Klarna has been growing rapidly.[49] The aim, as with any such tech firm, is to become the most popular app for purchases and the payment mechanism to which users link their bank accounts.[50] Klarna has over one hundred million active customers.[51] It began by raising venture capital from local firms and later secured funding from some of the world's most important venture capital companies, such as Sequoia Capital. The tech overlords SoftBank led a June 2021 fundraising round that valued Klara at US$45.6 billion, although its valuation has plummeted since.[52] The company's Stockholm headquarters employs workers from fifty-five countries.[53] Klarna has expanded from Sweden to the rest of the Nordics and across the world. The company is now almost as valuable as Nordea, the biggest "standard" bank in the Nordics.[54] It anticipates significant growth in the United States, where online spending is high and credit cards still dominate.

Digital tech firms tend to be scalable, in that they have the potential to grow rapidly. They often have low marginal costs for new users and they benefit from network effects: once one of your friends is using a social network, you are more likely to do so. They can sometimes gain as they grow, making better use of data and so making it hard for other firms to compete against them. The literature on digital firms suggests that they can develop quasi-monopoly status by combining network effects with the advantages of digital tech. Most of the rents from this form of innovation go to the firm or financiers, with less going to the workers themselves (unless they have stock options).

For some economists, the rise of digital tech firms such as Klarna and Spotify is problematic. Their potential market power and the concentration of production in a small number of places leads to inequality between workers, between places, and within places. Some researchers argue that the rise of digital tech may be one factor behind the rise in inequality in countries like Sweden since the 1980s. This view is consistent with two facts. The first is the decline of the labor share of production. With digital technology, a small number of workers can serve larger markets, and so the labor share of production declines. While the evidence on employment polarization is surprisingly weak, there is good evidence that digital technology has been responsible for a decline in the labor share. One of the world's leading economists, David Autor, and coauthors show in a classic 2020 paper that the labor share has been declining most in industries that are highly concentrated.[55]

A second fact relates to markups, or the amount that firms can charge for products over the marginal production cost. In a perfectly competitive market, markups are low, as firms selling more expensive products are undercut by cheaper rivals. But where firms have greater market power, they can charge more. Leading firms in digital technology sectors can charge high markups for their goods, something clear to anyone who has paid a premium for an Apple product over a cheaper product from a less exclusive brand. Research for the OECD shows that markups are higher, and increasingly so, in digital sectors.[56] Digital tech allows firms to prevent competition and concentrate value. Because these markups often come from scale, they encourage financiers to make large bets in the development of digital tech firms, even if the firms operate at a loss for some time.

Tech firms can also cause inequality between places. In the view of Maryann Feldman, Frederick Guy, and Simona Iammarino—three highly respected economic geographers and business scholars—the growth of a strong tech sector in the United States has been one of the major drivers of geographical inequality there.[57] Tech firms are also reliant on a set of agglomeration economies. They need highly skilled labor, links with specialist firms such as legal firms, and rapid access to knowledge. These agglomeration economies encourage geographic concentration. Yet at the same time, many tech firms have scalable business models, in that a firm can expand rapidly; it is tradable, in that products and services created in one place can be consumed at little additional cost elsewhere; and tech firms—such as Google, Facebook, and even Spotify—can achieve near-monopoly status.

The result is a stark concentration of income and wealth in a small area. And within that area, Feldman and colleagues argue, there are significant disparities in income between those working in the most innovative firms and those employed elsewhere. Inequality between places also increases. Cities with a strong tech economy charge forward, while those with fewer new firms are left behind.[58] In Sweden, these arguments are borne out by the concentration of the tech sector in Stockholm, which has been accompanied by rising house prices and gross wage inequality.

SILICON STOCKHOLM

Stockholm is the epicenter of Sweden's tech industry. A million people live on an archipelago at the center of an urban region of another 1.5 million. It is the capital, the site of Swedish government, and the home of many of the key innovation institutions of Sweden. Vinnova, the Swedish innovation agency, is based there. Leading universities—the Stockholm School of Economics, the KTH Royal Institute of Technology, and Stockholm University—are all located in one neighborhood. Klarna is based in central Stockholm's Norrmalm neighborhood, and Spotify's main office is a few blocks away in Vasastan. Local policymakers estimate that one-fifth of the city's population works in tech. In addition, Stockholm has a life sciences cluster, and around seventeen thousand people work for major firms such as AstraZeneca and startups.[59]

Why did Stockholm develop as a hub of tech? And what does that evolution mean for residents? The answer to the first question is a combination of luck and judgment. The city had strong institutions, including a well-educated population with good English and information-technology skills. The small size of the Swedish economy meant firms had to seek external markets early if they wanted to grow. The city is well-run, manageable, and a nice place to live. Although Stockholm offers no major tax breaks (because, as one city official told me, it "competes on competence"), there were strong incentives for the emergence of a developmental coalition. A percentage of local income taxes goes to the local government, providing incentives for it to attract high-wage work.

Economic geography is clear on the forces that encourage the clustering of knowledge-intensive industries, but the reasons why any specific city or region flourishes are often murky. In Stockholm, a few large, highly successful firms were seeds planted in fertile ground. [60] The initial success of Spotify was crucial. Several of the initial founders and staff of Spotify had experience working in contexts of high-risk entrepreneurship and innovation, so they started with a set of cultural norms, expectations, and knowledge about the process. They served as high-profile Swedish role models in the tech industry, providing advice, seed capital, role models, and exemplars.

Along with Klarna, Spotify helped anchor a self-sustaining tech cluster in Stockholm. Because tech hubs are so crucial to prosperity, their development is one of the most important subjects in economic geography. Scholars refer to their functioning as an "entrepreneurial ecosystem." The reference to nature is deliberate, because, like a natural ecosystem, an established entrepreneurial ecosystem should be able to adapt and evolve over time with minimal outside intervention, driven by interactions between networked firms, entrepreneurs, financiers, universities, and individuals.

Around these firms developed a supportive infrastructure. Swedish venture capital traces its roots to a joint partnership in the 1970s between the national government and the banks, though it was less successful after problems in the early 2000s. High-profile successes attracted more firms, and profitable exits provided venture capital money that could be recirculated into the system. Swedish serial investors served as angel investors, mentoring early-stage firms and reinvesting the profits of success locally. For example, one of the cofounders of Klarna, Niklas Adalberth, went on to found the Norrsken Foundation, an impact investment firm designed to achieve social aims through scalable firms. Others were more commercially minded. An early Klarna investor, Jane Walerud, later helped finance other leading Swedish tech firms such as the eye-tracking software firm Tobii.

Stockholm's tech sector developed the sort of open and supportive networks necessary for success in innovation-intensive industries, giving firms access to skilled staff and expertise. Such networks also help avoid management problems. Among the major problems of scaling up an innovative firm are the so-called Penrose effects. The celebrated economist Edith Penrose observed that the skills required to create an innovative product, market it, start a firm, and then scale it up are all very different.[61] But the founders and management of firms are often unwilling or unaware of this problem and don't want to stand aside as the company matures. Venture capitalists can help firms introduce appropriate management at different stages of the growth process. But doing so requires networks of specialists, often in a relatively small location. The early success of a few Swedish firms made it easier for later firms to find these specialists. In this case, networks became self-reinforcing.

Stockholm also had the basic requirements of a highly competitive cluster. The city's famously high quality of life and strong public services helped attract and retain workers. Leading universities provided applied research to be commercialized and a supply of skilled workers. The city's reputation attracted international workers who could be confident of finding work in other firms if their initial position didn't work out. These framework conditions were important for the development of Stockholm's high-tech sector, but they were not sufficient. Only after the success of the first wave of high-tech companies did the cluster began to function as a self-reinforcing ecosystem.

The clearest evidence of the scale and success of tech in Stockholm comes from venture capital data. Venture capital can be problematic for local economies. Venture capitalists make bets in scalable companies likely to achieve significant growth. Before making investments, they carefully screen firms, and after investment they work closely with them to achieve rapid growth. Because this process is intensive and relies on face-to-face contact, it is easier if firms are local. This leads to cumulative causation: venture capitalists want to invest near potential investments, and potential investments want to locate near venture capital. The result is the formation of clusters of tech and venture capital firms.

Venture capital is also a clear mediator between the state and the national innovation system. As argued by Josh Lerner, a Harvard economist, and Joacim Tåg from the Hanken School of Economics, venture capital relies on a set of institutional preconditions. First, it requires a legal environment that allows contracts to be written and enforced in reliable and efficient way. The tax system needs to reward the effort and risk put into entrepreneurship. To allow venture capitalists to make exits, there need to be stock markets that allow them to sell their investments. Labor-market regulations need to allow firms to hire and fire without too great a penalty. Finally, because firms need to commercialize advanced technology, there need to be strong links between universities and business. Lerner and Tåg find that these five criteria were met in Sweden only in the late 1990s.[62]

For venture capital, institutions matter. Investors need to be sure that their contracts are enforceable, that the legal system allows deals to be scrutinized clearly, and that they can place representatives on company boards. Better-developed financial markets provide the opportunity for profitable exits.[63] The tax system shapes both the supply and the type of entrepreneurs, as it determines the relative opportunity cost of formal employment. Social security systems incur a cost that must be borne by employers.

Sweden outperforms the rest of the Nordic countries—and all of Europe except Estonia— in per capita venture-capital investment, at $700. Crunchbase ranked it fifth in the world, behind Singapore, Israel, Estonia, and the United States—and significantly above the sixth-placed United Kingdom ($472 per capita).[64] Using data from 2013, the economic geographer Patrick Adler showed the concentration of Swedish venture capital investment in Stockholm.[65] There were one hundred investments in 2013 across ninety-one companies. Stockholm, home to 26 percent of the Swedish population, took 75.9 percent of the total investment made, and 67.9 percent of total venture-capital investment went to digital startups in a single postcode in central Stockholm, just west of KTH and near the Stockholm School of Economics and Stockholm University.

Sweden's high levels of personal taxation and its small size should, according to some, reduce the incentives to create new firms. The successes of the Swedish model might be attributed to luck. But the country's assets include a well-educated population with good technical and English-language skills. The research infrastructure is good, as are the basics of the economy—fast broadband, good public services, high-quality government. Technologies are adopted rapidly, often facilitated by the state.

This is not to say that Swedish success can continue. Many Swedish unicorns are taken over and run by entrepreneurs in other countries.[66] No Swedish firm has broken into the very big time— there is no Swedish Amazon, Google, Facebook, Uber, or Netflix.

The tech ecosystem has generally enhanced living standards for Stockholm's residents. It is hard to compare inequality between places, as boundaries vary and subnational data is poor. But estimates suggest that income inequality is much lower in Stockholm than in any US city and even lower than in other Swedish cities, such as Malmö.[67] Regional inequality was historically high, declining in the period after the Industrial Revolution, and then experiencing an uptick in the 1980s.[68] While interregional differentials have increased, they remain relatively low.[69] A system of fiscal transfers from rich areas to poor provides an equalizing mechanism, while the wage-bargaining system prevents wage differentials from growing large. Areas of natural-resource wealth outside the major cities mean that other areas of the country can grow rich on other forms of production.[70] There are also feasible, tech-led development strategies outside the capital. For example, Northvolt, an electric battery company founded by a former Tesla executive, has grown rapidly, building a factory in northern Sweden designed to produce the greenest battery ever.

Yet as inequality has been increasing at the high end of the distribution, there are also signs that this system is starting to fray. The richest regions, led by Stockholm, grew fastest in the period 2000–2019, and the population of lagging regions faces challenges of population aging.[71]

SWEDEN, THE STATE, AND DISRUPTIVE TECH

Sweden's success shows that a strong state is no barrier to radical innovation in the digital economy. While it was possible to argue twenty years ago that the state prevented entrepreneurial success, this no longer seems to be the case. Research suggests that public R&D spending can attract both private-sector R&D spending and venture capital activity.[72] This trend is hinted at in the development pairs of the 1960s, procurement for innovation in later years, and even in the historical development of Swedish venture capital. The first Swedish venture capital firm, Foretagskapital, was set up in 1973 as a partnership between the government and Swedish banks.[73] Large firms were often developed through public procurement and long-term partnerships between state and particular firms, although these have been hard to maintain.[74] The Swedish state has always had a more active relationship with the economy than simply laying a playing field. Indeed, a competent state supports the development of radical tech firms. Consider the three factors raised as issues by the founders of Spotify: availability of coders from local educational institutions, affordable housing, and changes in tax codes. Only one of these concerns is related to tax, and it is not about the tax rate but rather about the minutiae. Indeed, the chair of Klarna has explicitly argued in favor of Sweden's welfare state, as he argues it allows young people to invest in skills and take risks.[75]

Sweden combines an institutional structure allowing the development of new firms with a set of institutions that share the benefits. The country remains relatively regionally equal, with decentralized government, centralized wage coordination, fiscal transfers, and a diversity of economic models. A strong system of regional government, along with natural resource wealth, helps ensure that peripheral areas are less economically disadvantaged than they might be in other countries. This government funding is generative, in the sense that it contributes to growth; diffusive or distributive, in the sense that it lets people benefit from growth; and redistributive, in that there are transfers to different areas.

But even egalitarian Sweden has faced challenges. The reforms that allowed disruptive tech to thrive have begun to fray the social model. Inequality has been rising rapidly, driven by the growing wealth of the top 1 percent. Most countries saw inequality rise in the 1980s and 1990s; Sweden is unusual in that inequality continued to increase in the 2000s. At present, this looks like a form of "good" inequality that supports prosperity for others. But if it persists, the Swedish model may, in the long run, break down.

Conclusion

INNOVATION AND SHARED PROSPERITY

How can countries translate innovation into high living standards? For many policymakers, this is a second-order concern. For them, innovation is an end in itself, rather than a means to an end. But, as I have argued, there is little point in a highly innovative economy unless it benefits workers. To bring about this outcome, we need to extend our understanding of innovation policy, learn from examples beyond Silicon Valley, Oxbridge, and Shenzhen, and think harder about the distributional consequences of what are often major investments of public money. We should be learning from places where innovation translates to higher living standards.

We can learn a lot from the experience of countries such as Switzerland, Austria, Taiwan, and Sweden, which achieve high levels of innovation and have, at times, managed to share the benefits. These countries have plenty of problems. Austria, Sweden, and Switzerland have faced problems with populism and intolerance; Swedish income equality is rising, and social mobility is counter-posed by higher wealth inequality; Taiwan's inequality statistics are massaged by incomes from China, the share of national income going to the top 1 percent is growing rapidly, and house prices are squeezing young workers. All these countries still suffer from major disparities based on gender, race, and migration status. And they all face the challenges of sustaining their models in the face of global competition. There are, unfortunately, no utopias.

But examples do not have to be perfect to be helpful. These countries provide causes for optimism and examples of ways in which innovation can be used to achieve a broadly shared prosperity.

HOW TO SHARE THE BENEFITS OF INNOVATION

At this point critical readers may be worried about the extent to which we can learn lessons from countries with distinct histories and institutional architectures. First, critics might object that because these are small states, we cannot learn much from them. These countries are certainly small, but the idea that other countries can learn nothing from them is wrong. After all, policymakers in mid-sized countries such as my own, the United Kingdom, try and learn from much larger countries, such as the United States. Small size carries both advantages and costs. Small countries may find it easier to adapt their systems and experiment. As Peter Katzenstein argued in the mid-1980s, the "low-voltage politics" of small states allows coordination and institutional reform.[1] And small countries are forced to adopt a strategy based on openness to international markets.

The second argument is a trick of distraction. Some people may point to Austria's problems with corruption, Switzerland's shady bankers, or the problems of a Taiwanese model in which wealth inequality has been increasing. These criticisms are often valid, but they do not make other features of the models irrelevant. If we search for perfect examples of places that are highly innovative and share the benefits, we will be searching for a very long time. Instead, we should take what we can from these models, warts and all, but avoid portraying them as clichés or misguided ideas of paradise.

A third criticism is fairer: these countries are rich, but—with the exception of Taiwan—they have been slow growing; they are innovative, but not leaders in the latest waves of technology. These countries have also seen their growth stall. For example, although Austrians enjoy high average wages, their earnings have increased by less than the European average. But slow growth does not equal failure, and growth inevitably slows when countries reach the technological frontier. Most people would rather live a country that is rich and slow growing than one that is poor but experiencing rapid growth.

A fourth criticism is that policies that work in specific institutional contexts may not work elsewhere. This point is important and correct: naive and context-blind replication of policy in very different places leads to failed policies, wasted resources, and cynicism. Policymakers are pressed for time and for resources, so the temptation to make fast policy by following ready-made examples elsewhere is always going to be a problem.

But the danger of naive policy transfer is a cause for caution, not grounds for an outright rejection of the practice. Misguided policy transfer from countries such as Switzerland is no worse than simply uncritically adopting the US model. Here I aim to provide general lessons for adapting policy to specific local economic, social, and institutional conditions. The critical audience in the United Kingdom, for example, could learn much from Swiss efforts at vocational education—about its quality, prestige, and links with advanced industries. But they should not attempt to replicate the Swiss model exactly in the United Kingdom. Trying to transplant something that worked in one system into another without modifications would be foolhardy.

These four criticisms all hint at one of the foundational principles of public policy research: we need to think hard about the external validity of our models and consider carefully the contexts in which we apply them. No policy, let alone an innovation policy, works consistently across time and space—as faddish innovation policymakers have too often failed to realize.[2] Instead we should separate the unique circumstances of each individual country from the specific policies and development strategies it has followed.[3]

THE STATE, INNOVATION, AND SHARED PROSPERITY

My four cases show the role of the state in linking innovation with shared prosperity. First, the state does more than promote innovation; it also sets the framework to ensure the benefits are broadly shared. A narrow focus on innovation for its own sake risks missing the overall point of policy. Innovation policy needs to take account of skills, housing, welfare, and other social and economic concerns. Wage-setting and labor-market regulatory structures in Sweden and Austria help distribute the benefits of those countries' success in innovation. Taiwanese education policy has supported innovation and at times helped share the benefits (although the state's role in housing markets and the limited welfare state have not benefited workers).

Second, sharing the benefits of innovation requires the development of institutions that enable its diffusion. Such institutions include skill systems that help workers use and adapt new technologies, applied research institutions that tailor innovations to the needs of small firms, and dense networks through which knowledge diffuses. Scholars of innovation policy have tended to focus on systems and the structures that achieve innovation; less attention has been paid to the institutions that help innovation and new technologies diffuse through the wider economy, or to linking success in innovation-intensive industries with redistributional structures.

Finally, policies for innovation and shared prosperity are mutually reinforcing. This is clear in the cases I've considered. The high

Swiss quality of life attracts skilled international workers who contribute to the country's economic success. Competent government in
Sweden increases equity and also, by raising skill levels, innovation.
These economies don't succeed despite their social models; they
succeed because of them. Moreover, equity in the innovation process
can create a virtuous circle. For example, better vocational training
allows workers to benefit from innovation and also allows the diffusion of innovation; including disadvantaged groups in the STEM
workforce benefits those workers and also creates more innovation;
countries whose innovation ecosystems are geographically distributed are more innovative than those with a few dominant hubs.
Inequality of access to innovation reduces innovation overall.

These three arguments provide a rationale for government intervention. But they don't tell us how these countries do it. Many books
would, at this point, offer a new model of innovation policy. They
might offer a concept that "disrupts" innovation policy and a recipe
for success. But there is no generalized formula. While it is tempting
to portray national innovation systems as homogeneous, no serious
analysis would support this conclusion. Moreover, differences
between innovation systems are even starker at the local or regional
level, as comparisons of superstar cities in different regions demon-
strate. A firm in Switzerland deals with a very different context from
one in the United States, let alone one in China. But a firm in Basel
also faces a different context from one in Geneva. Policy is best when
it is informed by global evidence but tailored to local circumstances.
This means striking a balance between analytical simplicity, which
helps clarify ideas, and local nuance. There are no easy, formulaic
approaches to successful innovation policy.

Instead of offering a new model for innovation policy, I consider
the types of institutions that seem to matter. Each of these countries
I examine here has, or has had, a specific institutional structure
focused on the generation of innovation but also has strong institutions focused on diffusion and redistribution.

INSTITUTIONS: GENERATIVE, DIFFUSIVE, AND REDISTRIBUTIVE

Political economists use the concept of growth regimes, each of which, as Peter Hall notes, is "distinguished by the distinctive ways in which it generates economic growth and distributes its fruits."[4] Scholars in innovation talk instead about innovation systems that exist at the national and regional levels. The basic insight here is that firms do not operate in isolation but produce new innovations in tandem with a set of relationships, demand conditions, and supply constraints—for skills, intermediate goods, and so on—that are created, in part, by the state. This pattern is clear in all four of my case studies. The role of the state is either highly directed, as in Taiwan and Austria, or more laissez-faire, as in Switzerland. But in all cases, the institutional structure in each country shapes outcomes in important ways.

David Soskice has argued that the US dominance in radical innovation comes from a set of "generative institutional structures." These institutions, concerned with research, finance, labor markets, market size, and legal structures, have given rise to the particular form of US innovation, with radical tech firms able to scale up and defend their dominance through continual upgrading, defensive purchases of other companies, and legal capture. One key implication of this outcome is the importance of the structure of institutions and their interrelationships: venture capital is useless without investable firms, and money invested on R&D is wasted unless there are routes to commercialization and diffusion.

Clearly, some institutional structures are useful because they are generative, allowing radical innovation to develop: world-leading universities that produce technologies unseen elsewhere; venture capitalist firms that fund high-risk, high-return activities; agencies, such as DARPA in the United States, that fund blue-sky research on topics of scientific significance; angel investors reinvesting profits made from early innovations in new start-ups; PhD skill systems that provide the most imaginative researchers with the time, guidance, and resources to make major leaps. Weak antitrust legislation may belong in this category, in the sense that it allows firms to scale up, although it has many negative effects. Other important institutions include those in leading-edge research, high-impact entrepreneurship, and other forms of commercialization. Strong institutions need to generate innovation, not just invention.

The US has a specific generative institutional structure, but each of the countries I have studied has its own variety. In Taiwan, research labs feed chip-manufacturing success, and finance was steered toward good job creation. Swedish venture capital helps steer firms toward radical innovation, while Nordic markets provide Swedish companies with opportunities to scale; leading Swiss universities such as ETH produce applied innovation for leading-edge sectors. Some institutions focus on radical innovation, but others concentrate on the upgrading of local sectors. Austrian R&D focused on the low-tech industries of the past, and the result was productivity growth and occupational upgrading.

But the institutions that matter for increasing living standards are not just generative. Diffusive institutional structures ensure that innovations and new technologies are distributed through the economy. They include networks of small firms that apply existing technologies to specific institutional niches; vocational skills systems that train workers to adapt existing technologies to specific commercial needs; skills systems that train workers for the second-stage work of commercializing innovations; business networks that help diffuse technologies; financial markets that provide capital for firms likely to achieve only limited growth; and powerful local government, which can help firms grow and bring the benefits of advanced sectors into different regions.

These institutions provide mechanisms through which the benefits of innovation can reach workers. Diffusive institutional structures help distribute rents from innovation across a wider group of

Table 6   Institutions key to promoting innovation, by country

	Switzerland	Austria	Taiwan	Sweden
Generative institutions	World-leading research universities Openness to skilled foreign workers Deep pools of capital Competitive taxation	Universities focused on local strengths Large firms with long-term experience in local economies Focused national government policy	Multinational firms Science parks Government finance focused on leading sectors	Radical tech companies Venture-capital funding Angel investors recycling finance and expertise World-leading universities
Diffusive institutions	Universities of applied science Vocational education system Competitive, nonfrontier SMEs Cantonal governance structures	Local business networks Competitive, nonfrontier SMEs	STEM focused education system Highly competitive small firms	Vocational education system National technology-focused policy Decentralized regional government
Redistributive institutions	Corporatist labor-market institutions	Corporatist labor-market institutions Strong welfare state		Fiscal transfers to less advantaged regions Wage coordination policies Strong welfare state

people. They ensure that workers have the capabilities to benefit from innovation and thereby ensure that new technologies are diffused through the wider economy. The higher levels of the Swiss vocational education system offer one example, facilitating innovation and the diffusion of technology from elsewhere, and ensuring that workers benefit. All four countries offer forms of vocational education and have some focus on STEM. Another example is applied or translational research infrastructure, in particular infrastructure that serves local needs, such as *Fachhochschulen*. Swedish tax credits that subsidized the purchase of personal computers helped people adopt new technology, thereby increasing diffusion, sparking new ideas, and allowing people to develop the skills they needed to benefit from further productivity increases. The wider support infrastructure of economic development that allows firms across different regions to develop in innovation-intensive niches is also important.

Diffusive or distributional institutions solve a core problem with innovation and new technology: that access is unequal and focused on the wrong goals. It is crucial to give people the opportunity to be part of the innovation workforce—to participate in the delivery of innovation. Scare stories about technological change and the labor market tend to identify innovation and new technology as a problem for society. Of course, this is sometimes true. But the central problem is more often inequality of access to innovation, resulting in unequal distribution of benefits. We need to provide greater access to innovation and new technology, not less.

Institutions that shape the distribution of the benefits of innovation are also important. Inevitably, some innovations concentrate economic value, but things can be done to mitigate this trend. Some of these institutions operate in the labor market. For example, centralized wage bargaining, works councils that negotiate wages, and minimum wages convey some of the benefits of innovation to workers, even if those workers are not necessarily at the cutting edge. Other institutions in this category include redistributive institutions such as an appropriately designed tax system, a welfare state that brings people into economic activity, and strong, high-quality public services. Good schools, strong public services, health-care systems that work, and sensible immigration policies all help share the benefits of innovation while also sustaining it.

One key feature of the institutions most successful at generating, diffusing, and redistributing the benefits of innovation is that they achieve some sort of geographic equity. For innovation to reach people, it has to happen close to where they are. Urban economics models assume that people are willing and able to relocate— and migration should be celebrated for the economic and social role it can play. But mobility is not for everyone: people are kept in place by dense webs of family ties, networks, and so on. The costs of migration make it most appealing to those with the weakest ties and the most to gain—the young and the talented. In advanced economies, a slim majority of people move.[5] One common feature of Sweden, Switzerland, and Austria is that highly innovative firms operate even in relatively peripheral areas. Local economies compensate for the lack of agglomeration in various ways, including the development of localized clusters of skilled workers, research institutes focused on local economies, strong public services, and access to natural resources.

IS INNOVATION WITH EQUITY POSSIBLE?

I started this book with the concern that high levels of innovation are simply incompatible with broadly shared prosperity. The United States is the global leader in radical innovation and home to most of the world's leading firms. Partly as a result, it is rich but riven with inequality. China is following this lead. China is not yet rich, although some regions of it are, and inequality is relatively high.[6] These countries are leading, but they are also unequal. Focusing on them leads to the conclusion that inequality is the price of successful innovation.

But there are three arguments against this view. One is that the relationship is circumstantial: the US lead does not necessarily come solely from the processes that make it unequal. The institutions, financial markets, leading universities, scalable companies, and competitive labor market that seem to drive US innovation are not all linked to inequality. So it might be that inequality is circumstantial, caused by specific characteristics of the US tax system and financial markets, and the lack of diffusive institutions. Yet the scalability of US tech is a reason both for its success and for the inequality that results. Market size can concentrate income, as it allows digital tech firms to scale. The case of Sweden—which has achieved success in rapid-growth industries—offers only an imperfect counterexample here, because although inequality remains low there, it has been rising rapidly.

A second argument is more persuasive. We need to distinguish between the rapidly scaling firms of the tech economy and the very different forms of innovation that occur in other sectors of the economy. This argument, which draws on Breznitz, Meisenzahl, Mokyr, and others, contrasts the rapidly scaling stars of the tech economy, which make radical innovations (although plenty of tweaking takes place afterwards), with the incremental innovation that takes place in, for example, automobile firms.[7] Austria has achieved growth in traditional industries through innovation. Ownership may matter here. Firms in slow-growing sectors may have more diffuse ownership than rapidly scaling tech firms, which are more likely to concentrate wealth and income. This means that the rewards of innovation in tech firms are more unequal.

A third argument is related to the nature of inequality. Switzerland and Sweden have achieved high-growth, radical innovation while sustaining high incomes for middle-class earners. But they are both highly unequal at the top of the income distribution. No country, as far as I am aware, has managed to sustain growth in highly innovative firms without this sort of inequality developing. One form of inequality is "good'—as far as inequality can be said to be good—

provided it does not lock in advantage. Swedish industrial dynasties go back centuries, but it isn't clear that they have caused major problems for the country. They have often supported industrial upgrading, bringing others up with them.

So if we ask whether it is possible to lead in innovation without creating high levels of inequality, the answer is that it depends. The rapid growth of new tech firms is accompanied by growing inequality, and this can—in a narrow sense—be seen as a reward for growth. Some countries develop institutions that combine rapid growth in tech firms with rising incomes for mid- and low-skill workers; others don't. The problem isn't the nature of innovation but the institutions that share the benefits.

ANTI-INNOVATION POLITICS

The focus on generating innovation, and the consequent lack of attention to the distribution of the gains, is a problem for policy. Many of the most important works on innovation policy emphasize the role of the state in creating innovation. Mariana Mazzucato argues in *Entrepreneurial State* that because the state supports the research that underpins advanced products, governments should be more assertive in their taxation of innovative firms. It is an indictment of much governance in advanced countries that this call was seen as so controversial. The state's role in innovation has been the subject of debate for some time: a case in which the public returns on R&D exceed those of the private sector is commonly regarded as market failure. But I don't think this argument goes far enough. We should be thinking more, and more clearly, about the type of jobs and the distribution of the gains that come from major investments of public money.

Governments invest vast resources in innovation, and they have a moral duty and a practical imperative to make sure that the benefits are widely distributed. But there is also a pragmatic reason for doing so: if we don't share the benefits of innovation, we risk nurturing the backlash against it. The last decade has been marked by a rise in antisystem politics. Most advanced economies, including those I have studied, have suffered from challenges of populism and discontent. Populist politicians, and others, rail against the key institutions of the knowledge economy. For example, universities—a core institution for innovation—have been criticized rather than supported; the immigrants needed to work in innovative industries have been attacked rather than encouraged; unions lobby against the use of new technologies that might, in the long run, benefit their members; and housing markets in the most successful tech hubs have been restricted so that the benefits of high-tech growth go to landowners, not workers.

It is hardly surprising that many people feel they have no stake in the innovation economy. They are often right. If you live in a tech hub such as Oxford or San Francisco, how have you benefited from the city's growth? You might have a job created by the tech economy, but many other cities have high employment without it. Your wages may be slightly higher, but so are your rents; and your chances of owning your own home are probably lower. Many workers end up squeezed out of successful cities, commuting long distances to work and to see their friends and family. So if an opportunistic politician tells you that universities exist only to benefit other people, you might find yourself agreeing. It would hardly be surprising if you voted for a candidate who is anti-growth and anti-innovation.

Innovation is crucial for economic growth and rising living standards. But if the innovation economy remains exclusive and its rewards concentrated, it will sow the seeds of its own failure. A backlash against pro-innovation policies has been under way across many countries, with some justification. The exclusion of some groups from the innovation economy—because of who they are, the skills they have, or where they live—is a waste of talent and resources. In some places, too few people benefit. Making sure the high-tech economy is inclusive is the best way to share the benefits, but also the best way to sustain innovation overall.

Notes

INTRODUCTION

1. You might think that my argument misses out the importance of finance and high-value business services, but it does not: these industries are services, but they still do a lot of R&D. In the United Kingdom, HSBC and Lloyds both spend over £1 billion annually on R&D.

2. In fact, we make this exact argument—that investments in R&D do not always lead to growth—in Arman, H., Iammarino, S., Ibarra-Olivo, J. E., & Lee, N. (2022). Systems of innovation, diversification, and the R&D trap: A case study of Kuwait. *Science and Public Policy, 49*(2), 179–190.

3. OECD (2015). *In it together: Why less inequality benefits all.* OECD Publishing.

4. Chancel, L. (2019). *Ten facts about inequality in advanced economies.* WID.world Working Paper, No. 2019/15.

5. OECD (2019). *Under pressure: The squeezed middle class.* OECD Publishing. https://doi.org/10.1787/689afed1-en.

6. OECD (2022). Gender wage gap (indicator). https://doi.org/10.1787/7cee77aa-en.

7. McNeil, A., Luca, D. & Lee, N. (2022). *The long shadow of local decline: Birthplace economic conditions, political attitudes, and long-term individual economic outcomes in the UK.* International Inequalities Institute Working Paper, no. 76, London School of Economics and Political Science.

8. See Aghion, P., Akcigit, U., Bergeaud, A., Blundell, R., & Hémous, D. (2019). Innovation and top income inequality. *Review of Economic Studies, 86*(1), 1–45; Florida, R., & Mellander, C. (2016). The geography of inequality: Difference and determinants of wage and income inequality across US metros. *Regional Studies, 50*(1), 79–92; Lee, N., Sissons, P., & Jones, K. (2016). The geography of wage inequality in British cities. *Regional Studies, 50*(10), 1714–1727.

9. Blanchet, T., Chancel, L., & and Gethin, A. 2022. Why is Europe more equal than the United States? *American Economic Journal: Applied Economics, 14*(4): 480–518.

10. Donovan, S. A., & Bradley, D. H. (2019). *Real wage trends, 1979 to 2018.* Congressional Research Service.

11. Feldman, M. P., Guy, F., Iammarino, S., & Ioramashvili, C. (2021). *Gathering round Big Tech: How the market for acquisitions reinforces regional inequalities in the US.* Kenan Institute of Private Enterprise Research Paper, no. 21–01.

12. Saxenian, A. (1996). *Regional advantage: Culture and competition in Silicon Valley and Route 128.* Harvard University Press.

13. Harrison, B. (1988). *The Great U-Turn: Corporate restructuring and the polarizing of America.* Basic Books.

14. Peck, J., & Theodore, N. (2015). *Fast policy: Experimental statecraft at the thresholds of neoliberalism.* University of Minnesota Press.

15. Figures given for 2019, to avoid complexities introduced by the COVID pandemic. OECD (2023). General government spending (indicator). https://doi.org/10.1787/cc9669ed-en.

16. Blanchet et al., Why is Europe more equal than the United States?

CHAPTER 1

1. Baregheh, A., Rowley, J., & Sambrook, S. (2009). Towards a multidisciplinary definition of innovation. *Management Decision, 47*(8), 1323–1339.

2. Schumpeter, J. (1934). *The theory of economic development: An inquiry into profits, capital, credit, interest, and the business cycle.* Harvard University Press.

3. Schumpeter, *The theory of economic development.*

4. Richard Jones has a good rephrasing of an old quote: "Research is the process of turning money into ideas, innovation is turning ideas into money." Jones, R. (2021, August 2). Reflections on the UK's new innovation strategy. *Soft Machines.* www.softmachines.org/wordpress/?p=2591.

5. Arthur, W. B. (2009). *The nature of technology: What it is and how it evolves.* Simon & Schuster.

6. OECD (2018). The measurement of scientific, technological and innovation activities. *Oslo Manual 2018.* OECD, p. 20.

7. Schumpeter, J. A. (2002). The economy as a whole: Seventh chapter of *The theory of economic development.* Translated by Ursula Backhaus. *Industry and Innovation, 9*(1–2), 93.

8. Fagerberg, J., Srholec, M., & Verspagen, B. (2010). Innovation and economic development. In *Handbook of the Economics of Innovation* (Vol. 2) (pp. 833–872). North-Holland, 839.

9. Usher, A. P. 1951. Historical implications of *The theory of economic development. Review of Economics and Statistics, 33*(2), 160.

10. Breznitz, D. (2021). *Innovation in real places: Strategies for prosperity in an unforgiving world.* Oxford University Press.

11. Smith, K. (2005). Measuring innovation. In J. Fagerberg, D. Mowery, & R. Nelson (Eds.), *The Oxford handbook of innovation* (pp. 148–177). Oxford University Press. https://doi.org/10.1093/oxfordhb/9780199286805.003.0006.

12. Meisenzahl, R R., & Mokyr, J. (2011). The rate and direction of invention in the British Industrial Revolution: Incentives and institutions. In J. Lerner& S. Stern (Eds.), *The rate and direction of inventive activity revisited* (pp. 443–479). University of Chicago Press.

13. Breznitz, *Innovation in real places,* 3.

14. Greenstone, M., & Looney, A. (2011). A dozen economic facts about innovation. *The Hamilton Project.* Brookings Institution. www.brookings.edu/wp-content/uploads/2016/06/08_innovation_greenstone_looney.pdf.

15. Coenen, L., Hansen, T., & Rekers, J. V. (2015). Innovation policy for grand challenges: An economic geography perspective. *Geography Compass, 9*(9), 483–496.

16. Some argue that the Haldane principle is a myth from the 1960s. See Edgerton, D. (2018). Haldane principle's "centenary" is a good time to bury its myth. *Research Fortnight.* December 12.

17. HM Government. (2021). *National AI Strategy.* HMSO, 5.

18. HM Government (2020). *UK Research and Development Roadmap.* HMSO, 7.

19. Hall, B. H. Innovation and diffusion. In J. Fagerberg, D. Mowery, & R. Nelson (Eds.), *The Oxford handbook of innovation* (pp. 459–483). Oxford University Press.

20. Rekers, J. V. (2016). What triggers innovation diffusion? Intermediary organizations and geography in cultural and science-based industries. *Environment and Planning C: Government and Policy, 34*(6), 1058–1075.

21. Breznitz, D., & Murphree, M. (2011). *Run of the Red Queen: Government, innovation, globalization, and economic growth in China.* Yale University Press.

22. Grillitsch, M., Rekers, J. V., & Tödtling, F. (2019). When drivers of clusters shift scale from local towards global: What remains for regional innovation policy?. *Geoforum, 102*, 57–68.

23. Marshall, A. (1890). *The Principles of Economics.* MacMillan, 198.

24. Storper, M. (1997). *The regional world: Territorial development in a global economy.* Guilford Press.

25. Saxenian, A. (2007). *The new argonauts: Regional advantage in a global economy.* Harvard University Press.

26. Solon, O. (2013). Bill Gates: Capitalism means male baldness research gets more funding   than malaria. *Wired.* March 14.

27. Nelson, R. R. (2011). *The moon and the ghetto* revisited. *Science and Public Policy, 38*(9), 681–690.

28. Verspagen, B. (2005). Innovation and economic growth. In J. Fagerberg, D. Mowery, & R. Nelson (Eds.), *The Oxford handbook of innovation* (pp. 487–513). Oxford University Press . https://doi.org/10.1093/oxfordhb/9780199286805.003.0018.

29. Schumpeter, J. (1942). *Capitalism, socialism, and democracy.* Harper & Brothers, 82–83.

30. Schumpeter, *Capitalism, socialism, and democracy, 82.*

31. OECD (2021). *OECD R&D tax incentives database,* 2021 edition. www.oecd.org/sti/rd-tax-stats-database.pdf.

32. Lundvall, B. Å., & Borrás, S. (2005). Science, technology and innovation policy. In J. Fagerberg, D. Mowery, & R. Nelson (Eds.), *The Oxford handbook of innovation* (pp. 599–631). Oxford University Press.

33. Lundvall & Borrás, Science, technology and innovation policy.

34. Hall, P. A. (2022). Growth regimes. *Business History Review,* 1–25. https://doi.org/10.1017/S0007680522000034.

35. Institutional approaches and "policy mix" approaches can often lapse into abstract theorizing rather than clear-headed analysis. For a superb exception, see Flanagan, K., Uyarra, E., & Laranja, M. (2011).

Reconceptualising the "policy mix" for innovation. *Research Policy, 40*(5), 702–713.

36. Taylor, M. Z. (2016). *The politics of innovation: Why some countries are better than others at science and technology.* Oxford University Press.

37. Castaldi, C., and Mendonça, S. (2022). Regions and trademarks: Research opportunities and policy insights from leveraging trademarks in regional innovation studies. *Regional Studies, 56*(2), 177–189. https://doi.org/10.1080/00343404.2021.2003767.

CHAPTER 2

1. Van Reenen, J. (1996). The creation and capture of rents: Wages and innovation in a panel of UK companies. *Quarterly Journal of Economics, 111*(1), 195–226.

2. Kline, P., Petkova, N., Williams, H., & Zidar, O. (2019). Who profits from patents? Rent-sharing at innovative firms. *Quarterly Journal of Economics, 134*(3), 1343–1404. Note, however, that rewards are not necessarily equally shared within the firm. There are still significant gender (and other) disparities.

3. Aghion, P., Akcigit, U., Hyytinen, A., & Toivanen, O. (2018, May). On the returns to invention within firms: Evidence from Finland. *AEA Papers and Proceedings 108,* 208–212.

4. Kline et al., Who profits from patents?

5. Aghion et al., On the returns to invention within firms.

6. Lucking, B., Bloom, N., & Van Reenen, J. (2019). Have R&D spillovers declined in the 21st century? *Fiscal Studies, 40*(4), 561–590.

7. Mazzucato, M. (2013). *The entrepreneurial state: Debunking private vs public myths.* Anthem Press.

8. Frey, C. B., & Osborne, M. A. (2017). The future of employment: How susceptible are jobs to computerisation? *Technological Forecasting and Social Change, 114,* 254–280.

9. Arntz, M., Gregory, T., & Zierahn, U. (2016). *The risk of automation for jobs in OECD Countries: A comparative analysis.* OECD Social, Employment, and Migration Working Papers, no. 189, 0_1.

10. Bank of England (2023). *A millennium of macroeconomic data.* www.bankofengland.co.uk/statistics/research-datasets.

11. Goos, M., & Manning, A. (2007). Lousy and lovely jobs: The rising polarization of work in Britain. *Review of Economics and Statistics, 89*(1), 118–133; Autor, D. H., Levy, F., & Murnane, R. J. (2003). The skill content

of recent technological change: An empirical exploration. *Quarterly Journal of Economics, 118*(4), 1279–1333.

12. Mazzolari, F., & Ragusa, G. (2013). Spillovers from high-skill consumption to low-skill labor markets. *Review of Economics and Statistics, 95*(1), 74–86.

13. Zilian, L. S., Zilian, S. S., & Jäger, G. (2021). Labour market polarisation revisited: Evidence from Austrian vacancy data. *Journal for Labour Market Research, 55*(1), 1–17.

14. Murphy, E. C., & Oesch, D. (2018). Is employment polarisation inevitable? Occupational change in Ireland and Switzerland, 1970–2010. *Work, Employment and Society, 32*(6), 1099–1117.

15. OECD (2017). *OECD employment outlook 2017.* OECD Publishing, https://doi.org/10.1787/empl_outlook-2017-en.

16. Fernández-Macías, E. (2012). Job polarization in Europe? Changes in the employment structure and job quality, 1995–2007. *Work and Occupations, 39*(2), 157–182.

17. Vipond, H. (2020). A shoemaker's tale: Technology and disruption. Atlantic Fellows for Social Equity. https://afsee.atlanticfellows.lse.ac.uk/en-gb/blogs/a-shoemakers-tale-technology-and-disruption.

18. Deming, D. J., & Noray, K. (2020). Earnings dynamics, changing job skills, and STEM careers. *Quarterly Journal of Economics, 135*(4), 1965–2005.

19. Makkonen, T., & Lin, B. (2012). Continuing vocational training and innovation in Europe. *International Journal of Innovation and Learning, 11*(4), 325–338.

20. Moretti, Enrico. (2010). Local multipliers. *American Economic Review, 100*(2), 373–377.

21. Kemeny, T., & Osman, T. (2018). The wider impacts of high-technology employment: Evidence from US cities. *Research Policy, 47*(9), 1729–1740.

22. Lee, N., & Clarke, S. (2019). Do low-skilled workers gain from high-tech employment growth? High-technology multipliers, employment and wages in Britain. *Research Policy, 48*(9), 103803.

23. Hall, B. H. Innovation and diffusion. In J. Fagerberg, J., D. Mowery, and R. Nelson (Eds.) *The Oxford handbook of innovation* (pp. 459–483). Oxford University Press.

24. Solow, R. (2001). Information technology and the recent productivity boom in the US. Remarks at the National Competitiveness Network (NCN) Summit. http://web.mit.edu/cmi-videos/solow/text.html.

25. Hall, Innovation and diffusion.

26. Haldane, A. (2018). The UK's productivity problem: Hub no spokes. Academy of Social Sciences Annual Lecture. www.bankofengland.co.uk/-/media/boe/files/speech/2018/the-uks-productivity-problem-hub-no-spokes-speech-by-andy-haldane.pdf.

27. Hägerstrand, T. (1968). *Innovation diffusion as a spatial process.* University of Chicago Press.

28. Lengyel, B., Bokányi, E., Di Clemente, R., Kertész, J., & González, M. C. (2020). The role of geography in the complex diffusion of innovations. *Scientific Reports, 10*(1), 1–11.

29. Kemeny, T., Petralia, S., & Storper, M. (2022). Disruptive innovation and spatial inequality. *Regional Studies,* 1–18. https://doi.org/10.1080/003 43404.2022.2076824.

30. Bloom, N., Hassan, T. A., Kalyani, A., Lerner, J., & Tahoun, A. (2021). *The diffusion of disruptive technologies.* NBER Working Paper, no. w28999.

31. Borras, S., & Edquist, C. (2015). Education, training and skills in innovation policy. *Science and Public Policy, 42*(2), 215–227.

32. Rosenberg, N. (1972). Factors affecting the diffusion of technology. *Explorations in Economic History, 10*(1), 3.

33. Vona, F., & Consoli, D. (2015). Innovation and skill dynamics: A life-cycle approach. *Industrial and Corporate Change 24*(6), 1393–1415.

34. Consoli, D., Fusillo, F., Orsatti, G., & Quatraro, F. (2021). Skill endowment, routinisation and digital technologies: Evidence from US metropolitan areas. *Industry and Innovation, 28,* 1–29.

35. Lewis, P. (2020). Developing technician skills for innovative industries: Theory, evidence from the UK life sciences industry, and policy implications. *British Journal of Industrial Relations, 58*(3), 617–643.

36. Finegold, D., & Soskice, D. (1988). The failure of training in Britain: Analysis and prescription. *Oxford Review of Economic Policy, 4*(3), 21–53.

37. Finegold, D. (1999). Creating self-sustaining, high-skill ecosystems. *Oxford Review of Economic Policy, 15*(1), 61.

38. Finegold, Creating self-sustaining, high-skill ecosystems..

39. Saxenian, A. (2007). *The new argonauts: Regional advantage in a global economy.* Harvard University Press; Storper, M., Kemeny, T., Makarem, N., & Osman, T. (2015). *The rise and fall of urban economies: Lessons from San Francisco and Los Angeles.* Stanford University Press.

40. Redding, S. (1996). The low-skill, low-quality trap: Strategic complementarities between human capital and R & D. *Economic Journal, 106*(435), 458–470.

41. These middle classes aren't actually as large as those of Israel (where 72 percent of the population is middle-income), Czech Republic (71 percent), Norway (71 percent), Slovakia (70 percent) or the Netherlands (70 percent). Source: OECD (2019). *Under pressure: The squeezed middle class*. OECD Publishing. https://doi.org/10.1787/689afed1-en.

42. Blanchet, T., Chancel, C,, & Gethin, A. (2022). Why is Europe more equal than the United States? *American Economic Journal: Applied Economics, 14*(4): 480–518.

CHAPTER 3

1. Household disposable income: OECD (2023). Income inequality (indicator). https://doi.org/10.1787/7f420b4b-en.

2. Alvaredo, F., Atkinson, A. B., Piketty, T., and Saez, E. (2022). *World inequality database*. WID.world. https://wid.world/data.

3. Most of these are pretax income figures. In 2019, government spending was 32.7 percent of GDP in Switzerland and 38.3 percent in the United States. OECD (2021). OECD data, general government spending. https://data.oecd.org/gga/general-government-spending.htm.

4. The obvious question is the extent to which Switzerland is a tax haven. Some cantons, such as Zug, certainly make it look that way. But the country has been cooperating with the OECD, and Swiss banks can no longer hide money as they once did. See Walker, O. (2022). Swiss banks' struggles to move on from murky past hit by documents leak. *Financial Times.* 22 February.

5. OECD (2023). Gross domestic product (GDP) (indicator). https://doi.org/10.1787/dc2f7aec-en.

6. Taylor, M. Z. (2016). *The politics of innovation: Why some countries are better than others at science and technology.* Oxford University Press.

7. Hutton, G. (2022). *Financial services: Contribution to the UK economy.* United Kingdom: House of Commons. https://researchbriefings.files.parliament.uk/documents/SN06193/SN06193.pdf.

8. Steinberg, J. (2015). *Why Switzerland?* Cambridge University Press, 18.

9. Steinberg, *Why Switzerland?*, 13, 38.

10. Steinberg, *Why Switzerland?*, 39, 38.

11. Ladner, A. (2011). Switzerland: Subsidiarity, power-sharing, and direct democracy. In F. Hendriks, A. Lidström, & J. Loughlin (Eds.),

The Oxford handbook of local and regional democracy in Europe (pp. 196–218). Oxford University Press. https://doi.org/10.1093/oxfordhb/9780199562978.003.0009.

12. Federal Assembly [Switzerland] (2023). *Women's suffrage in Switzerland: 100 years of struggle*. www.parlament.ch/en/über-das-parlament/political-women/conquest-of-equal-rights/women-suffrage.

13. Stohr, C. (2018). Multiple core regions: Regional inequality in Switzerland, 1860–2008. *Research in Economic History, 34,* 135–198.

14. Steinberg, *Why Switzerland?*, 57. Feudal laws existed, but they were hard to enforce and had little of the power that they did other countries. Steinberg, *Why Switzerland?*, 18.

15. Stohr, Multiple core regions.

16. European Observation Network for Territorial Development and Cohesion (ESPON) multimodal transport accessibility data shows that the area is not as well connected as the Benelux countries or western Germany, but the north, in particular, has excellent access to wider markets. See Kluge, L., & Spiekerman, K. (2017). *Scenarios for accessibility by the sea, road, rail, air and multimodal*. ESPON.www.espon.eu/access-scenarios.

17. Meili, R., & Shearmur, R. (2019). Diverse diversities: Open innovation in small towns and rural areas. *Growth and Change, 50*(2), 492–514.

18. Federal Statistical Office [Switzerland] (2022). *Commuting*. www.bfs.admin.ch/bfs/en/home/statistics/mobility-transport/passenger-transport/commuting.html.

19. Bairoch, P. (1989). Les spécifitiés des chemins de fer suisses des origins à nos jours. *SZG, 39*(1), 36–28. Cited in Steinberg, *Why Switzerland?*, 171.

20. Steinberg, *Why Switzerland?*, 26.

21. Steinberg, *Why Switzerland?*, 179.

22. Steinberg, *Why Switzerland?*, 26.

23. Landes, D. S. (1984) *Revolution in time: Clocks and the making of the modern world*. Harvard University Press.

24. Glasmeier, A. (1991). Technological discontinuities and flexible production networks: The case of Switzerland and the world watch industry. *Research Policy, 20*(5), 469–485.

25. Glasmeier, Technological discontinuities, 477.

26. Mudambi, R. (2005). *Branding time: Swatch and global brand management*. Temple University IGMS Case Series, no. 05–001.

27. Raffaelli, R. (2019). Technology reemergence: Creating new value for old technologies in Swiss mechanical watchmaking, 1970–2008. *Administrative Science Quarterly, 64*(3), 576–618.

28. Gapper, J. (2017). Swiss watches risk becoming antiques. *Financial Times.* March 29.

29. Raffaelli, Technology reemergence.

30. Steinberg, *Why Switzerland?*

31. Coulter, M. (2023). Swiss Google workers stage walkout as job cuts hit Europe. Reuters, 15.3.2023.

32. Steinberg, *Why Switzerland?*, 84.

33. OECD (2023). Wage levels (indicator). https://doi.org/10.1787/0a1c27bc-en.

34. OECD (2021). Household disposable income (indicator). https://doi.org/10.1787/de435f6e-en. Data given for current prices and PPP.

35. The Swiss labor force is not widely unionized. At 14.4 percent in 2018, union membership is below the OECD average of 15.9 percent, far lower than in other coordinated states such as Denmark (67.5 percent) and just below that of Germany (16.6 percent). Swiss union membership has been on a long-term downward trend. See Visser, J. (2019). *ICTWSS database. version 6.1.* Amsterdam Institute for Advanced Labour Studies (AIAS).

36. The 2016 PISA scores for Switzerland are: reading 492 (492), mathematics 521 (490), science 506 (493). See PISA (2018). *PISA database.* OECD. www.oecd.org/pisa/data/2018database.

37. Lalive, R., & Lehmann, T. (2017).*The labor market in Switzerland, 2000–2016.* IZA World of Labor, 402. http://dx.doi.org/10.15185/izawol.402.

38. Lalive & Lehmann, *The labor market in Switzerland.*

39. OECD (2023). Gender wage gap (indicator). https://doi.org/10.1787/7cee77aa-en.

40. See Durrer, S. (2019) *Gender equality in Switzerland.* Confédération Suisse. www.ohchr.org/sites/default/files/Documents/Issues/Development/SR/visit-to-switzerland/foge_GE.pdf.

41. Niggli, M., & Rutzer, C. (2021) *A gender gap to more innovation in Switzerland.* University of Basel, https://innoscape.ch/en/publications/gender.

42. OECD (2020). *Education at a glance: Country note; Switzerland.* OECD. www.oecd.org/berlin/publikationen/EAG2020_CN_CHE.pdf.

43. To illustrate this policy, one of the rising stars of Swiss academia told me he had started in an apprenticeship.

44. OECD (2019). *OECD Economic Surveys: Switzerland 2019*. OECD Publishing. https://doi.org/10.1787/7e6fd372-en.

45. Korber, M., & Oesch, D. (2019). Vocational versus general education: Employment and earnings over the life course in Switzerland. *Advances in Life Course Research, 40*, 1–13.

46. OECD (2020). How much is spent per student on educational institutions? In *Education at a glance 2020: OECD indicators*. OECD Publishing. https://doi.org/10.1787/5e4ecc25-en.

47. See, for example, Thomas, K. (2014). Why does Switzerland do so well in university rankings? *Guardian*. 1 October.

48. International Labour Organisation [ILO] (n.d.). Statistics on collective bargaining. Available from: https://ilostat.ilo.org/topics/collective-bargaining.

49. Müller, T., Vandele, K., & Zwysen, W. (2021). Wages and collective bargaining: Is social Europe really back on the agenda? In European Trade Union Institute [ETUI] (Ed.), *Benchmarking working Europe 2021* (pp. 84–106). ETUI.

50. OECD (2022). *OECD regions and cities at a glance: Country note; Switzerland*. OECD. www.oecd.org/cfe/Switzerland-Regions-and-Cities-2020.pdf.

51. European Commission (2023). Eurydice: Switzerland; Key features of the education system. https://eurydice.eacea.ec.europa.eu/national-education-systems/switzerland/overview; Pfister, C., Koomen, M., Harhoff, D., & Backes-Gellner, U. (2021). Regional innovation effects of applied research institutions. *Research Policy, 50*(4), 104197. https://doi.org/10.1016/j.respol.2021.104197.

52. Lehnert, P., Pfister, C., & Backes-Gellner, U. (2020). Employment of R&D personnel after an educational supply shock: Effects of the introduction of universities of applied sciences in Switzerland. *Labour Economics, 66,* 101883; Pfister et al., Regional innovation effects of applied research; Schlegel, T., Pfister, C., Harhoff, D., & Backes-Gellner, U. (2022). Innovation effects of universities of applied sciences: An assessment of regional heterogeneity. *Journal of Technology Transfer, 47,* 63–118.

53. Swiss history has not always been encouraging. For Steinberg, "The basic realities of Swiss economic life can be summed up into linked paradoxes: because they were poor, they specialised in luxury goods, and because they specialised they were easily ruined." Steinberg, *Why Switzerland?*, 193.

CHAPTER 4

1. Schulze, M. S., & Wolf, N. (2012). Economic nationalism and economic integration: The Austro-Hungarian Empire in the late nineteenth century. *Economic History Review, 65*(2), 652–673.

2. Judt, T. (2006). *Postwar: A history of Europe since 1945*. Penguin.

3. Judt, *Postwar*, 95.

4. Bischof, G., Pelinka, A., & Stiefel, D. (Eds.). (2000). *The Marshall Plan in Austria* (Vol. 8). Transaction Publishers.

5. Beller, S. 2006. *A concise history of Austria*. Cambridge University Press.

6. Stampfer, M., Pichler, R., & Hofer, R. (2010). The making of research funding in Austria: Transition politics and institutional development, 1945–2005. *Science and Public Policy, 37*(10), 765–780.

7. Judt, *Postwar*, 369.

8. Beller, *A concise history of Austria*.

9. Beller, *A concise history of Austria*.

10. Afonso, A., & Mach, A. (2012). Coming together but staying apart: Continuity and change in the Austrian and Swiss varieties of capitalism. In U. Becker, L. Noordegraaf-Eelens, L. Tsipouri, & V. Stenius (Eds.), *The changing political economies of small West European countries* (pp. 99–124). Amsterdam University Press.

11. Astleithner, F., & Flecker, J. (2018). From the golden age to the gilded cage? Austrian trade unions, social partnership and the crisis. In H. Dribbush, S. Lehndorff, & T. Schulten (Eds.), *Rough waters: European trade unions in a time of crises* (pp. 185-208). European Trade Union Institute.

12. Until 2021, manual and nonmanual workers were treated differently.

13. See European Trade Union Institute (2023). Worker participation: Austria. www.worker-participation.eu/National-Industrial-Relations/Countries/Austria.

14. Podvrsic, A., Becker, J., Piroska, D., Profant, T., & Hodulák, V. (2020). *Mitigating the COVID-19 effect: Emergency economic policymaking in Central Europe*. ETUI Working Paper, no. 2020.07.

15. Astleithner & Flecker, From the golden age to the gilded cage?, 185.

16. Astleithner & Flecker, From the golden age to the gilded cage?, 185.

17. Böheim, R. (2017). *The labor market in Austria, 2000–2016*. IZA World of Labor. https://wol.iza.org/articles/the-labor-market-in-austria/long.

18. Busemeyer, M. R. (2009). Asset specificity, institutional complementarities and the variety of skill regimes in coordinated market economies. *Socio-economic Review, 7*(3), 375–406.

19. Durazzi, N., & Geyer, L. (2020). Social inclusion in the knowledge economy: Unions' strategies and institutional change in the Austrian and German training systems. *Socio-economic review, 18*(1), 103–124.

20. Dornmayr, H. and Nowak, S. (2019) Lehrlingsausbildung im Überblick, cited in Schlögl, P., Mayerl, M., Löffler, R., & Schmölz, A. (2020). Supra-company apprenticeship training in Austria: A synopsis of empirical findings on a possibly early phase of a new pillar within VET. *Empirical Research in Vocational Education and Training, 12*(1), 1–17.

21. Thelen, K. (2014). *Varieties of liberalization and the new politics of social solidarity.* Cambridge University Press.

22. OECD. (2018). *Good jobs for all in a changing world of work: The OECD Jobs Strategy.* OECD Publishing.

23. OECD (2023). GDP per hour worked (indicator). https://doi.org/10.1787/1439e590-en.

24. Hermann, C., & Flecker, J. (2015). Mastering the crisis but not the future: The Austrian model in the financial and economic crisis. In S. Lehndorff (Ed.), *Divisive integration: The triumph of failed ideas in Europe* (pp. 195–209). European Trade Union Institute..

25. Böheim, *The labor market in Austria.*

26. Eurostat (2021). Gender pay gap situation in Europe. https://ec.europa.eu/info/policies/justice-and-fundamental-rights/gender-equality/equal-pay/gender-pay-gap-situation-eu_en.

27. Böheim, R., & Gust, S. (2021). *The Austrian pay transparency law and the gender wage gap.* IZA Discussion Paper, no. 14206.

28. Böheim, *The labor market in Austria,* 263.

29. Thelen, *Varieties of liberalization,* 363.

30. See Eder, M. (2021). Billionaire Peter Thiel hires Austria's disgraced former chancellor. Bloomberg, 30 December. www.bloomberg.com/news/articles/2021-12-30/billionaire-thiel-gives-austria-s-former-wunderkind-a-job.

31. Frey, E. (2016). Metals specialist Berndorf shines light on Austria's hidden strength. *Financial Times.* November 3. www.ft.com/content/f1bd4d80-8baf-11e6-8cb7-e7ada1d123b1.

32. Alvaredo, F., Atkinson, A. B., Piketty, T., and Saez, E. (2022). *World inequality database.* WID.world. https://wid.world/data.

33. Blanchet, T., Chancel, L., & Gethin, A. (2019). *How unequal is Europe? Evidence from distributional national accounts, 1980-2017.* WID.world Working Paper, no. 6.

34. Rocha-Akis, S. (2021). *The income distribution in Austria.* Österreichisches Institut für Wirtschaftsforschung.

35. Blanchet, T., Chancel, L., & Gethin, A. (2022) Why is Europe more equal than the United States? *American Economic Journal: Applied Economics, 14*(4), 480-518.

36. Christl, M., Köppl–Turyna, M., Lorenz, H., & Kucsera, D. (2020). Redistribution within the tax-benefits system in Austria. *Economic Analysis and Policy, 68,* 250-264.

37. World Intellectual Property Organisation [WIPO](2022). Global Innovation Index 2022: What is the future of innovation-driven growth? WIPO. www.wipo.int/global_innovation_index/en/2022.

38. Taylor, M. Z. (2016). *The politics of innovation: Why some countries are better than others at science and technology.* Oxford University Press.

39. Carvalho, A. (2018). Wishful thinking about R&D policy targets: What governments promise and what they actually deliver. *Science and Public Policy, 45*(3), 373-391.

40. Total R&D spending fell from €312 billion to €311 billion. Eurostat (2021). R&D expenditure in the EU at 2.3% of GDP in 2020. https://ec.europa.eu/eurostat/en/web/products-eurostat-news/-/ddn-20211129-2.

41. OECD (2018). *OECD reviews of innovation policy: Austria 2018.* OECD Publishing. https://doi.org/10.1787/9789264309470-en.

42. OECD, *OECD reviews of innovation policy,* 52.

43. Stampfer, M., Pichler, R., & Hofer, R. (2010). The making of research funding in Austria: Transition politics and institutional development, 1945-2005. *Science and Public Policy, 37*(10), 765-780.

44. Janger, J. (2019). The Austrian example. *Research Professional.* 26 June.

45. OECD (2021). *R&D Tax incentives: Austria, 2021.* OECD Directorate for Science, Technology and Innovation. December.

46. OECD, *R&D Tax incentives: Austria, 2021.*

47. Austrian Research Promotion Agency (FFG). (2019). *Objectives and Mission.* www.ffg.at/en/FFG/objectives-and-mission.

48. Dachs, B., & Drach, A. (2019). Forschung und Entwicklung von Unternehmen in langfristiger Perspektive: Starkes Wachstum, alte Akteure? *Perspektiven der Wirtschaftspolitik, 20*(4), 340-351.

49. Atkins, R. (2015). Austria's sights move beyond the European markets. *Financial Times.* 20 October.

50. Voestalpine (2021). *Corporate responsibility report 2021.* https://reports.voestalpine.com/2021/cr-report/environment/energy.html.

51. OECD (2015). *Frascati manual 2015: Guidelines for collecting and reporting data on research and experimental development, the measurement of scientific, technological and innovation activities.* OECD, https://doi.org/10.1787/9789264239012-en pp.28.

52. International Labour Organization. (2023). *ILO modelled estimates database.* ilostat.ilo.org/data.

53. Rodrik, D., & Stantcheva, S. (2021). Fixing capitalism's good jobs problem. *Oxford Review of Economic Policy, 37*(4), 826.

54. Tödtling, F., & Sedlacek, S. (1997). Regional economic transformation and the innovation system of Styria. *European Planning Studies, 5*(1), 43-63. https://doi.org/10.1080/09654319708720383.

55. Geldner, N. (1998). Successful structural change in Styria. *Austrian Economic Quarterly, 3*(2), 95-100.

56. Tödtling & Sedlacek, Regional economic transformation.

57. Tödtling & Sedlacek, Regional economic transformation.

58. Kaufmann, A., & Tödtling, F. (2002). How effective is innovation support for SMEs? An analysis of the region of Upper Austria. *Technovation, 22*(3), 147-159.

59. Sturn, D. (2000). Decentralized industrial policies in practice: The case of Austria and Styria. *European Planning Studies, 8*(2), 169-182.

60. Sturn, Decentralized industrial policies; Tödtling & Sedlacek, Regional economic transformation.

61. MacNeill, S. & Steiner, M. (2010). Leadership of cluster policy: Lessons from the Austrian province of Styria. *Policy Studies, 31*(4), 441-455. https://doi.org/10.1080/01442871003723374.

62. Eder, J., & Trippl, M. (2019). Innovation in the periphery: Compensation and exploitation strategies. *Growth and Change, 50*(4), 1511-1531.

63. Hansen, T., & Winther, L. (2014). Competitive low-tech manufacturing and challenges for regional policy in the European context: Lessons from the Danish experience. *Cambridge Journal of Regions, Economy and Society, 7*(3), 466.

64. Trippl, M., & Otto, A. (2009). How to turn the fate of old industrial areas: A comparison of cluster-based renewal processes in Styria and the Saarland. *Environment and Planning A, 41*(5), 1217-1233.

65. Federal Government, Republic of Austria (2020). *RTI Strategy 2030: Strategy for research, technology and innovation of the Austrian federal government.*

CHAPTER 5

1. There are some big health warnings with this sort of comparison, but the source is: International Monetary Fund (2023). GDP per capita (PPP), current international dollar prices. International Monetary Fund (IMF) (2022). *IMF database: GDP per capita.* https://data.imf.org.

2. Chinn, D. L. (1982). Growth, equity, and Gini coefficients: The case of Taiwan. *Economic Development and Cultural Change, 30*(4), 65–79.

3. Gold, T. B. (2016). Retrocession and authoritarian KMT rule (1945–1986). In G. Schubert (Ed.), *Routledge handbook of contemporary Taiwan* (pp. 36–50). Routledge.

4. Gold, T. B. (2016). Entrepreneurs, multinationals, and the state. In E. A. Winckler & S. Greenhalgh (Eds.), *Contending approaches to the political economy of Taiwan* (pp. 191–221). Routledge.

5. Yeung, H. W. C. (2016). *Strategic coupling: East Asian industrial transformation in the new global economy.* Cornell University Press.

6. Wong, J. (2016). The developmental state and Taiwan: Origins and adaptation. In G. Schubert (Ed.), *Routledge handbook of contemporary Taiwan* (pp. 201–217). Routledge.

7. Gold, Retrocession and authoritarian KMT rule.

8. In 2003, the government introduced the "New Ten" major projects: to make Taiwanese universities competitive on international league tables; to establish arts centers in northern, central, and southern Taiwan; to upgrade internet connections; to hold a "Taiwan exhibition" showcasing the best of the country; to improve rail and road infrastructure; and to build a new intercontinental container port, metro systems, better sewers, and desalination plants.

9. Wong, The developmental state and Taiwan.

10. Gold, Retrocession and authoritarian KMT rule.

11. Wade, R. H. (2017) The developmental state: Dead or alive? *Development and Change, 49*(2), 518–546.

12. Rodrik, D. (1996). Understanding economic policy reform. *Journal of Economic Literature, 34*(1), 9–41.

13. Rodrik, D. (2006). Goodbye Washington consensus, hello Washington confusion? A review of the World Bank's economic growth in the

1990s: Learning from a decade of reform. *Journal of Economic Literature,* *44*(4), 973–987.

14. Wade, The developmental state, 7.

15. Wade, The developmental state, 27–28.

16. Taylor, M. Z. (2016). *The politics of innovation: Why some countries are better than others at science and technology.* Oxford University Press.

17. Wong, The developmental state and Taiwan.

18. Breznitz, D. (2007). *Innovation and the state.* Yale University Press.

19. Breznitz, *Innovation and the state.*

20. Wade, R. (1990). *Governing the market.* Princeton University Press.

21. Wong, The developmental state and Taiwan.

22. Breznitz, *Innovation and the state.*

23. Yeung, *Strategic coupling,* 56.

24. Hille, K., & Cane, A. (2006). TSMC rejigs chip production to reduce costs. *Financial Times.* January 3. www.ft.com/content/469896f2-7c85-11da-936a-0000779e2340.

25. Nuttall, C. (2008). Intel sees leadership in a shrinking world. *Financial Times.* July 1. 2006. www.ft.com/content/18debbc7-1bbf-3742-b4b5-f2e366aa1ef0.

26. Kwong, R. (2010) TSMC Plans record $4.8bn investment. *Financial Times.* 28 January. www.ft.com/content/9c1f836a-0be2-11df-96b9-00144feabdc0.

27. Hille, K. (2021). TSMC: how a Taiwanese chipmaker became a linchpin of the global economy. *Financial Times.* March 24. www.ft.com/content/05206915-fd73-4a3a-92a5-6760ce965bd9.

28. Wang, J. H. (2007). From technological catch-up to innovation-based economic growth: South Korea and Taiwan compared. *Journal of Development Studies, 43*(6), 1084–1104.

29. Taylor, *The politics of innovation.*

30. Acemoglu, D., & Robinson, J. A. (2002). The political economy of the Kuznets curve. *Review of Development Economics, 6*(2), 183–203.

31. Fei, J., Ranis, G. and Kuo, S. W. Y. (1979). *Growth with equity: The Taiwan case.* World Bank.

32. Ranis, G. (1978). Equity with growth in Taiwan: How "special" is the "special case"? *World Development, 6*(3), 397–409.

33. Ranis, Equity with growth, 401.

34. Chinn, Growth, equity, and Gini coefficients.

35. Roy, D. (2003). *Taiwan: A political history.* Cornell University Press.

36. This leads to a paradoxical claim in much of the literature: even during the White Terror, the Guomindang allowed limited representation. Taiwan still performs relatively well on World Bank measures of political voice and accountability. See Kaufmann, D., and Kraay, A. (2021). *Worldwide governance indicators*. World Bank.

37. Roy, *Taiwan*.

38. Amsden, A. H. (1991). Taiwan from an international perspective. *Asian Affairs: An American Review, 18*(2), 86.

39. See Fields, K. (1995). *Enterprise and the state in Korea and Taiwan.* University of Chicago Press; Wang, From technological catch-up to innovation-based economic growth.

40. Lue, J-D. (2013). Promoting work: A review of active labour market policies in Taiwan. *Journal of Asian Public Policy, 6*(1), 81–98. https://doi .org/10.1080/17516234.2013.765184.

41. Shi, S. J. (2012). Shifting dynamics of the welfare politics in Taiwan: From income maintenance to labour protection. *Journal of Asian Public Policy, 5*(1), 82–96.

42. Liu, J., Lai, M. Y., & Liu, Z. S. (2022). Trade liberalization, domestic reforms, and income inequality: Evidence from Taiwan. *Review of Development Economics, 26*(3), 1286–1309. https://doi.org/10.1111/rode.12875.

43. Lue, Promoting work.

44. Shi, Shifting dynamics.

45. Hanushek, E. A., & Woessmann, L. (2008). The role of cognitive skills in economic development. *Journal of Economic Literature, 46*(3), 607–668.

46. Goldin, C. & Katz, L. (2010). *The race between education and technology.* Harvard University Press.

47. Barro, R., & Lee, J. (2013). A new data set of educational attainment in the world, 1950–2010. *Journal of Development Economics, 104*, 184–198.

48. Hanushek & Woessmann, The role of cognitive skills.

49. Ranis, Equity with growth in Taiwan.

50. Wang, W-C. (2009). Information economy and inequality: Wage polarisation, unemployment, and occupational transition in Taiwan since 1980. *Journal of Asian Economics, 20*, 128.

51. Amsden, A., & Chu, W-W. (2003). *Beyond late development: Taiwan's upgrading policies.* MIT Press.

52. Tsai, S. L., & Kanomata, N. (2011). Educational expansion and inequality of educational opportunity: Taiwan and Japan. *Sociological Theory and Methods, 26*(1), 179–195.

53. Ministry of Education, Republic of China (2008), cited in Tsai & Kanomata, Educational expansion.

54. Ashton, D., Green, F., Sung, J., & James, D. (2002). The evolution of education and training strategies in Singapore, Taiwan and S. Korea: A development model of skill formation. *Journal of Education and Work, 15*(1), 5–30.

55. Green, F., Ashton, D., James, D., & Sung, J. (1999). The role of the state in skill formation: Evidence from the Republic of Korea, Singapore, and Taiwan. *Oxford Review of Economic Policy, 15*(1), 82–96.

56. Green et al., The role of the state in skill formation.

57. Chang, M., Blanchette, J. and Hass., R. (2022). *Can semiconductor manufacturing return to the US?* Podcast. Brookings Institution. www .brookings.edu/podcast-episode/can-semiconductor-manufacturing-return-to-the-us.

58. Wade, *Governing the market,* 112.

59. Green et al., The role of the state in skill formation.

60. Andersson, M., & Klinthäll, M. (2015). "Growth with equity" and regional development: Distributional consequences of agglomeration in Taiwan. *Journal of the Asia Pacific Economy, 20*(2), 271–289.

61. See, for example, Quartly, J. (2020). The Gini in Taiwan's bottle. *Taiwan Business Topics.* November 19. https://topics.amcham.com .tw/2020/11/taiwan-gini-coefficient.

62. Huang, B., Morgan, P. J., & Yoshino, N. (2019). *Demystifying rising inequality in Asia.* Asian Development Bank Institute.

63. In my interviews for this chapter, Taiwanese were universally skeptical when I told them that it was a low-inequality country. Sadly, I found they were right.

64. Chu, C., Chen, C-Y., Lin., M-J., and Su, H-L. (2022). *Distributional national accounts of Taiwan, 1991–2017.* World Inequality Database Working Paper, no. 2022/15.

65. Alvaredo, F., Atkinson, A. B., Piketty, T., and Saez, E. (2022). *World inequality database.* WID.world. https://wid.world/data.

66. Wang, J. H. (2007). From technological catch-up to innovation-based economic growth: South Korea and Taiwan compared. *Journal of Development Studies, 43*(6), 1084–1104.

67. See Wood, A. (1998). Globalisation and the rise in labour market inequalities. *Economic Journal, 108*(450), 1463–1482.

68. Estimates from Investment Commission, Ministry of Economic Affairs, various years. Cited in Lue, Promoting work.

69. Lee, Y. F. L. (2008). Economic growth and income inequality: The modern Taiwan experience. *Journal of Contemporary China, 17*(55), 361–374.

70. Lee, Economic growth and income inequality. The service employment category is titled "Service Workers & Shop/Market Sales Workers & Clerks."

71. Data for Japan, South Korea, the People's Republic of China, Indonesia, Singapore, Malaysia, India, Hong Kong, and Bangladesh from Zhuang, J., Kanbur, R., and Rhee, C. (2014). *Rising inequality in Asia and policy implications.* ADBI Working Paper, no. 463. www.adbi.org/working-paper/2014/02/21/6172.rising.inequality.asia.policy.implications.

72. Economist (2020). Why commercial ties between Taiwan and China are beginning to fray. *Economist.* November 19.

73. Lee, Economic growth and income inequality.

74. Wang, W. C. (2009). Information economy and inequality: Wage polarization, unemployment, and occupation transition in Taiwan since 1980. *Journal of Asian Economics, 20*(2), 120–136.

75. Andersson, M., & Klinthäll, M. (2012). The opening of the North–South divide: Cumulative causation, household income disparity and the regional bonus in Taiwan, 1976–2005. *Structural Change and Economic Dynamics, 23*(2), 170–179.

76. Lue, Promoting work.

77. Hlasny, V. (2017). *Different faces of inequality across Asia: Decomposition of income gaps across demographic groups.* ADBI Working Paper, no. 688. www.adb.org/publications/different-faces-inequality-across-asia.

78. Andersson, & Klinthäll, "Growth with equity."

79. Accounting and Accounting Office of the Executive Yuan [Taiwan] (2020). *Comprehensive analysis of the results of the annual household income and expenditure survey.* https://ws.dgbas.gov.tw/win/fies/a11.asp?year%20=%20106.

80. Andersson & Klinthäll, "Growth with equity."

81. Calculation based on author's analysis of Luxembourg income study. (*Luxembourg income study (LIS) database* (2021). LIS.). Data excludes households with inactive heads.

82. Lin, T. C., Hsu, S. H., & Lin, Y. L. (2019). The effect of housing prices on consumption and economic growth: The case of Taiwan. *Journal of the Asia Pacific Economy, 24*(2), 292–312.

83. Chien-Hsun Chen, (2018). The housing affordability crisis and government policy actions in Taiwan. *Economic Alternatives, 3*, 334–347.

84. Turton, M. (2021). Notes from Central Taiwan: Are housing prices a national security crisis? *Taipei Times*. December 13.

85. Yu, W-H. (2015). *Women and employment in Taiwan*. Brookings Institution. www.brookings.edu/opinions/women-and-employment-in-taiwan.

86. Taipei Times (2021). Taiwan no. 1 in Asia, world no. 6 for gender equality. *Taipei Times*. www.taipeitimes.com/News/taiwan/archives/2021/01/09/2003750242.

87. Hlasny, *Different faces of inequality across Asia*.

88. Yu, *Women and employment in Taiwan*.

89. Liu, J., Lai, M. Y., & Liu, Z. S. (2022). Trade liberalization, domestic reforms, and income inequality: Evidence from Taiwan. *Review of Development Economics, 26*(3), 1286–1309.

90. Wang, From technological catch-up to innovation-based economic growth.

91. Ing-wen, T. (2016). Inaugural address. Office of the President Republic of China (Taiwan), https://english.president.gov.tw/Page/252.

92. Chuang, Y. C., & Lai, W. W. (2017). Returns to human capital and inequality: The case of Taiwan. *Journal of Economic Development, 42*(3), 61-88.

93. Chow, P. C. (2021). Taiwan in international economic relations. In J. Dreyer & J. deLisle (Eds.), *Taiwan in the era of Tsai Ing-wen* (pp. 84–107). Routledge.

CHAPTER 6

1. Ahmed, M. (2015). Stockholm: The unicorn factory. *Financial Times*. March 31.

2. Adler, P., Florida, R., King, K., & Mellander, C. (2019). The city and high-tech startups: The spatial organization of Schumpeterian entrepreneurship. *Cities, 87,* 121–130.

3. Matthews, D. (2018). The White House, definitely not scared of socialism, issues report on why socialism is bad. Vox.com. October 23. www.vox.com/policy-and-politics/2018/10/23/18013872/white-house-socialism-report-cea-mao-lenin-bernie-sanders.

4. Schön, L. (2012). *An economic history of modern Sweden*. Routledge.

5. Brandal, N., Bratberg, Ø., & Thorsen, D. (2013). *The Nordic model of social democracy*. Springer.

6. Schön, *An economic history of modern Sweden.*

7. Schön, *An economic history of modern Sweden.*

8. Schön, *An economic history of modern Sweden.*

9. Schön, *An economic history of modern Sweden.*

10. Braunerhjelm, P., & Henrekson, M. (2013). Entrepreneurship, institutions, and economic dynamism: Lessons from a comparison of the United States and Sweden. *Industrial and Corporate Change, 22*(1), 107–130.

11. Economist (2013). Northern lights: A special report on the Nordic countries. *Economist.* www.economist.com/sites/default/files/20130202_nordic_countries.pdf.

12. Braunerhjelm & Henrekson, Entrepreneurship, institutions, and economic dynamism.

13. Braunerhjelm & Henrekson, Entrepreneurship, institutions, and economic dynamism.

14. Eurostat (2022). Real GDP per capita (indicator). https://ec.europa.eu/eurostat/databrowser/view/sdg_08_10/default/table.

15. Steinmo, S. (2010). *The evolution of modern states: Sweden, Japan, and the United States.* Cambridge University Press.

16. Therborn, G. (2020). Sweden's turn to economic inequality, 1982–2019. *Structural Change and Economic Dynamics, 52,* 159–166.

17. Björklund, A., & Waldenström, D. (2021). *Facts and myths in the popular debate about inequality in Sweden.* Research Institute for Industrial Economics (IFN) Working Paper , no. 1392.

18. Björklund & Waldenström, *Facts and myths.*

19. Björklund & Waldenström, *Facts and myths.*

20. OECD (2022). Income inequality (indicator). https://doi.org/10.1787/7f420b4b-en.

21. OECD (2021). *OECD Economic Surveys: Sweden 2021.* OECD Publishing. https://doi.org/10.1787/f61d0a54-en. Almost half of parliamentarians are women (47.3 percent), compared to 30.7 percent across the OECD.

22. Cowell, F., Karagiannaki, E., & McKnight, A. (2018). Accounting for cross-country differences in wealth inequality. *Review of Income and Wealth, 64*(2), 332–356. Note, however, that these figures on wealth inequality exclude pensions.

23. OECD (2021). *Government at a Glance 2021.* OECD Publishing. https://doi.org/10.1787/1c258f55-en.

24. Causa, O., & Hermansen, M. (2020). Income redistribution through taxes and transfers across OECD countries. In J. Gabriel Rodriguez & J.

Bishop (Eds.), *Inequality, redistribution and mobility* (pp. 29-74). Emerald Publishing.

25. Causa & Hermansen, Income redistribution.

26. World Bank (2019). *Ease of doing business.* World Bank, Doing Business Project. https://data.worldbank.org/indicator/IC.BUS.EASE.XQ.

27. Steinmo, *The evolution of modern states.*

28. Causa & Hermansen, Income redistribution.

29. Steinmo, *The evolution of modern states.*

30. Oesch, D., & Piccitto, G. (2019). The polarization myth: Occupational upgrading in Germany, Spain, Sweden, and the UK, 1992–2015. *Work and Occupations, 46*(4), 441–469.

31. Von Borries, A., Grillitsch, M., & Lundquist, K. J. (2022). *Geographies of low-income jobs: The concentration of low-income jobs, the knowledge economy and labor market polarization in Sweden, 1990–2018.* Lund University, CIRCLE–Centre for Innovation Research, Papers in Innovation Studies, no. 2022/4.

32. Von Borries, Grillitsch, & Lundquist, *Geographies of low-income jobs.*

33. Tomson, D. L. (2000). *The rise of Sweden democrats: Islam, populism and the end of Swedish exceptionalism.* Brookings Institution. www.brookings.edu/research/the-rise-of-sweden-democrats-and-the-end-of-swedish-exceptionalism.

34. Eger, M. A. (2010). Even in Sweden: The effect of immigration on support for welfare state spending. *European Sociological Review, 26*(2), 203–217.

35. Dahlberg, M., Edmark, K., & Lundqvist, H. (2012). Ethnic diversity and preferences for redistribution. *Journal of Political Economy, 120*(1), 41–76.

36. OECD (2018). *PISA Results: Sweden.* www.oecd.org/pisa/publications/PISA2018_CN_SWE.pdf.

37. OECD (2022). *OECD main science and technology indicators highlights, March 2022.* OECD. www.oecd.org/sti/msti-highlights-march-2022.pdf.

38. OECD (2013). *OECD reviews of innovation policy: Sweden 2012.* OECD Publishing. https://doi.org/10.1787/9789264184893-en.

39. Berggren, C., & Laestadius, S. (2003). Co-development and composite clusters: The secular strength of Nordic telecommunications. *Industrial and Corporate Change, 12*(1), 91–114.

40. Berggren & Laestadius, Co-development and composite clusters.

41. Knowledge at Wharton (2015). *How Stockholm became a unicorn factory.* University of Pennsylvania. https://knowledge.wharton.upenn.edu/article/how-stockholm-became-a-unicorn-factory.

42. Berggren & Laestadius, Co-development and composite clusters.

43. OECD, *OECD reviews of innovation policy: Sweden 2012.*

44. Economist. (2006). Farewell Nordic model: The end of another European dream. *Economist.* November 16.

45. Henrekson, M. (2005). Entrepreneurship: A weak link in the welfare state? *Industrial and Corporate Change, 14*(3), 446, emphasis added.

46. Heyman, F., Norbäck, P. J., Persson, L., & Andersson, F. (2019). Has the Swedish business sector become more entrepreneurial than the US business sector? *Research Policy, 48*(7), 1809–1822.

47. Spotify (2022). About Spotify. https://newsroom.spotify.com/company-info.

48. Wong, J. I. (2016). Sweden must change quickly: Spotify threatens to leave the country, Quartz. April 14. https://qz.com/661319/sweden-must-change-quickly-spotify-threatens-to-leave-the-country.

49. Venkataramakrishnanm, S. (2021). Klarna and Stripe announce "buy now, pay later" partnership. *Financial Times.* October 26. www.ft.com/content/841e0d03-f547-4a1f-b1f4-ef9a8ac7ab1f.

50. Milne, R. (2021). SoftBank investment helps Klarna to $45.6bn valuation. *Financial Times.* June 10. www.ft.com/content/9f73b352-723f-471b-b098-5f090279b5bb.

51. Venkataramakrishnanm, S. (2022). Klarna's widening losses driven by rapid expansion. *Financial Times.* February 28.www.ft.com/content/8ff87375-476b-4322-bc33-a483a471b8fc.

52. Venkataramakrishnanm., S. (2022). Klarna's valuation crashes to under $7bn in tough funding round. *Financial Times.* February 17. www.ft.com/content/66b65d68-d62e-4aec-a1ad-a7d9e2ba0435.

53. Mallaby, S. (2022). Venture capital's new race for Europe. *Financial Times.* February 3. www.ft.com/content/6fc9455a-75fc-4952-a4ff-203e5579aefa.

54. Milne, R. (2021). Klarna targets acquisitions as it raises fresh $1bn of investment. *Financial Times.* March 1. www.ft.com/content/419be00f-0a00-4fed-b4a6-bb55263033bc.

55. Autor, D., Dorn, D., Katz, L. F., Patterson, C., & Van Reenen, J. (2020). The fall of the labor share and the rise of superstar firms. *Quarterly Journal of Economics, 135*(2), 645–709.

56. Calligaris, S., Criscuolo, C., & Marcolin, L. (2018). *Mark-ups in the digital era.* OECD Science, Technology and Industry Working Papers, no. 2018(10), 0_1–26.

57. Feldman, M., Guy, F., & Iammarino, S. (2021). Regional income disparities, monopoly and finance. *Cambridge Journal of Regions, Economy and Society, 14*(1), 25–49.

58. Feldman, Guy, & Iammarino, Regional income disparities. They also note another problematic feature: monopoly rents in the tech sector tend to be concentrated, making it harder for other firms to innovate and eventually leading to firms charging higher prices. But this doesn't seem relevant to the Swedish case, because tech firms simply aren't big enough or in core sectors.

59. Alvedalen, J., & Carlsson, B. (2021). *Scaling up in entrepreneurial ecosystems: A comparative study of entrepreneurial ecosystems in life science.* Lund University, CIRCLE–Centre for Innovation Research, Papers in Innovation Studies, no. 2021/10. http://wp.circle.lu.se/upload/CIRCLE/workingpapers/202110_alvedalen.pdf.

60. Alvedalen & Carlsson, Scaling up.

61. Penrose, E. (1959). *The theory of the growth of the firm.* Oxford University Press.

62. Lerner, J., & Tåg, J. (2013). Institutions and venture capital. *Industrial and Corporate Change, 22*(1), 153–182.

63. Lerner & Tåg, Institutions and venture capital.

64. Glasner, J. (2021). These countries have the most startup investment for their size. *Crunchbase News.* November 2; Crunchbase (2022). The Crunchbase unicorn board. https://news.crunchbase.com/unicorn-company-list.

65. Adler et al., The city and high-tech startups.

66. Milne, R. (2019). Can $5bn Klarna avoid the fate of other Swedish unicorns? *Financial Times.* August 7. www.ft.com/content/1312b0ea-b904-11e9-8a88-aa6628ac896c.

67. OECD (2022). *Metropolitan areas: Income distribution statistics.* https://stats.oecd.org/Index.aspx?DataSetCode = CITIES#.

68. Enflo, K. & Missiaia, A. (2020). Between Malthus and the industrial take-off: Regional inequality in Sweden, 1571–1850. *Economic History Review, 73*(2), 431–454.

69. André, C., Beom, J., Pak, M. & Purwin, A. (2021). *Keeping regional inequality in check in Sweden.* OECD Economics Department Working Papers, no. 1689. https://doi.org/10.1787/e4bec28f-en.

70. Hansen, T. & Coenen, L. (2017) Unpacking resource mobilisation by incumbents for biorefineries: The role of micro-level factors for technological innovation system weaknesses, *Technology Analysis and Strategic Management, 29*(5), 500–513. https://doi.org/10.1080/09537325.2016.1249838.

71. André et al., *Keeping regional inequality in check.*

72. Gompers, P., & Lerner, J. (1998). Venture capital distributions: Short-run and long-run reactions. *Journal of Finance, 53*(6), 2161–2183.

73. Lerner & Tåg, Institutions and venture capital.

74. OECD (2012). *Economic survey of Sweden.* OECD Publishing. www.oecd-ilibrary.org/economics/oecd-economic-surveys-sweden-2012_eco_surveys-swe-2012-en.

75. Ahmed, Stockholm: The unicorn factory.

CONCLUSION

1. Katzenstein, P. J. (1985). *Small states in world markets: Industrial policy in Europe.* Cornell University Press.

2. See Edler, J., Cunningham,P., Gok, A., & Shapira, P. (2016). *Handbook of innovation policy impact.* Edward Elgar.

3. Chinn, D. L. (1982). Growth, equity, and Gini coefficients: The case of Taiwan. *Economic Development and Cultural Change, 30*(4), 65–79.

4. Hall, P. (2022). Growth regimes. *Business History Review, 1,* 5.

5. McNeil, A., Lee, N., & Luca, D. (2022). *The long shadow of local decline: Birthplace economic conditions, political attitudes, and long-term individual economic outcomes in the UK.* International Inequalities Institute Working Paper, no. 76, London School of Economics and Political Science.

6. A rough comparison shows GDP per capita (PPP) in Beijing as similar to average GDP per capita in Japan. The United States is, as far as we can tell, more unequal, according to World Bank data. But this sort of comparison is a statistical minefield and should be treated with great caution.

7. Breznitz, D. (2021). *Innovation in real places: Strategies for prosperity in an unforgiving world.* Oxford University Press; Meisenzahl, R. R., & Mokyr, J. (2011). The rate and direction of invention in the British Industrial Revolution: Incentives and institutions. In J. Lerner & S. Stern (Eds.), *The rate and direction of inventive activity revisited* (pp. 443–479). University of Chicago Press.

References

Accounting and Accounting Office of the Executive Yuan [Taiwan] (2020). *Comprehensive analysis of the results of the annual household income and expenditure survey.* https://ws.dgbas.gov.tw/win/fies/a11 .asp?year%20=%20106.

Acemoglu, D., & Robinson, J. A. (2002). The political economy of the Kuznets curve. *Review of Development Economics, 6*(2), 183–203.

Adler, P., Florida, R., King, K., & Mellander, C. (2019). The city and high-tech startups: The spatial organization of Schumpeterian entrepreneurship. *Cities, 87,* 121–130.

Afonso, A., & Mach, A. (2012). Coming together but staying apart: Continuity and change in the Austrian and Swiss varieties of capitalism. In U. Becker, L. Noordegraaf-Eelens, L. Tsipouri, & V. Stenius (Eds.), *The changing political economies of small West European countries* (pp. 99–124). Amsterdam University Press.

Aghion, P., Akcigit, U., Bergeaud, A., Blundell, R., & Hémous, D. (2019). Innovation and top income inequality. *Review of Economic Studies, 86*(1), 1–45.

Aghion, P., Akcigit, U., Hyytinen, A., & Toivanen, O. (2018). On the returns to invention within firms: Evidence from Finland. In

American Economic Association: Papers and Proceedings, 108,
208–12.

Ahmed, M. (2015). Stockholm: The unicorn factory. *Financial Times.*
March 31.

Alvedalen, J., & Carlsson, B. (2021). *Scaling up in entrepreneurial ecosystems: A comparative study of entrepreneurial ecosystems in life science.*
Lund University, CIRCLE–Centre for Innovation Research, Papers in
Innovation Studies, no. 2021/10. http://wp.circle.lu.se/upload/CIRCLE
/workingpapers/202110_alvedalen.pdf.

Alvaredo, F., Atkinson, A. B., Piketty, T., and Saez, E. (2022). *World
inequality database.* WID.world. https://wid.world/data.

Amsden, A. H. (1991). Taiwan from an international perspective. *Asian
Affairs: An American Review, 18*(2), 81–97.

Amsden, A., and Chu, W-W. (2003). *Beyond late development: Taiwan's
upgrading policies.* MIT Press.

Andersson, M., & Klinthäll, M. (2012). The opening of the North–South
divide: Cumulative causation, household income disparity and the
regional bonus in Taiwan, 1976–2005. *Structural Change and Economic Dynamics, 23*(2), 170–179.

——— (2015). "Growth with equity" and regional development: Distributional consequences of agglomeration in Taiwan. *Journal of the Asia
Pacific Economy, 20*(2), 271–289.

André, C., Beom, J., Pak, M. & Purwin, A. (2021). *Keeping regional
inequality in check in Sweden.* OECD Economics Department Working Papers, no. 1689.

Arman, H., Iammarino, S., Ibarra-Olivo, J. E., & Lee, N. (2022). Systems
of innovation, diversification, and the R&D trap: A case study of
Kuwait. *Science and Public Policy, 49*(2), 179–190.

Arntz, M., Gregory, T., & Zierahn, U. (2016). *The risk of automation
for jobs in OECD Countries: A comparative analysis.* OECD Social,
Employment, and Migration Working Papers, 189, 0_1.

Arthur, W. B. (2009). *The nature of technology: What it is and how it
evolves.* Simon & Schuster.

Asheim, B. T., Smith, H. L., & Oughton, C. (2011). Regional innovation
systems: Theory, empirics and policy. *Regional Studies, 45*(7), 875–891.

Ashton, D., Green, F., Sung, J., & James, D. (2002). The evolution of
education and training strategies in Singapore, Taiwan and South
Korea: A development model of skill formation. *Journal of Education
and Work, 15*(1), 5–30.

Astleithner, F., & Flecker, J. (2018). From the golden age to the gilded cage? Austrian trade unions, social partnership and the crisis. In H. Dribbush, S. Lehndorff, & T. Schulten (Eds.), *Rough waters: European trade unions in a time of crises* (pp. 185-208). European Trade Union Association. www.etui.org/publications/books/rough-waters-european-trade-unions-in-a-time-of-crises.

Atkins, R. (2015). Austria's sights move beyond the European markets. *Financial Times*. 20 October.

Austrian Research Promotion Agency (FFG). (2019). *Objectives and Mission*. www.ffg.at/en/FFG/objectives-and-mission.

Autor, D., Dorn, D., Katz, L. F., Patterson, C., & Van Reenen, J. (2020). The fall of the labor share and the rise of superstar firms. *Quarterly Journal of Economics, 135*(2), 645–709.

Autor, D. H., Levy, F., & Murnane, R. J. (2003). The skill content of recent technological change: An empirical exploration. *Quarterly Journal of Economics, 118*(4), 1279–1333.

Bank of England (2023). *A millennium of macroeconomic data*. www.bankofengland.co.uk/statistics/research-datasets.

Baregheh, A., Rowley, J., & Sambrook, S. (2009). Towards a multidisciplinary definition of innovation. *Management Decision, 47*(8), 1323–1339.

Barro, R. & Lee, J.-W. (2013). A new data set of educational attainment in the world, 1950–2010. *Journal of Development Economics, 104*, 184–198.

Beller, S. (2006) *A concise history of Austria*. Cambridge University Press.

Berggren, C., & Laestadius, S. (2003). Co-development and composite clusters: The secular strength of Nordic telecommunications. *Industrial and Corporate Change, 12*(1), 91–114.

Bischof, G., Pelinka, A., & Stiefel, D. (2000). *The Marshall Plan in Austria* (Vol. 8). Transaction Publishers.

Björklund, A., & Waldenström, D. (2021). *Facts and myths in the popular debate about inequality in Sweden*. Research Institute for Industrial Economics (IFN) Working Paper, no. 1392.

Blanchet, T., Chancel, L., & Gethin, A. (2019). *How unequal is Europe? Evidence from distributional national accounts, 1980–2017*. World Inequality Database Working Paper, no. 6.

——— (2022). Why is Europe more equal than the United States? *American Economic Journal: Applied Economics, 14*(4): 480–518.

Bloom, N., Hassan, T. A., Kalyani, A., Lerner, J., & Tahoun, A. (2021). *The diffusion of disruptive technologies*. NBER Working Paper, no. w28999.

Böheim, R. (2017). *The labor market in Austria, 2000–2016*. IZA World of Labor. https://wol.iza.org/articles/the-labor-market-in-austria/long.

Böheim, R., & Gust, S. (2021). The Austrian pay transparency law and the gender wage gap. IZA Discussion Paper, no. 14206.

Borras, S., & Edquist, C. (2015). Education, training and skills in innovation policy. *Science and Public Policy, 42*(2), 215–227.

Bozkaya, A., & Kerr, W. R. (2014). Labor regulations and European venture capital. *Journal of Economics and Management Strategy, 23*(4), 776–810.

Braithwaite, T. (2021). Behind every racy fintech, a sensible German saver. *Financial Times*. May 28. www.ft.com/content/f535f974-38c6-42df-86b4-646e025ed2da.

Brandal, N., Bratberg, Ø., & Thorsen, D. (2013). *The Nordic model of social democracy*. Springer.

Braunerhjelm, P., & Henrekson, M. (2013). Entrepreneurship, institutions, and economic dynamism: Lessons from a comparison of the United States and Sweden. *Industrial and Corporate Change, 22*(1), 107–130.

Breznitz, D. (2007). *Innovation and the state*. Yale University Press.

——— (2021). *Innovation in real places: Strategies for prosperity in an unforgiving world*. Oxford University Press.

Breznitz, D., & Murphree, M. (2011). *Run of the Red Queen: Government, innovation, globalization, and economic growth in China*. Yale University Press.

Busemeyer, M. R. (2009). Asset specificity, institutional complementarities and the variety of skill regimes in coordinated market economies. *Socio-economic Review, 7*(3), 375–406.

Calligaris, S., Criscuolo, C., & Marcolin, L. (2018). *Mark-ups in the digital era*. OECD Science, Technology and Industry Working Papers, no. 2018(10), 0_1–26.

Carvalho, A. (2018). Wishful thinking about R&D policy targets: What governments promise and what they actually deliver. *Science and Public Policy, 45*(3), 373–391.

Castaldi, C., & Mendonça, S. (2022). Regions and trademarks: Research opportunities and policy insights from leveraging trademarks in regional innovation studies, *Regional Studies, 56*(2), 177–189. https://doi.org/10.1080/00343404.2021.2003767.

Causa, O. and M. Hermansen (2020). Income redistribution through taxes and transfers across OECD countries. In J. Gabriel Rodriguez &

J. Bishop (Eds.), *Inequality, redistribution and mobility* (pp. 29-74). Emerald Publishing.

Chancel, L. (2019). *Ten facts about inequality in advanced economies.* World Inequality Database Working Paper, no. 15, 2019.

Chang, M., Blanchette, J. and Hass., R. (2022). *Can semiconductor manufacturing return to the US?* Podcast. Brookings Institution. www.brookings.edu/podcast-episode/can-semiconductor-manufacturing-return-to-the-us.

Chen, C. (2018). The housing affordability crisis and government policy actions in Taiwan. *Economic Alternatives, 3,* 334–347.

Chinn, D. L. (1982). Growth, equity, and Gini coefficients: The case of Taiwan. *Economic Development and Cultural Change, 30*(4), 65–79.

Chow, P. C. (2021). Taiwan in international economic relations. In J. Dreyer & J. deLisle (Eds.), *Taiwan in the era of Tsai Ing-wen* (pp. 84–107). Routledge.

Christl, M., Köppl–Turyna, M., Lorenz, H., & Kucsera, D. (2020). Redistribution within the tax-benefits system in Austria. *Economic Analysis and Policy, 68,* 250–264.

Chu, C., Chen, C-Y., Lin., M-J., & Su, H-L. (2022). *Distributional national accounts of Taiwan, 1991–2017.* World Inequality Database Working Paper, no. 2022/15.

Chuang, Y. C., & Lai, W. W. (2017). Returns to human capital and inequality: The case of Taiwan. *Journal of Economic Development, 42*(3), 61–88.

Coenen, L., Hansen, T., & Rekers, J. V. (2015). Innovation policy for grand challenges: An economic geography perspective. *Geography Compass, 9*(9), 483–496.

Consoli, D., Fusillo, F., Orsatti, G., & Quatraro, F. (2021). Skill endowment, routinisation and digital technologies: Evidence from US metropolitan areas. *Industry and Innovation, 28*(8), 1017–1045.

Coulter, M. (2023). Swiss Google workers stage walkout as job cuts hit Europe. Reuters. March 15.

Cowell, F., Karagiannaki, E., & McKnight, A. (2018). Accounting for cross-country differences in wealth inequality. *Review of Income and Wealth, 64*(2), 332–356.

Crafts, N. (1996). "Post-neoclassical endogenous growth theory": What are its policy implications? *Oxford Review of Economic Policy, 12*(2), 30–47.

Dachs, B., & Drach, A. (2019). Forschung und Entwicklung von Unternehmen in langfristiger Perspektive: Starkes Wachstum, alte Akteure? *Perspektiven der Wirtschaftspolitik, 20*(4), 340–351.

Dahlberg, M., Edmark, K., & Lundqvist, H. (2012). Ethnic diversity and preferences for redistribution. *Journal of Political Economy, 120*(1), 41–76.

Deming, D. J., & Noray, K. (2020). Earnings dynamics, changing job skills, and STEM careers. *Quarterly Journal of Economics, 135*(4), 1965–2005.

Donovan, S. A., & Bradley, D. H. (2019). *Real wage trends, 1979 to 2018.* Congressional Research Service.

Durazzi, N., & Geyer, L. (2020). Social inclusion in the knowledge economy: Unions' strategies and institutional change in the Austrian and German training systems. *Socio-economic review, 18*(1), 103–124.

Economist (2006). Farewell Nordic model: The end of another European dream. *Economist.* November 16.

———— (2013). Northern lights: A special report on the Nordic countries. *Economist.* www.economist.com/sites/default/files/20130202_nordic_countries.pdf.

———— (2020). Why commercial ties between Taiwan and China are beginning to fray. *Economist.* November 19.

Eder, J., & Trippl, M. (2019). Innovation in the periphery: Compensation and exploitation strategies. *Growth and Change, 50*(4), 1511–1531.

Eder, M. (2021). Billionaire Peter Thiel hires Austria's disgraced former chancellor. Bloomberg, 30 December. www.bloomberg.com/news/articles/2021-12-30/billionaire-thiel-gives-austria-s-former-wunderkind-a-job.

Edgerton, D. (2018). Haldane principle's "centenary" is a good time to bury its myth. *Research Fortnight.* December 12.

Edler, J., Cunningham, P., Gok, A. & Shapira, P. (2016). *Handbook of innovation policy impact.* Edward Elgar.

Eger, M. A. (2010). Even in Sweden: The effect of immigration on support for welfare state spending. *European Sociological Review, 26*(2), 203–217.

Enflo, K. & Missiaia, A. (2020). Between Malthus and the industrial take-off: Regional inequality in Sweden, 1571–1850. *Economic History Review, 73*(2), 431–454.

European Commission (2023). Eurydice: Switzerland; Key features of the education system. https://eurydice.eacea.ec.europa.eu/national-education-systems/switzerland/overview.

European Trade Union Institute (2023). Worker participation: Austria. www.worker-participation.eu/National-Industrial-Relations/Countries/Austria.

Eurostat (2021). Gender pay gap situation in Europe. https://ec.europa
.eu/info/policies/justice-and-fundamental-rights/gender-equality
/equal-pay/gender-pay-gap-situation-eu_en.

—— (2021). R&D expenditure in the EU at 2.3% of GDP in 2020.
https://ec.europa.eu/eurostat/en/web/products-eurostat-news/-
/ddn-20211129-2.

—— (2022). Real GDP per capita (indicator). https://ec.europa.eu
/eurostat/databrowser/view/sdg_08_10/default/table.

Fagerberg, J., Srholec, M., & Verspagen, B. (2010). Innovation and economic development. In *Handbook of the Economics of Innovation*
(Vol. 2) (pp. 833–872). North-Holland.

Federal Assembly [Switzerland] (2023). *Women's suffrage in Switzerland:
100 years of struggle.* www.parlament.ch/en/über-das-parlament
/political-women/conquest-of-equal-rights/women-suffrage.

Federal Government, Republic of Austria (2020). *RTI Strategy 2030:
Strategy for research, technology and innovation of the Austrian
federal government.* https://era.gv.at/public/documents/4489/RTI_
Strategy_2030-1-1.pdf.

Federal Statistical Office [Switzerland] (2022). *Commuting.* www.bfs
.admin.ch/bfs/en/home/statistics/mobility-transport/passenger-
transport/commuting.html.

Fei, J., Ranis, G. and Kuo, S. W. Y. (1979). *Growth with equity: The
Taiwan case.* World Bank.

Feldman, M., Guy, F., & Iammarino, S. (2021). Regional income disparities, monopoly and finance. *Cambridge Journal of Regions, Economy
and Society, 14*(1), 25–49.

Feldman, M. P., Guy, F., Iammarino, S., & Ioramashvili, C. (2021).
*Gathering round Big Tech: How the market for acquisitions reinforces
regional inequalities in the US.* Kenan Institute of Private Enterprise
Research Paper, no. 21–01.

Fernández-Macías, E. (2012). Job polarization in Europe? Changes in the
employment structure and job quality, 1995–2007. *Work and Occupations, 39*(2), 157–182.

Fields, K. (1995). *Enterprise and the state in Korea and Taiwan.* University of Chicago Press.

Finegold, D. (1999). Creating self-sustaining, high-skill ecosystems.
Oxford Review of Economic Policy, 15(1), 60–81.

Finegold, D., & Soskice, D. (1988). The failure of training in Britain: Analysis and prescription. *Oxford Review of Economic Policy, 4*(3), 21–53.

Flanagan, K., Uyarra, E., & Laranja, M. (2011). Reconceptualising the "policy mix" for innovation. *Research Policy, 40*(5), 702–713.

Florida, R., & Mellander, C. (2016). The geography of inequality: Difference and determinants of wage and income inequality across US metros. *Regional Studies, 50*(1), 79–92.

Forbes (2023). World billionaire list. *Forbes.* www.forbes.com/billionaires.

Frey, C. B., & Osborne, M. A. (2017). The future of employment: How susceptible are jobs to computerisation? *Technological Forecasting and Social Change, 114*, 254–280.

Frey, E. (2016). Metals specialist Berndorf shines light on Austria's hidden strength. *Financial Times.* November 3. www.ft.com/content /f1bd4d80-8baf-11e6-8cb7-e7ada1d123b1.

Fritsch, M., & Wyrwich, M. (2021). Does successful innovation require large urban areas? Germany as a counterexample. *Economic Geography, 97*(3), 284–308.

Gapper, J. (2017). Swiss watches risk becoming antiques. *Financial Times.* March 29. www.ft.com/content/0ff2327e-13bf-11e7-80f4-13e067d5072c.

Geldner, N. (1998). Successful structural change in Styria. *Austrian Economic Quarterly, 3*(2), 95–100.

Glasmeier, A. (1991). Technological discontinuities and flexible production networks: The case of Switzerland and the world watch industry. *Research Policy, 20*(5), 469–485.

Glasner, J. (2021). These countries have the most startup investment for their size. *Crunchbase News.* November 2.

Gold, T. B. (2016). Entrepreneurs, multinationals, and the state. In E. A. Winckler & S. Greenhalgh (Eds.), *Contending approaches to the political economy of Taiwan* (pp. 191–221). Routledge.

——— (2016). Retrocession and authoritarian KMT rule (1945–1986). In G. Schubert (Ed.), *Routledge Handbook of Contemporary Taiwan* (pp. 36–50). Routledge.

Gompers, P., & Lerner, J. (1998). Venture capital distributions: Short-run and long-run reactions. *Journal of Finance, 53*(6), 2161–2183.

Goos, M., & Manning, A. (2007). Lousy and lovely jobs: The rising polarization of work in Britain. *Review of Economics and Statistics, 89*(1), 118–133.

Green, F., Ashton, D., James, D., & Sung, J. (1999). The role of the state in skill formation: Evidence from the Republic of Korea, Singapore, and Taiwan. *Oxford Review of Economic Policy, 15*(1), 82–96.

Greenstone, M., & Looney, A. (2011). *A dozen economic facts about innovation.* The Hamilton Project. Brookings Institution. www.brookings.edu /wp-content/uploads/2016/06/08_innovation_greenstone_looney.pdf.

Grillitsch, M., Rekers, J. V., & Tödtling, F. (2019). When drivers of clusters shift scale from local towards global: What remains for regional innovation policy? *Geoforum, 102,* 57–68.

Haldane, A. (2018). The UK's productivity problem: Hub no spokes. Academy of Social Sciences Annual Lecture. www.bankofengland .co.uk/-/media/boe/files/speech/2018/the-uks-productivity-problem-hub-no-spokes-speech-by-andy-haldane.pdf.

Hall, B. H. (2005). Innovation and diffusion. In J. Fagerberg, J., D. Mowery, & R. Nelson (Eds.), *The Oxford handbook of innovation* (pp. 459-483). Oxford University Press.

Hall, P. A. (2022). Growth regimes. *Business History Review,* 1–25. https://doi.org/10.1017/S0007680522000034.

Hansen, T. & Coenen, L. (2017). Unpacking resource mobilisation by incumbents for biorefineries: The role of micro-level factors for technological innovation system weaknesses, *Technology Analysis and Strategic Management, 29*(5), 500–513, https://doi.org/10.1080/09537 325.2016.1249838.

Hansen, T., & Winther, L. (2014). Competitive low-tech manufacturing and challenges for regional policy in the European context: Lessons from the Danish experience. *Cambridge Journal of Regions, Economy and Society, 7*(3), 449–470.

Hanushek, E. A., & Woessmann, L. (2008). The role of cognitive skills in economic development. *Journal of Economic Literature, 46*(3), 607–668.

Henrekson, M. (2005). Entrepreneurship: A weak link in the welfare state? *Industrial and Corporate Change, 14*(3), 437–467.

Hermann, C., & Flecker, J. (2015). Mastering the crisis but not the future: The Austrian model in the financial and economic crisis. In S. Lehndorff (Ed.), *Divisive integration: The triumph of failed ideas in Europe* (pp. 195–209). European Trade Union Institute.

Heyman, F., Norbäck, P. J., Persson, L., & Andersson, F. (2019). Has the Swedish business sector become more entrepreneurial than the US business sector? *Research Policy, 48*(7), 1809–1822.

Hille, K. (2021). TSMC: how a Taiwanese chipmaker became a linchpin of the global economy. *Financial Times.* March 24. www.ft.com/content /05206915-fd73-4a3a-92a5-6760ce965bd9.

Hille, K. & Cane, A. (2006). TSMC rejigs chip production to reduce costs. *Financial Times.* January 3. www.ft.com/content/469896f2-7c85-11da-936a-0000779e2340.

Hlasny, V. (2016). *Different faces of inequality across Asia: Decomposition of income gaps across demographic Groups.* ADBI Working Paper, no. 688.

HM Government (2020). *UK Research and Development Roadmap.* HMSO.

——— (2023). HM Government. (2021). *National AI Strategy.* HMSO.

Huang, B., Morgan, P. J., & Yoshino, N. (2019). *Demystifying rising inequality in Asia.* Asian Development Bank Institute.

Hutton, G. (2022). *Financial services: Contribution to the UK economy.* House of Commons. https://researchbriefings.files.parliament.uk/documents/SN06193/SN06193.pdf.

International Labour Organization. (2023). *ILO modelled estimates database.* ilostat.ilo.org/data.

International Monetary Fund (IMF) (2022). *IMF database: GDP per capita.* https://data.imf.org.Janger, J. (2019). The Austrian example. *Research Professional.* 26 June.

Jones, R. (2021, August 2). Reflections on the UK's new innovation strategy. *Soft Machines.* www.softmachines.org/wordpress/?p=2591.

Liu, J., Lai, M. Y., & Liu, Z. S. (2022). Trade liberalization, domestic reforms, and income inequality: Evidence from Taiwan. *Review of Development Economics, 26*(3), 1286–1309.

Lue, J-D. (2013). Promoting work: A review of active labour market policies in Taiwan. *Journal of Asian Public Policy,* 6:1, 81–98. https://doi.org/10.1080/17516234.2013.765184.

Judt, T. (2006). *Postwar: A history of Europe since 1945.* Penguin.

Katzenstein, P. J. (1985). *Small states in world markets: Industrial policy in Europe.* Cornell University Press.

Kaufmann, A., & Tödtling, F. (2002). How effective is innovation support for SMEs? An analysis of the region of Upper Austria. *Technovation, 22*(3), 147–159.

Kaufmann, D., and Kraay, A. (2021). *Worldwide governance indicators.* World Bank.

Kemeny, T., & Osman, T. (2018). The wider impacts of high-technology employment: Evidence from US cities. *Research Policy, 47*(9), 1729–1740.

Kemeny, T., Petralia, S., & Storper, M. (2022). Disruptive innovation and spatial inequality. *Regional Studies,* 1–18. https://doi.org/10.1080/00343404.2022.2076824.

Kline, P., Petkova, N., Williams, H., & Zidar, O. (2019). Who profits from patents? Rent-sharing at innovative firms. *Quarterly Journal of Economics, 134*(3), 1343–1404.

Kluge, L., & Spiekerman, K. (2017). *Scenarios for accessibility by the sea, road, rail, air and multimodal.* ESPON.

Knowledge at Wharton (2015). *How Stockholm became a unicorn factory.* University of Pennsylvania. https://knowledge.wharton.upenn.edu /article/how-stockholm-became-a-unicorn-factory.

Korber, M., & Oesch, D. (2019). Vocational versus general education: Employment and earnings over the life course in Switzerland. *Advances in Life Course Research, 40,* 1–13.

Kwong, R. (2010) TSMC Plans record $4.8bn investment. *Financial Times.* 28 January. www.ft.com/content/9c1f836a-0be2-11df-96b9-00144feabdc0.

Ladner, A. (2011). Switzerland: Subsidiarity, power-sharing, and direct democracy. In F. Hendriks, A. Lidström, & J. Loughlin (Eds.), *The Oxford handbook of local and regional democracy in Europe* (pp. 196-218). Oxford University Press. https://doi.org/10.1093/oxfordhb /9780199562978.003.0009.

Lalive, R. & Lehmann, T. (2017). *The labor market in Switzerland, 2000-2016.* IZA World of Labor, no. 402. http://dx.doi.org/10.15185 /izawol.402.

Landes, D. S. (1984). *Revolution in time: Clocks and the making of the modern world.* Harvard University Press.

Lee, N., & Clarke, S. (2019). Do low-skilled workers gain from high-tech employment growth? High-technology multipliers, employment and wages in Britain. *Research Policy, 48*(9), 103803.

Lee, N., Sissons, P., & Jones, K. (2016). The geography of wage inequality in British cities. *Regional Studies, 50*(10), 1714–1727.

Lee, Y. F. L. (2008). Economic growth and income inequality: The modern Taiwan experience. *Journal of Contemporary China, 17*(55), 361–374.

Lehnert, P., Pfister, C., & Backes-Gellner, U. (2020). Employment of R&D personnel after an educational supply shock: Effects of the introduction of universities of applied sciences in Switzerland. *Labour Economics, 66,* 101883.

Lengyel, B., Bokányi, E., di Clemente, R., Kertész, J., & González, M. C. (2020). The role of geography in the complex diffusion of innovations. *Scientific Reports, 10*(1), 1–11.

Lerner, J., & Tåg, J. (2013). Institutions and venture capital. *Industrial and Corporate Change, 22*(1), 153–182.

Lewis, P. (2020). Developing technician skills for innovative industries: Theory, evidence from the UK life sciences industry, and policy implications. *British Journal of Industrial Relations, 58*(3), 617–643.

Lin, T. C., Hsu, S. H., & Lin, Y. L. (2019). The effect of housing prices on consumption and economic growth: The case of Taiwan. *Journal of the Asia Pacific Economy, 24*(2), 292–312.

Liu, J., Lai, M. Y., & Liu, Z. S. (2022). Trade liberalization, domestic reforms, and income inequality: Evidence from Taiwan. *Review of Development Economics.* https://doi.org/10.1111/rode.12875.

Lucking, B., Bloom, N., & Van Reenen, J. (2019). Have R&D spillovers declined in the 21st century? *Fiscal Studies, 40*(4), 561–590.

Lue, J-D. (2013). Promoting work: A review of active labour market policies in Taiwan. *Journal of Asian Public Policy, 6*(1), 81–98.

Lundvall, B. Å., & Borrás, S. (2005). Science, technology and innovation policy. In J. Fagerberg, D. Mowery, & R. Nelson (Eds.), *The Oxford handbook of innovation*, pp. 599–631). Oxford University Press.

MacNeill, S. & Steiner, M. (2010). Leadership of cluster policy: lessons from the Austrian province of Styria, *Policy Studies, 31*(4), 441–455. https://doi.org/10.1080/01442871003723374.

Makkonen, T., & Lin, B. (2012). Continuing vocational training and innovation in Europe. *International Journal of Innovation and Learning, 11*(4), 325–338.

Mallaby, S. (2022). Venture capital's new race for Europe. *Financial Times.* February 4. www.ft.com/content/6fc9455a-75fc-4952-a4ff-203e5579aefa.

Marshall, A. (1890). *The principles of economics.* MacMillan.

Matthews, D. (2018). The White House, definitely not scared of socialism, issues report on why socialism is bad. Vox.com. October 23. www.vox.com/policy-and-politics/2018/10/23/18013872/white-house-socialism-report-cea-mao-lenin-bernie-sanders.

Mazzolari, F., & Ragusa, G. (2013). Spillovers from high-skill consumption to low-skill labor markets. *Review of Economics and Statistics, 95*(1), 74–86.

Mazzucato, M. (2013). *The entrepreneurial state: Debunking private vs public myths.* Anthem Press.

——— (2018). *The value of everything: Making and taking in the global economy.* Hachette UK.

McNeil, A., Luca, D. & Lee, N., (2022). *The long shadow of local decline: Birthplace economic conditions, political attitudes, and long-term individual economic outcomes in the UK*. International Inequalities Institute Working Paper, no. 76, London School of Economics and Political Science.

Meili, R., & Shearmur, R. (2019). Diverse diversities: Open innovation in small towns and rural areas. *Growth and Change, 50*(2), 492–514.

Meisenzahl, R. R., & Mokyr, J. (2011). The rate and direction of invention in the British Industrial Revolution: Incentives and institutions. In J. Lerner & S. Stern (Eds.), *The rate and direction of inventive activity revisited* (pp. 443–479). University of Chicago Press.

Milne, R. (2019). Can $5bn Klarna avoid the fate of other Swedish unicorns? *Financial Times*. August 7. www.ft.com/content/1312b0ea-b904-11e9-8a88-aa6628ac896c.

——— (2021). Klarna targets acquisitions as it raises fresh $1bn of investment. March 1. *Financial Times*. www.ft.com/content/419be00f-0a00-4fed-b4a6-bb55263033bc.

——— (2021). SoftBank investment helps Klarna to $45.6bn valuation. *Financial Times*. June 10. www.ft.com/content/9f73b352-723f-471b-b098-5f090279b5bb.

Moretti, Enrico. (2010). Local multipliers. *American Economic Review, 100*(2), 373–377.

Mudambi, R. (2005). *Branding time: Swatch and global brand management*. Temple University IGMS Case Series, no. 05–001.

Murphy, E. C., & Oesch, D. (2018). Is employment polarisation inevitable? Occupational change in Ireland and Switzerland, 1970–2010. *Work, Employment and Society, 32*(6), 1099–1117.

Nelson, R. R. (2011). *The moon and the ghetto* revisited. *Science and Public Policy, 38*(9), 681–690.

Niggli, M. & Rutzer, C. (2021). *A gender gap to more innovation in Switzerland*. Innoscape. https://innoscape.ch/en/publications/gender.

Nuttall, C. (2008). Intel sees leadership in a shrinking world. *Financial Times*. July 1. 2006. www.ft.com/content/18debbc7-1bbf-3742-b4b5-f2e366aa1ef0.

OECD (2012). *Economic survey of Sweden*. OECD. www.oecd-ilibrary.org/economics/oecd-economic-surveys-sweden-2012_eco_surveys-swe-2012-en.

——— (2013). *OECD Reviews of Innovation Policy: Sweden 2012*. OECD Publishing. https://doi.org/10.1787/9789264184893-en.

———— (2015). *Frascati manual 2015: Guidelines for collecting and reporting data on research and experimental development, the measurement of scientific, technological and innovation activities.* OECD.

———— (2015). *In it together: Why less inequality benefits all.* OECD Publishing.

———— (2017). *OECD employment outlook 2017.* OECD Publishing. https://doi.org/10.1787/empl_outlook-2017-en.

————(2018). *Good jobs for all in a changing world of work: The OECD Jobs Strategy.* OECD Publishing.

———— (2018). *OECD reviews of innovation policy: Austria 2018.* OECD Publishing. https://doi.org/10.1787/9789264309470-en.

———— (2018). *PISA Results: Sweden.* www.oecd.org/pisa/publications /PISA2018_CN_SWE.pdf.

———— (2018). The measurement of scientific, technological and innovation activities. *Oslo Manual 2018.* OECD.

———— (2019). *Under pressure: The squeezed middle class.* OECD Publishing https://doi.org/10.1787/689afed1-en.

———— (2021). *Economic Survey of Sweden.* OECD Publishing. www.oecd-ilibrary.org/economics/oecd-economic-surveys-sweden-2012_eco_surveys-swe-2012-en.

———— (2021). Household disposable income (indicator). https://doi.org /10.1787/de435f6e-en.

———— (2021). *OECD Economic Surveys: Sweden 2021.* OECD Publishing. https://doi.org/10.1787/f61d0a54-en.

———— (2021). *OECD R&D tax incentives database,* 2021 edition. www.oecd .org/sti/rd-tax-stats-database.pdf.

———— (2021) *Main Science and Technology Indicators, Volume 2020 Issue 2,* OECD Publishing. https://doi.org/10.1787/eea67efc-en.

———— (2021). OECD data, general government spending. https://data.oecd .org/gga/general-government-spending.htm.

———— (2021). *R&D Tax incentives: Austria, 2021.* OECD Directorate for Science, Technology and Innovation. December.

———— (2022). Gender wage gap (indicator). https://doi.org/10.1787 /7cee77aa-en.

———— (2022). Income inequality (indicator). https://doi.org/10.1787 /7f420b4b-en.

———— (2022). *Metropolitan areas: Income distribution statistics.* https:// stats.oecd.org/Index.aspx?DataSetCode = CITIES#.

——— (2022). *OECD main science and technology indicators highlights, March 2022*. OECD. www.oecd.org/sti/msti-highlights-march-2022.pdf.

——— (2023). GDP per hour worked (indicator). https://doi.org/10.1787/1439e590-en.

——— (2023). General government spending (indicator). https://doi: 10.1787/a31cbf4d-en.

——— (2023). Gross domestic product (GDP) (indicator). https://doi.org/10.1787/dc2f7aec-en.

——— (2023). Income inequality (indicator). https://doi.org/10.1787/7f420b4b-en.

——— (2023). Wage levels (indicator). https://doi.org/10.1787/0a1c27bc-en.

Oesch, D., & Piccitto, G. (2019). The polarization myth: Occupational upgrading in Germany, Spain, Sweden, and the UK, 1992–2015. *Work and Occupations, 46*(4), 441–469.

Peck, J., & Theodore, N. (2015). *Fast policy: Experimental statecraft at the thresholds of neoliberalism*. University of Minnesota Press.

Penrose, E. (1959). *The theory of the growth of the firm*. Oxford University Press.

Pfister, C., Koomen, M., Harhoff, D., & Backes-Gellner, U. (2021). Regional innovation effects of applied research institutions. *Research Policy, 50*(4), 104197.

PISA (2018). *PISA database*. OECD. www.oecd.org/pisa/data/2018database.

Podvrsic, A., Becker, J., Piroska, D., Profant, T., & Hodulák, V. (2020). *Mitigating the COVID-19 effect: Emergency economic policy-making in Central Europe*. ETUI Working Paper, no. 2020.07.

Quartly, J. (2020). The Gini in Taiwan's bottle. *Taiwan Business Topics*. November 19. https://topics.amcham.com.tw/2020/11/taiwan-gini-coefficient.

Raffaelli, R. (2019). Technology reemergence: Creating new value for old technologies in Swiss mechanical watchmaking, 1970–2008. *Administrative Science Quarterly, 64*(3), 576–618.

Ranis, G. (1978). Equity with growth in Taiwan: How "special" is the "special case"? *World Development, 6*(3), 397–409.

Redding, S. (1996). The low-skill, low-quality trap: Strategic complementarities between human capital and R & D. *Economic Journal, 106*(435), 458–470.

Rekers, J. V. (2016). What triggers innovation diffusion? Intermediary organizations and geography in cultural and science-based industries.

Environment and Planning C: Government and Policy, 34(6), 1058–1075.

Rocha-Akis, S. (2021). *The income distribution in Austria.* Österreichisches Institut für Wirtschaftsforschung.

Rodrik, D. (1996). Understanding economic policy reform. *Journal of Economic Literature, 34*(1), 9–41.

Rodrik, D. (2006). Goodbye Washington consensus, hello Washington confusion? A review of the World Bank's economic growth in the 1990s: Learning from a decade of reform. *Journal of Economic literature, 44*(4), 973–987.

Rodrik, D., & Stantcheva, S. (2021). Fixing capitalism's good jobs problem. *Oxford Review of Economic Policy, 37*(4), 824–837.

Rosenberg, N. (1972). Factors affecting the diffusion of technology. *Explorations in Economic History, 10*(1), 3–33.

Roy, D. (2003). *Taiwan: A political history.* Cornell University Press.

Saxenian, A. (1996). *Regional advantage: Culture and competition in Silicon Valley and Route 128.* Harvard University Press.

——— (2007). *The new argonauts: Regional advantage in a global economy.* Harvard University Press.

Schlegel, T., Pfister, C., Harhoff, D., & Backes-Gellner, U. (2021). Innovation effects of universities of applied sciences: An assessment of regional heterogeneity. *Journal of Technology Transfer, 47,* 63–118.

Schlögl, P., Mayerl, M., Löffler, R., & Schmölz, A. (2020). Supra-company apprenticeship training in Austria: A synopsis of empirical findings on a possibly early phase of a new pillar within VET. *Empirical Research in Vocational Education and Training, 12*(1), 1–17.

Schön, L. (2012). *An economic history of modern Sweden.* Routledge.

Schulze, M. S., & Wolf, N. (2012). Economic nationalism and economic integration: The Austro-Hungarian Empire in the late nineteenth century. *Economic History Review, 65*(2), 652–673.

Schumpeter, J. A. (1934). *Business cycle: The theory of economic development.* Oxford University Press.

——— (1934). *The theory of economic development: An inquiry into profits, capital, credit, interest, and the business cycle.* Harvard University Press.

——— (1942). *Capitalism, socialism, and democracy.* Harper & Brothers.

——— (2002). The economy as a whole: Seventh chapter of *The theory of economic development.* Translated by Ursula Backhaus. *Industry and Innovation, 9*(1–2), 93.

Shi, S. J. (2012). Shifting dynamics of the welfare politics in Taiwan: From income maintenance to labour protection. *Journal of Asian Public Policy, 5*(1), 82–96.

Smith, K. (2005). Measuring Innovation. In J. Fagerberg, D. Mowery, & R. Nelson (Eds.), *The Oxford handbook of innovation* (pp. 148–177). Oxford University Press.

Solon, O. (2013). Bill Gates: Capitalism means male baldness research gets more funding than malaria. *Wired.* March 14.

Solow, R. (2001). Information technology and the recent productivity boom in the US. Remarks at the National Competitiveness Network (NCN) Summit. http://web.mit.edu/cmi-videos/solow/text.html.

Soskice, D. (2021). The United States as radical innovation driver: The politics of declining dominance? In J. S. Hacker, A. Hertel-Fernandez, P. Pierson, & K. Thelen (Eds.), *The American political economy: Politics, markets, and power* (pp. 323-351). Cambridge University Press.

Stampfer, M., Pichler, R., & Hofer, R. (2010). The making of research funding in Austria: Transition politics and institutional development, 1945–2005. *Science and Public Policy, 37*(10), 765–780.

Steinberg, J. (2015). *Why Switzerland?* Cambridge University Press.

Steinmo, S. (2010). *The evolution of modern states: Sweden, Japan, and the United States.* Cambridge University Press.

Stohr, C. (2018). Multiple core regions: Regional inequality in Switzerland, 1860–2008. *Research in Economic History. 34,* 135–198.

Storper, M. (1997). *The regional world: Territorial development in a global economy.* Guilford Press.

Storper, M., Kemeny, T., Makarem, N., & Osman, T. (2015). *The rise and fall of urban economies: Lessons from San Francisco and Los Angeles.* Stanford University Press.

Sturn, D. (2000). Decentralized industrial policies in practice: The case of Austria and Styria. *European Planning Studies, 8*(2), 169–182.

Taipei Times (2021). Taiwan no. 1 in Asia, world no. 6 for gender equality. *Taipei Times.* www.taipeitimes.com/News/taiwan/archives/2021/01/09/2003750242.

Taylor, M. Z. (2016). *The politics of innovation: Why some countries are better than others at science and technology.* Oxford University Press.

Tether, B., Mina, A., Consoli, D., & Gagliardi, D. (2005). *A literature review on skills and innovation: How does successful innovation impact on the demand for skills and how do skills drive innovation?* Department for Trade and Industry.

Thelen, K. (2014). *Varieties of liberalization and the new politics of social solidarity*. Cambridge University Press.

Therborn, G. (2020). Sweden's turn to economic inequality, 1982–2019. *Structural Change and Economic Dynamics, 52*, 159–166.

Tödtling, F., & Sedlacek, S. (1997). Regional economic transformation and the innovation system of Styria. *European Planning Studies, 5*(1), 43–63. https://doi.org/10.1080/09654319708720383.

Tomson, D. L. (2000). *The rise of Sweden Democrats: Islam, populism and the end of Swedish exceptionalism*. Brookings Institution. www.brookings.edu/research/the-rise-of-sweden-democrats-and-the-end-of-swedish-exceptionalism.

Trippl, M., & Otto, A. (2009). How to turn the fate of old industrial areas: A comparison of cluster-based renewal processes in Styria and the Saarland. *Environment and Planning A, 41*(5), 1217–1233.

Tsai, S. L., & Kanomata, N. (2011). Educational expansion and inequality of educational opportunity: Taiwan and Japan. *Sociological Theory and Methods, 26*(1), 179–195.

Turton, M. (2021). Notes from Central Taiwan: Are housing prices a national security crisis? *Taipei Times*, 13.12.2021.

Urquiola, M. (2020). *Markets, minds, and money: Why America leads the world in university research*. Harvard University Press.

Usher, A. P. (1951). Historical implications of *The theory of economic development. Review of Economics and Statistics, 33*(2), 158–162.

Van Reenen, J. (1996). The creation and capture of rents: Wages and innovation in a panel of UK companies. *Quarterly Journal of Economics, 111*(1), 195–226.

Venkataramakrishnanm, S. (2021). Klarna and Stripe announce "buy now, pay later" partnership. *Financial Times*. October 26. www.ft.com/content/841e0d03-f547-4a1f-b1f4-ef9a8ac7ab1f.

——— (2022). Klarna's valuation crashes to under $7bn in tough funding round. *Financial Times*. February 17. www.ft.com/content/66b65d68-d62e-4aec-a1ad-a7d9e2ba0435.

——— (2022). Klarna's widening losses driven by rapid expansion. *Financial Times*. February 28. www.ft.com/content/8ff87375-476b-4322-bc33-a483a471b8fc.

Verspagen, B. (2005). Innovation and economic growth. In J. Fagerberg, D. Mowery, & R. Nelson (Eds.), *The Oxford handbook of innovation* (pp. 487–513). Oxford University Press.

Vipond, H. (2020). A shoemaker's tale: Technology and disruption. Atlantic Fellows for Social Equity. https://afsee.atlanticfellows.lse.ac.uk/en-gb/blogs/a-shoemakers-tale-technology-and-disruption.

Visser, J. (2019). *ICTWSS database. version 6.1.* Amsterdam Institute for Advanced Labour Studies (AIAS).

Voestalpine (2021). *Corporate responsibility report 2021.* https://reports.voestalpine.com/2021/cr-report/environment/energy.html.

Vona, F., & Consoli, D. (2015). Innovation and skill dynamics: A life-cycle approach. *Industrial and Corporate Change, 24*(6), 1393–1415.

Von Borries, A., Grillitsch, M., & Lundquist, K. J. (2022). *Geographies of low-income jobs: The concentration of low-income jobs, the knowledge economy and labor market polarization in Sweden, 1990-2018.* Lund University, CIRCLE–Centre for Innovation Research, Papers in Innovation Studies, no. 2022/4.

Wade, R. (1990). *Governing the market.* Princeton University Press.

———— (2017). The developmental state: Dead or alive? *Development and Change, 49*(2), 518–546.

Walker, O. (2022). Swiss banks' struggles to move on from murky past hit by documents leak. *Financial Times.* 22 February. www.ft.com/content/f4c3be6c-6c98-47e0-9d7c-74b4d4064ba5.

Wallerstein, M. (1990). Centralized bargaining and wage restraint. *American Journal of Political Science, 34*(4), 982–1004.

Wang, J. H. (2007). From technological catch-up to innovation-based economic growth: South Korea and Taiwan compared. *Journal of Development Studies, 43*(6), 1084–1104.

Wang, W-C. (2009). Information economy and inequality: Wage polarization, unemployment, and occupation transition in Taiwan since 1980. *Journal of Asian Economics, 20*(2), 120–136.

Wong, J. (2016). The developmental state and Taiwan: Origins and adaptation. In G. Schubert (Ed.), *Routledge handbook of contemporary Taiwan* (pp. 201–217). Routledge.

Wong, J. I. (2016). Sweden must change quickly: Spotify threatens to leave the country, Quartz. April 14. https://qz.com/661319/sweden-must-change-quickly-spotify-threatens-to-leave-the-country.

Wood, A. (1998). Globalisation and the rise in labour market inequalities. *Economic Journal, 108*(450), 1463–1482.

World Bank (2019). *Ease of doing business.* World Bank, Doing Business Project. https://data.worldbank.org/indicator/IC.BUS.EASE.XQ.

World Intellectual Property Organisation [WIPO](2022). Global Innovation Index 2022: What is the future of innovation-driven growth? WIPO. www.wipo.int/global_innovation_index/en/2022.

Yeung, H. W. C. (2016). *Strategic coupling: East Asian industrial transformation in the new global economy.* Cornell University Press.

Yu, W-H. (2015). *Women and employment in Taiwan.* Brookings Institution. www.brookings.edu/opinions/women-and-employment-in-taiwan.

Zhuang, J., Kanbur, R., and Rhee, C. (2014). *Rising inequality in Asia and policy implications.* ADBI Working Paper, no. 463. www.adbi .org/working-paper/2014/02/21/6172.rising.inequality.asia.policy .implications.

Zilian, L. S., Zilian, S. S., & Jäger, G. (2021). Labour market polarisation revisited: Evidence from Austrian vacancy data. *Journal for Labour Market Research, 55*(1), 1–17.

Index

Page numbers in **bold** refer to figures, page numbers in *italic* refer to tables.

institutional structures, 169–170, *171*; growth, 13; and inequality, 64–65, 64; intensity, 91, 100, 102–104, 125–126; public returns on, 175; ranking, 38, *39–40*; rewards, 46; spending, 2–4, *3*, 13, 24, 34–35, 38, *39*, 56, 64, 91, 98, 100–107, 101, 111, 149–151, 162; target setting, 101–102, 104, 115; tax subsidies, 104, 106–107
researcher numbers, 38, *39*
rewards, 9, 46, 174
rich countries, types of, 1–2
risk taking, 9
Roche, 77–78
Rosenberg, Nathan, 61
Russia, invasion of Ukraine, 114

Schumpeter, Joseph, 21–22, 23, 24, 33–34
Schüssel, Wolfgang, 103
science policy, 28–29, 35
scientific progress, 25
Sedlacek, Sabine, 108
shared prosperity, 10, 12, 13, 55, 98–99, 165, 165–168, 173–175
Shih, Hsin-Yu, 125
Silicon Valley, 12, 15, 31, 62–63; innovation model, 6, 7, 8
Singapore, 3, 31, 116, 124, 132, 133, 134, *134*, 138
skill development, 14, 55, 60, 62, 67, 84–87, 129–132, 167–168
skills, 15, 44, 50, 54–55, 61–63
small states, 165
social-partnership model, 91, 94–98
social spending, 147–148
soft innovation, 41, 77, 108
Solow model, 34
Soskice, David, 35–36, 62, 169
South Korea, 6–7, 13, 31, 100, 116, 121, 124, 128, 132, 133–134, 134, *134*, 138
spatial inequality, 136–137, 156–157
Spotify, 154, 158, 162
stakeholder capitalism, 119
state, the, role of, 13–14, 18, 121, 124, 132, 141, 150–151, 162–163, 167–168, 169, 175
Steinberg, Jonathan, 70
Stockholm, Sweden, 140–141, 148, 157, 157–162

Stockport, 43–44
Stohr, Christian, 72–73
Storper, Michael, 60
Styria, Austria, 108–114, 109, 110, 112
Su, Hsuan-Li, 133
Sweden, 13, 15, 16, 17, 68, 140–141, 140–163, 164, 168, 169, 173, 175; background, 141–149, 145, *147*; diffusive institutional structures, *171*, 172; digital tech success, 153–157, 157–162; disruptive innovation, 141; economic and industrial policy, 142–143; economic reform, 144; education, 149; employment rate, 145–146; GDP, 143, 144; gender inequalities, 146; generative institutional structures, 170, *171*; Gini coefficient, 147; government spending, 147; inequality, 140, 144–147, 145, *147*, 149, 156–157, 161–162, 163, 164; innovation model, 149–151, 162–163; labor market, 142, 143, 148, 156, 160, 167; migration, 148; Nordic model, 141–149, 149; R&D spending, 149–150, 162; redistributive institutional structures, *171*; relative poverty, 144; social spending, 147–148; state funding, 150–151; Stockholm, 140–141, 148, 157, 157–162; taxation, 143–144, 148, 152, 153, 160, 161; telecoms sector, 150; unicorn firms, 140–141; venture capital, 140, 155, 158–159, 159–161, 162; wealth inequality, 146, 146–147, *147*, 149, 164; welfare state, 141, 142, 147–148, 151, 151–153
Switzerland, 13, 15, 16, 16–17, 68–89, *147*, 164, 165, 166, 168, 169, 173; background, 69–73; cost of living, 81; diffusion and adaptation, 84–87; diffusive institutional structures, *171*, 172; disposable household income, 69; GDP, 69; gender inequalities, 83–84; generative institutional structures, 170, *171*; Gini coefficient, 68, 80; gross disposable income, 80–81; household incomes, 65, *66*; income distribution, 68, 69; income inequality, 80, 83; industrial base, 69–70; industrialization, 72–73; innovation model, 68–69, 69–70, 73–74, 84, 88–89; innovation

Founded in 1893,
UNIVERSITY OF CALIFORNIA PRESS
publishes bold, progressive books and journals
on topics in the arts, humanities, social sciences,
and natural sciences—with a focus on social
justice issues—that inspire thought and action
among readers worldwide.

The UC PRESS FOUNDATION
raises funds to uphold the press's vital role
as an independent, nonprofit publisher, and
receives philanthropic support from a wide
range of individuals and institutions—and from
committed readers like you. To learn more, visit
ucpress.edu/supportus.